Religious Trends in Modern China

LECTURES ON THE HISTORY OF RELIGIONS

SPONSORED BY THE AMERICAN COUNCIL
OF LEARNED SOCIETIES

NEW SERIES · NUMBER THREE

DELIVERED AS THE HASKELL LECTURES, 1950
AT THE UNIVERSITY OF CHICAGO

Religious Trends IN MODERN CHINA

by *Wing-tsit Chan*

OCTAGON BOOKS

A DIVISION OF FARRAR, STRAUS AND GIROUX

New York 1978

Reprinted 1969
by special arrangement with Columbia University Press

Second Octagon printing 1978

OCTAGON BOOKS
A division of Farrar, Straus & Giroux, Inc.
19 Union Square West
New York, N.Y. 10003

Library of Congress Catalog Card Number: 71-96176
ISBN: 0-374-91406-0

Manufactured by Braun-Brumfield, Inc.
Ann Arbor, Michigan
Printed in the United States of America

To JANE and HENRY C. BROWNELL

WHO HAVE DEVOTED FORTY YEARS OF SERVICE

TO THE CHINESE PEOPLE

Foreword

In the new series of Lectures on the History of Religions, sponsored and organized since 1936 by the American Council of Learned Societies through its Committee on the History of Religions, the present volume is the third. The first was that of Martin P. Nilsson, *Greek Popular Religion* (1940), and the second that of Henri Frankfort, *Ancient Egyptian Religion* (1948).

Wing-tsit Chan, the present author, was born in Canton; he obtained the B.A. degree at Lingnan University, and his doctorate at Harvard University. Since 1942 he has been Professor of Chinese Culture and Philosophy at Dartmouth College, and he is a well-known lecturer and contributor to many publications and studies on Chinese letters and cultural history. In 1948, as a Guggenheim Fellow, he returned to his native country and used an opportunity that was fast disappearing through revolutionary changes to gather the specific materials presented in this book on *Religious Trends in Modern China.* As China experiences the conflicting and powerful impact of foreign ideologies, many trends more continuous with its own distinct cultural history tend to become obscured from our view. It is to such trends in the field of religion during the past half-century of extraordinary change that Professor Chan has devoted his attention in this study. Recognizing that his material would have its unique and perhaps irreplaceable importance, the Committee on the History of Religions, then under the chairmanship of Professor Herbert W. Schneider, invited Professor Chan to give a series of lectures on the subject, under its sponsorship at various American institutions during the year 1949–50.

The lectures were given, as a whole or in part, at Smith College, Cornell University, Oberlin College, Columbia University, the Friends' International House in Washington, D.C., and as The Haskell Lectures for 1950 at the University of Chicago. The Committee of the American Council of Learned Societies wishes to thank each and all of these institutions for their participation, and especially to express its appreciation to The Haskell Lectures committee in Chicago for its generous support and valued co-sponsorship of the lectures.

Furthermore, we are grateful to Columbia University Press for undertaking the publication of this volume as it did of the two previous books in the series. Some special editorial problems, presented by the Chinese materials of this volume, could only have been solved by the understanding and extensive cooperation of author and press.

Horace L. Friess
For the Committee

Columbia University
October, 1952

Preface

The present work is a slight expansion of a series of lectures given in 1950 under the sponsorship of the Committee on the History of Religions of the American Council of Learned Societies and the Haskell Lecture Committee. It is an attempt to discover recent Chinese religious trends from a long-range point of view. To the original five lectures I have added a chapter on Chinese Islam.

During my trip to China in 1948–49 on a Guggenheim Fellowship to pursue a project on Neo-Confucianism, I had the opportunity to use Chinese libraries, consult Chinese scholars, and visit temples. Conditions for study and travel were most difficult, for the Communists had taken over half of China and libraries were being closed. Fortunately, I was able to see most of the Chinese periodicals in which most, if not all, of the information about contemporary Chinese religions is to be found. Much of this literature, for the present at least, has become inaccessible to the West.

The purpose of the lectures is not to present a general history or survey of Chinese religions, for this was familiar to the audiences to which the lectures were addressed, but to discover the significant trends in Confucianism, Taoism, and Buddhism in the last fifty years. Therefore no description of religious literature, religious festivals, or temple arrangements is offered, although the general reader uninitiated in Chinese religion will find no difficulty in using this book, for the lectures were so designed that the general features and historical backgrounds of traditional Chinese religions are clearly outlined. I have especially emphasized the recent development of religious thought and philosophy, not only because the field has not been touched and needs to be covered, but also because it is in this field that the true tendencies of Chinese religions can best be discovered. These features and backgrounds and the intellectual and reform movements in Chinese religions in the last fifty years show unmistakably that certain tendencies have persisted in Chinese religions during the last several decades or even centuries. These tendencies have largely escaped the attention of Western observers, who generally allow the superstitious practices in Chinese religions to blind them. With deeper understanding and a broader perspective, we cannot fail to conclude that superstitions are passing phenomena, while certain tendencies are more lasting, some having persisted for the last two thousand years.

It is important to see these trends in order truly to understand Chinese religious life and thought. It is all the more important because Communist triumph in China seems on the surface to forecast the termination of religion in China. Viewed in the historical perspective and in the patterns of Chinese religious thought, however, Chinese religion has outlived many political systems and ideologies. Communism may change Chinese religion, but Chinese religion may change Communism too. The persistent religious trends should show us which direction these changes will follow when they take place. For example, it is almost universally accepted that the Christian missionary movement as we have known it has ended in China. In its traditional form and concept, it is definitely becoming a closed chapter. But seen in the light of strong Chinese religious tendencies, its present suspension may be a prelude to a brighter and richer movement. For several hundred years Chinese Buddhists defied the government, braved the natural hazards of the Himalayas, and went to India to "seek the Law" and to bring back holy scriptures, golden images, and Indian scholars, thus establishing and maintaining a long relationship between Chinese Buddhists and Indian missionaries on the basis of pure faith, genuine friendship, and cooperative partnership. In our own time, Chinese Moslems, once their isolation from world Islam was broken, inaugurated a similar movement and in the same spirit, though on a small scale. The present effort of Chinese Communists to isolate Christianity in China runs against this tendency. But sooner or later the isolation will be over, and in the light of Chinese religious history, both past and contemporary, it is reasonable to expect that a new type of Christian missionary movement will be started in China. The relation between Chinese Communism and Chinese religion did not fall within the scope of these lectures. However, I have indicated on pages 53, 90–91, 168, and 261–63 how Chinese religious trends may be affected by Communism.

With reference to transliteration of Chinese words, in spite of its gross inadequacies, I have used the Wade system (except for place names and personal names already familiar to the West) simply because the system is most generally used. Diacritical marks over Oriental words are given in the Bibliography and Glossary, but omitted in the text, in footnotes, and in the Index, except the umlaut where it is necessary to avoid ambiguity, as, for example, between *yu* and *yü* (but not between *hsu* and *hsü*, because there is no such distinction). Sinologists are not agreed on the use of the capital and the hyphen in transliteration. I have tried to evolve my own system and to remain consistent in it. For instance, I have capitalized independent words and titles in proper names, such as Lao Tzŭ, Tao-tê Hui, and

K'ung Chiao (but K'ung-chiao Hui when *chiao* becomes part of a compound). In titles of books or articles, only the first letter of the title and the first letter of proper names are capitalized. I have hyphenated Chinese phrases to bring out the meaning more clearly, but for the same reason, family names, honorifics, collective nouns, and nouns referring to bodies of writing are not hyphenated except when the context of the phrase demands hyphenation.

I want to thank the Committee on the History of Religions, under the chairmanship of Professor Herbert W. Schneider and his successor Professor Horace L. Friess, for the appointment to give these lectures, the Haskell Lecture Fund for sponsoring them and aiding in their publication, and Professor Arthur Jeffery of Columbia, Professor Kenneth K. S. Ch'en of Harvard, Canon Claude L. Pickens, Jr., of the Society of Friends of Moslems in China, Professor Clarence H. Hamilton of Oberlin, and Professor M. S. Bates of the Union Theological Seminary for their excellent suggestions.

Thanks are also due to the University of California Press for permission to quote from *China*, edited by Harley Farnsworth MacNair; the University of Hawaii for permission to quote from *The Essentials of Buddhist Philosophy*, by Junjiro Takakusu, edited by myself and Charles A. Moore; and the School of Theology of Boston University for permission to use the material on the harmony of Chinese religions which I presented at its Mid-Century Institute on Religion in a World of Tensions in 1951. Mrs. Miriam Bergamini, of Columbia University Press, edited the manuscript and my daughter Jean typed part of it. To them and to many scholars and librarians in China and in the United States I am grateful.

Above all, I want to thank Professor Friess for his painstaking work in arranging for the lectures and their publication and for his valuable advice on the manuscript. His keen interest, encouragement, and friendship have made the delivery of the lectures and the preparation of the manuscript an enjoyable experience.

WING-TSIT CHAN

Dartmouth College
March, 1952

Contents

Religious Trends in Modern China

I

What Is Living and What Is Dead in Confucianism

The religious situation in China is paradoxical in several ways. While Chinese government, education, and literature have been completely revolutionized in the last half century, the religious front has been comparatively quiet. By and large, the daily religious life of the people goes on quietly as it has for centuries. The Jade Emperor, the highest deity in the Taoist religion, still sits serenely in his seat and the Three Buddhas still stand calmly on lotus pedestals.

It seems, then, that religion has stayed aloof from the radical transformations that characterize twentieth-century China. And yet its apparent quietness should not conceal from us the tremendous changes that have been taking place in Chinese religion. Images are being thrown out of temples. Temples are being wrecked. Entire religious institutions are being abolished. And atheism, not faith, is cherished as the height of spiritual development. Thus on the one hand, there is stability in Chinese religion, but on the other, there is flux.

From certain points of view, this change is purely negative —anti-religious movements, emancipation from superstitions, decline of religious organizations. But from other points of view, the change is also positive and constructive. For there is a new life in religion. Even critics of Chinese religion have to concede that there have been new religious developments, new awakening, new growth.

These new developments are in themselves paradoxical. In the regenerating process, ancient beliefs and practices are being abandoned, and yet much that is perennial in traditional heritage is perpetuated. All in all, the religious situation is complicated and puzzling. On the following pages we shall outline the situation in the last fifty years, paying special attention to the recent trends in the three systems, Confucianism, Buddhism, and Taoism. We shall begin with the first.

THE DOWNFALL OF CONFUCIANISM

To people who confine their views to traditional institutions and to young Chinese students who still rebel against these institutions, Confucianism must be a thing of the past. As a religious institution, or rather as a secular institution that has sponsored and promoted traditional rites, Confucianism has definitely been overthrown. This has been a striking event in the last five decades.

As such an institution, Confucianism reached its height in Chinese history in 1906 when the Manchu rulers, in a desperate attempt to salvage their crumbling dynasty, issued an edict to place sacrifices to Confucius (551–479 B.C.) on equality with those to Heaven. It raised the traditional Secondary Sacrifice to Grand Sacrifice and made Confucius "Assessor of Heaven." [1]

This gesture is extremely significant in two ways. In the first place it represents the highest honor ever paid to the Ancient Teacher. Emperor P'ing inaugurated the custom of giving him posthumous titles by making him a "Duke" in A.D. 1; the highest title ever conferred on him was "King" (or "Prince") in 739, unless one considers the title "Perfect Sage," awarded in 1008, to rank even higher. That was as far as the Chinese were willing to go. An Imperial Academy petition in 1074 to honor Confucius with the title of "Emperor" was rejected by the Board of Rites.[2] The second significance is that the gesture implies an attempt to deify Confucius. It was the first and last official effort in Chinese history to make him a god. Although some scholars in the Western Han period (202 B.C. to A.D. 9) regarded him virtually as a deity,[3] by and large the Chinese people have not worshiped him as a power over the fortune of human existence but have rather honored him as an ideal example of man. The seasonal sacrifice to Confucius, whether in the capital, in Confucius' native Chufu, or in almost every prefecture, and the traditional daily rites of kneeling and bowing before his tablet in schools were performed out of respect for the "Perfect Sage."

But the desperate attempt did not save the Manchu empire. Nor did it save the Confucian institution. There was

[1] The rites for Confucius in the Ch'ing Dynasty (1644–1912) were based on those of T'ang (618–906) and later dynasties. The sacrifice to Confucius was of the secondary or middle grade, while sacrifice of the first grade, the Grand Sacrifice, was reserved for Heaven. See *Ta-Ch'ing t'ung-li* ("General Regulations of the Great Ch'ing Dynasty"), *chüan* (Part) 12.

[2] See *Sung shih* ("History of the Sung Dynasty"), *chüan* 105.

[3] Fung Yu-lan says, "In the modern text literature and apocryphal books of the Western Han period, Confucius was attributed with omniscience and omnipotence. . . . This is making Confucius a god." Fung Yu-lan, *Hsin li-hsueh* ("New Rational Philosophy"), p. 285; *idem, A Short History of Chinese Philosophy*, p. 207.

a movement to make Confucianism the state cult, but it failed completely.[4] In brief, the events were as follows: K'ang Yu-wei (1858–1927), the moving spirit of the Hundred Days Reform in 1898, declared that "half of the Confucian *Analects* was sufficient to restore world order," petitioned the Manchu emperor to establish Confucianism as the state religion, and preached the Confucian utopia of Great Com-

[4] The arguments for a state religion were: (1) China has always had a state religion. (2) Since other modern nations have a state religion, why not China? (3) Even those countries having no official state religion use the calendar and prayers of a particular religion, thus making that religion virtually a state religion. (4) A state religion does not interfere with freedom of belief because citizens are still free to follow any religion. (5) To have no state religion would be to have no foundation for national morality. (6) To abolish the Chinese state religion (Confucianism) would be to abolish Chinese culture, since Confucianism and Chinese culture are practically identical. (7) Without a state religion China even as a political entity would be in danger. (8) Freedom of belief is a negative policy, since it merely does not confine citizens to one religion. (9) Just as equality of brothers does not remove the seniority of the elder brother, so equality of religions does not preclude a state religion which is equivalent to an elder brother. See *K'ung-chiao Hui tsa-chih* ("Confucian Society Magazine"), I, No. 1 (February, 1913), 3–4; I, No. 2 (March, 1913), 8; I, No. 5 (June, 1913), 13, 33; I, No. 7 (August, 1913), 43–48; I, No. 9 (October, 1913), 3; see also *Pu-jen* ("Unable to Bear"), No. 3 (April, 1913), pp. 2–12; No. 7 (August, 1913), p. 3.

On the other side, the arguments ran like these: (1) A constitution should guarantee freedom of belief. (2) Religion and the state should be separated. (3) China has never had a state religion. (4) China has not been a religious country. (5) Religion has been superseded by science in the modern world. (6) Modern states have no state religion. (7) To follow the example of those countries with a state religion would be to imitate their worst aspect. (8) Religion is basically a moral matter and no constitution should interfere with the citizens' morals. (9) No constitution in the world contains a personal name; hence the name of Confucius should not be mentioned in the Chinese constitution. (10) To establish Confucianism as the state religion would be to antagonize the Buddhists in Mongolia and Tibet. (11) Confucianism is not a religion. (12) All religions should be equal, and the constitution should not accord a particular religion any special favor. (13) Confucianism is a historical product and its rise and fall need no help from the constitution. (14) The Manchu Dynasty fell in spite of its adherence to Confucianism. (15) Confucianism is incompatible with a republican form of government. See *Hsin ch'ing-nien* (hereafter cited as *La Jeunesse*), II, Nos. 2, 3, and 5 (October, 1916 to January, 1917), 4, 3, and 2, respectively; *Chia-yin* (hereafter cited as *The Tiger*), I, No. 1 (May, 1914) 15–19.

monwealth in America and Europe.[5] In 1907, Ch'en Huan-chang (1881–1931), then a graduate student at Columbia University, organized a Confucian Society in New York and on Confucius' birth anniversary performed traditional ceremonies in the United China Society in which Professor Hart of Columbia participated.[6] Ch'en also formed the Confucian Society in Shanghai in 1912, in Peking in 1913, and later in Chufu, with K'ang as president and Ch'en himself as executive secretary. Within a year the society grew to include 130 branches in China, Manchuria, Japan, Hong Kong, and Macao,[7] and in 1913 Ch'en began to edit and publish the *Confucian Society Magazine* in which a new calendar starting with the year of Confucius' birth was used. The society tried to pay special attention to youth, farmers, workers, merchants, women, and rural areas;[8] in 1913 it petitioned the Parliament of the Republic to adopt Confucianism as the state religion. Prominent intellectuals like Yen Fu (1853–1921) and Hsia Tseng-yu (1865–1924) led the movement by signing the petition;[9] other scholars supported it, including Chang Tung-sun, who declared that

[5] Huang Yen, ed., *K'ung-chiao shih-nien ta-shih* ("Ten Years of Important Events in Confucianism"), VII, 36. The Great Commonwealth refers to *Li chi* (*The Book of Propriety*), Chap. 9, in which Confucius is attributed to have said, "When the great Way prevailed, the world became a common state. Rulers were elected according to their virtue and ability, and good faith and peace were restored. There, people regarded not only their parents as parents and their own children as children. The old people were able to enjoy their old age, the adults to employ their talents, the young people to respect their elders, and widows, orphans, and cripples to have support. . . . This was the Period of the Great Commonwealth." For an English translation of *Li chi*, which has been variously translated as "The Book of Propriety," "The Book of Rites," "The Book of Ceremony," etc., see *The Li Ki*, trans. by James Legge, in *The Sacred Books of the East*, Vols. XXVII and XXVIII.

[6] *K'ung-chiao Hui tsa-chih*, I, No. 1 (February, 1913), 2.

[7] *Ibid.* See also Huang Yen, ed., *K'ung-chiao shih-nien ta-shih*, VII, 36.

[8] *Ching-shih pao* ("Welfare Magazine"), I, No. 1 (January, 1922), 51.

[9] *K'ung-chiao Hui tsa-chih*, I, No. 5 (June, 1913), 13.

"inasmuch as Confucianism is the crystallization of several thousand years of Chinese civilization, it practically amounts to a state religion," [10] and foreign scholars like Reginald F. Johnston, who joined the Confucian Society and stated that he was "in entire sympathy with the movement to make Confucianism the state religion, or rather to preserve it as such." [11] Piles of telegrams from military governors of almost every province poured into the capital in support of the movement. The Draft Constitution Committee, meeting at the Temple of Heaven in Peking in October, 1913, at first declined to legalize Confucianism as the state religion but finally compromised to the extent of stating in Article 19 that "in the education of citizens, the doctrines of Confucius shall be regarded as the basis of moral cultivation." [12] On February 8, 1914, President Yuan Shih-k'ai (1858–1916), bent on becoming an emperor, decreed the resumption of sacrifice to Heaven and Confucius which the establishment of the Republic in 1912 had suspended,[13] and in August, 1914, Yuan himself, dressed in academic cap and gown, officiated as the representative of the people.[14] Although Yuan's death in 1916 dealt a fatal blow to the movement, the Confucian Society continued its pressure on the new Parliament. All this story, in its details and ramifications, needs to be recorded for posterity. But for our purpose it suffices to note that the movement, in spite of the support of many scholars and government officials, failed quickly and completely.

The failure means, first of all, the end of the effort to make Confucianism a constitutional state religion. It is

[10] *Yung-yen* (*Justice*), I, No. 15 (July, 1913), 12.
[11] *K'ung-chiao Hui tsa-chih*, I, No. 3 (April, 1913), 38.
[12] Cf. Pan Wei-tung, *The Chinese Constitution*, p. 159.
[13] *Cheng-fu kung-pao* ("Government Gazette"), No. 631 (February 8, 1914).
[14] Wu Hsin-heng, "A Brief History of the Sacrifice to Confucius" (in Chinese), *Hsin Ya-hsi-ya* ("New Asia"), X, No. 2 (August, 1935), 99–127.

true that the constitution of 1923 says that "a citizen of the Republic of China shall be free to honor Confucius and to prefer any religion," [15] but "honoring" in this case means "respect," without any religious connotation. From the very outset, the general sentiment was overwhelmingly against a state religion. One of the most earliest to oppose it was K'ang's outstanding pupil Liang Ch'i-ch'ao (1873–1929), who declared that "those who want to preserve the Confucian religion merely put modern thought in Confucian terms and say that Confucius knew all about it. . . . They love Confucius; they do not love truth." [16] Chang T'ai-yen (1868–1936), "Great Master of Chinese Studies," whose scholarship and opinions were respected by radical and conservative alike, condemned the movement as backward, because "China has never had a state religion." [17] In saying so he was reflecting the general opinion, for to the Chinese the only thing that proponents could offer as evidence of a state religion was the imperial sacrifice to Heaven, which was regarded by their opponents as purely ceremonial and the emperor's private affair.[18] Ch'en Huan-chang asserted that Confucianism was made a state religion when Duke Wen of the state of Wei personally received instructions from the Confucian pupil, Tzu Hsia (507–400 B.C.), but this story lacks historical basis.[19] It was also argued that Confucianism was a state religion because Emperor Wu

[15] Cf. Pan Wei-tung, *The Chinese Constitution*, p. 192. See also Ch'ien Tuan-sheng, *The Government and Politics of China*, p. 437.

[16] "To Preserve the Confucian Religion is Not the Way to Love Confucius," (in Chinese), *Sien Min Choong Bou* (*Hsin-min ts'ung-pao*, "New People's Periodical"), No. 2 (January 15, 1902), 69.

[17] Chang T'ai-yen, "Refutation of the Proposal to Establish Confucianism as a Religion" (in Chinese), in *T'ai-yen wen-lu* ("Essays by Chang T'ai-yen"), 1st series, II, 56A.

[18] *K'ung-chiao Hui tsa-chih*, I, No. 5 (June, 1913), 119.

[19] *Ibid.*, I, No. 1 (February, 1912), 1. The source of this story is *chüan* 67 of Ssu-ma Ch'ien's *Shih chi* (*The Historical Records*). The story has been proved unreliable. See Ch'ien Mu, *Hsien-Ch'in chu-tzu hsi-nien* ("A Correlated Chronology of Ancient Philosophers"), pp. 124–25.

suppressed the non-Confucian schools and established the Confucian College of Doctors in 136 B.C. and adopted the Confucian Classics as basis for education. That the argument is unsound needs no clarification. While these measures made Confucianism supreme, they did not make it a state religion.[20] Ch'en concluded that since all Chinese religious rites were based on Confucian teachings, Confucianism was therefore a state religion. Such reasoning shows his desperate attempt to find an excuse for his cause. Having neither a historical nor a logical basis, the movement was bound to fail.

The failure means, in the second place, the termination of the sacrifice to Heaven and the sacrifice to Confucius. The sacrifice to Heaven, an old custom whereby the emperor annually officiated on behalf of his people, was not really a religious exercise. Much less was it aimed at "securing the propitiation of this supreme power to the end that it may withhold its avenging *kwei*" (specters).[21] Rather, it was chiefly ceremonial. It had no direct relation to the religious life of the people. Nor was the emperor ever thought of in the slightest degree as a high priest. But the ceremony did symbolize the close connection between the sacrifice and the monarchial system. It was therefore strenuously opposed, not on any religious ground, but with the political argument that it, being a private affair of the emperor, should have nothing to do with the Republic. The objection was based on the well-founded fear that resumption of the ceremony would herald the return of the monarchy. Yuan's sinister motive in restoring the sacrifice was too obvious to fool the

[20] *K'ung-chiao Hui tsa-chih,* I, No. 1 (February, 1912), 1. This supremacy is often called in the West the state cult of Confucianism. For a full story, see Hu Shih, "The Establishment of Confucianism as a State Religion during the Han Dynasty," *Journal of the North China Branch of the Royal Asiatic Society,* LX (1929), 20–41; Shryock, *The Origin and Development of the State Cult of Confucius.*

[21] de Groot, *The Religion of the Chinese,* p. 19.

Chinese. After his death, the issue was never raised again, proving once and for all that the issue was not religious but purely political.

As to the sacrifice to Confucius, as soon as Yuan became president in 1912, he maneuvered to revive it in the schools.[22] Although he failed, he did succeed in restoring it in the Temple of Confucius.[23] This continued until the Nationalist Government ordered its cessation in 1928. With this, the tradition of sacrifice to Confucius practically passed into history. It is true that as late as August, 1934, the Central Executive Committee of the Nationalist Party, the highest organ in control of the government as well as the party, decided that August 27 be observed by the entire nation as the birth anniversary of Confucius (later also designated as Teacher's Day), and instructed the government to appoint a high official, accompanied by delegates from the various departments, to sacrifice to the sage in his native Chufu.[24] In October of the same year, by government decree, the seventy-seventh direct lineal descendant of Confucius, K'ung

[22] *K'ung-chiao Hui tsa-chih,* I, No. 6 (July, 1913), 11–12; also Shryock, *op. cit.*, pp. 215–16.

[23] The first imperial sacrifice to Confucius took place in 195 B.C. when Emperor Kao Tsu paid sacrifice to Confucius' tomb in his native Chufu. The custom of government officials sacrificing to Confucius in the capital and in the prefectures began in A.D. 59. The first sacrifice to pupils of Confucius along with the sage began during the reign of Emperor Fei (A.D. 240–48) of Wei. In A.D. 267, the tradition of offering sacrificial animals to Confucius at the four seasons, both in the Imperial Academy and in Confucius' native state of Lu, was inaugurated by Emperor Wu (265–90) of Chin. In 282, the tradition of the crown prince sacrificing to Confucius was started. Instrumental music was first used in the sacrifice during the reign of Emperor Wen (424–53) of Sung. Ceremonial dance was introduced during the reign of Emperor Wu of Ch'i (483–93). During the North Ch'i period (550–77), libation of wine to Confucius was ordered on the first day of each month, as well as a special sacrifice twice a year, in spring and autumn, thus starting another new custom. In 647, Emperor T'ai Tsung (627–49) of T'ang decreed detailed ceremonies for the sacrifice to Confucius, including choral music, thus inaugurating an additional custom. See the section on rites in the various dynastic histories.

[24] Wu Hsin-heng, in *Hsin Ya-hsi-ya,* X, No. 2 (August, 1935), 123–25.

Te-ch'eng by name, was appointed "Sacrificial Officer of the Great Perfection, Ultimate Sage, Foremost Teacher," thus replacing the traditional title of the "Duke of Extended Sagehood" that had prevailed from 1055 down to the Republic. By the same decree, special privileges were accorded K'ung and other descendants.[25] But no Chinese thought of these actions as having any religious significance. As to the sacrifice itself, few people now paid any attention to it. Even the government itself sponsored it halfheartedly, perhaps with the dubious hope of counteracting the Japanese promotion of the Confucian religion in newly conquered Manchuria. It is true, too, that in the 1930s warlords like Ch'en chi-t'ang, Ho Chien, Sung Che-yuan, and Chang Tsung-ch'ang revived the sacrifice in their own provinces, unmistakably as a means of political control through the misuse of Confucius. By that time, however, the movement was so thoroughly discredited that no Chinese considering himself modern would associate with it.

Strange as it may sound, originally the effective opposition against making Confucianism the state religion and against sacrifice to Heaven and Confucius came from Confucian scholars themselves. I have already referred to the protests by Chang T'ai-yen. Chang was the first modern Confucian scholar to promote the study of ancient non-Confucian and anti-Confucian philosophies. Unwittingly, through such promotion he had already destroyed the supremacy of Confucianism in thought in general. Now he wittingly proceeded to destroy Confucianism as a religion in particular, declaring that "only ignorant people follow religion. . . . The greatness of Confucius lies with his preoccupation with social and governmental affairs."[26] Ts'ai Yuan-p'ei (1867–1940), soon to emerge as the dean of Chinese intellectuals, strongly

[25] *Chung-yang jih-pao* ("Central Daily News"), Peking, November 16, 1934.
[26] Chang T'ai-yen, *op. cit.*, p. 55B.

opposed making Confucianism the state religion. To him, Confucianism was not a religion at all.[27]

We must not forget that in the opposition to the state religion, Christians played a noble part. The Society for Religious Liberty, organized by Protestants and joined by Roman Catholics, Moslems, Taoists, and Buddhists, sent many telegrams to the Parliament protesting against making Confucianism the state religion.[28] There was also the celebrated case of Chung Jung-kuang, a Confucian scholar turned Christian, who, as Commissioner of Education for Kwangtung, not only agitated against a state religion but in 1912 abolished all religious rites in schools, an extremely radical move.[29] But Christians were then not influential enough to play a decisive role. We must not forget, either, that young intellectual rebels had a share in the defeat of the movement. As we shall see, Ch'en Tu-hsiu contributed some strong arguments. But in those days young intellectuals had not enjoyed the respect of legislators and government officials in whose hands the fate of the matter rested. It was the voices of Chang T'ai-yen, Ts'ai Yuan-p'ei, and other Confucian scholars equally prominent that were heard. The opposition soon spread over the entire country. By 1916, when K'ang Yu-wei again petitioned the government to sacrifice to Confucius and to respect the Confucian religion as supreme, no newspaper in North or South China supported him, and when the Parliament finally omitted Article 19 from the constitution and the Department of Interior ordered the cancellation of the kneeling ceremony before Confucian tablets, no newspaper objected.[30] The national sentiment was such that neither a state religion nor sacrifice to Heaven or Confucius would be tolerated. The failure of

[27] *La Jeunesse*, II, No. 5 (January, 1917), 2.
[28] *China Mission Year Book*, 1917, p. 37.
[29] *K'ung-chiao Hui tsa-chih*, I, No. 1 (February, 1912), 27.
[30] *La Jeunesse*, II, No. 2 (October, 1916), 4.

Confucianism to become a state religion was therefore complete.

This failure also means, in the third place, that Confucianism was denied status as a religion as such. In the opposition to it as a state religion, one of the chief arguments was that it was not a religion at all. Chang T'ai-yen argued that since Confucius himself confessed that he did not know anything about the great sacrifice,[31] he could not have founded a religion. "The reason why Confucius has remained a hero in China," he says, "is because he made history, developed literature, promoted scholarship, and equalized social classes. . . . In these four supreme achievements, Confucius has become the key to the preservation of the Chinese people and the growth of Chinese civilization. But he was not a religious founder." [32] In the same spirit, Ts'ai Yuan-p'ei emphatically stated that Confucius restrained himself in religious matters, and that since it had neither the form nor the content of a religion, Confucianism should not be made a state religion.[33] To put it even more strongly, Ch'en Tu-hsiu declared that "the doctrines of Confucius are not the words of a religionist." He further reminded us that the very term *k'ung-chiao,* the Confucian religion, was not invented until controversy arose among Confucianists, Buddhists, and Taoists in the Southern and Northern Dynasties (386–589).[34] When one recalls the familiar facts that Confucius did not answer questions about spirits and death, that he did not discuss spirits, that he seldom talked about the

[31] *Lun-yü* (*Analects*), III, 11. For English translations, see, among others, *The Confucian Analects,* trans. by James Legge in *The Chinese Classics,* 2nd ed. Vol. I; *The Analects of Confucius,* trans. by Arthur Waley; *The Best of Confucius,* trans. by James Ware (Garden City, N.Y., Halcyon House, 1950).

[32] Chang T'ai-yen, *op. cit.,* pp. 58A–B.

[33] *La Jeunesse,* II, No. 5 (January, 1917), 2.

[34] *Ibid.,* p. 4: "More on the Confucian Religion" (in Chinese).

Mandate of Heaven, that his doctrine about the Way of Heaven was not known to his pupils,[35] and that throughout Chinese history there has been no Confucian church, priesthood, or creed, one will realize that the words of Chang, Ts'ai, and Ch'en are extremely convincing.

Of course, K'ang Yu-wei and his followers tried their best to defend Confucianism as a religion. K'ang conceded that Confucianism emphasizes man while other systems emphasize the divine being, but he demanded to know why this fact should disqualify it as a religion. "Although Confucian teachings center around man," he declared, "they are based on the Mandate of Heaven and made clear by the powers of spirits." "Besides," he continued, "Confucius himself honored Heaven and served Shang-ti, the Lord on High." [36] Ch'en Huan-chang claimed that since all Chinese religious ideas and practices were founded on Confucian teachings, Confucianism was therefore a religion. He complained that opponents of the Confucian religion viewed religion in too narrow a sense. Some, he added, equated religion with superstition, and since Confucianism was free from superstition, they refused to accept it as a religion.[37]

As crusaders for a cause, both K'ang and Ch'en lacked objectivity in their views. There were other scholars, however, who evaluated Confucianism objectively and concluded that at least in some respects it was a religion. For example, Chang Tung-sun maintained that Confucianism met the four requirements of a religion in believing in Heaven and its Mandate, in advocating faith and attacking perverse doctrines, in possessing an ethical system, and in having con-

[35] *Analects*, XI, 11; VII, 20; V, 12.
[36] "On the Confucian Society" (in Chinese), *K'ung-chiao Hui tsa-chih*, I, No. 2 (March, 1913), 1–12.
[37] "Making Our Original State Religion as the State Religion Does Not Interfere with Religious Freedom" (in Chinese), *ibid.*, I, No. 1 (February, 1913), 1.

tributed tremendously to Chinese civilization.[38] Another writer offered six proofs for Confucianism as a religion: (1) Religion is based on faith, and Confucius said that at fifty he knew the Mandate of Heaven. (2) Religion presupposes a sense of Heavenly mission, and Confucius declared that since Heaven endowed him with virtue, none could harm him, and that if Heaven would not destroy culture, his enemy would not be able to harm him. (3) Religion affirms the power of divine beings, and Confucius praised the strong power of spirits. (4) Religion requires sacrifice as a means of disciplining one's mind and nature, and Confucius sacrificed to spirits as though they were actually present. (5) Religion advocates prayer, and Confucius said that he had prayed for a long time and that he who offended Heaven had no god to pray to. Finally (6), religion encourages vows, and Confucius swore that if he did anything wrong, Heaven might destroy him.[39] To another writer, since temples are built for the sacrifice to Confucius, the system at least has some aspect of a religion.[40]

All these arguments, reasonable and factual as they are, can only lead to the conclusion that Confucianism is religious, but they do not prove that Confucianism is a religion, certainly not a religion in the Western sense of an organized church comparable to Buddhism or Taoism. To this day, the Chinese are practically unanimous in denying Confucianism as a religion.

If the Chinese only rejected Confucianism as the state religion and denied it as a religion as such, the downfall of Confucianism would have been exciting but not critical. But the Chinese went on to destroy it altogether, even as a

[38] "My Views on Confucianism" (in Chinese), *Justice,* I, No. 15 (July, 1913), 38–40.
[39] "A Fair Appraisal of Confucianism" (in Chinese), *K'ung-chiao Hui tsa-chih,* I, No. 4 (May, 1913), 33–34. See also *Analects,* II, 4; VII, 22; IX, 5; VIII, 19; III, 12; VII, 34; III, 13; VI, 26.
[40] "On Religion" (in Chinese), *The Tiger,* I, No. 6 (June, 1915), 2.

cultural force. They pronounced the sentence that Confucianism was no longer a constructive force in modern life.

The *coup de grace* was delivered by the twin leaders of the Intellectual Renaissance that began in 1917—Ch'en Tu-hsiu (1879–1942) and Hu Shih. The most intensive anti-Confucian period was from 1911 to 1928, but the onslaught was carried on through the early 1930s. Hu Shih considers Ch'en and Wu-Yü (1874–1949) the most vigorous critics of Confucianism and says that both emphasized the idea that "the way of Confucius is not suitable to modern life." [41] This may have been true of the early period. In his attack on Confucianism, Wu was merciless. He condemned Confucian filial piety as a "big factory for the manufacturing of obedient subjects," [42] and Confucian moral teachings as "man-eating" mores.[43] Exercising more oratory than logic, he was indeed vociferous. But most of the time he was far away in Chengtu in the interior, a thousand miles from the centers of the New Thought Movement, and did not have the following among young intellectuals that Hu and Ch'en did. All three, however, concentrated on the point that Confucianism was not consonant with modern society. Ch'en says that "the essence of Confucianism is the principle of propriety" and that "it is the basis for the distinction of the superior and the inferior, the noble and the lowly, and so forth, and is therefore incompatible with the modern idea of equality." [44] Furthermore, he says, "The Confucian doctrine of filial piety, obedience, subordination of women, Confucian mores and Confucian elaborate funerals are all unsuitable to the contemporary world." [45] Finally, he declares that "Confucianism is absolutely inconsistent with republicanism. . . . Both Confucius and Mencius predicated

[41] Wu Yü, *Wu Yü wen-lu* ("Essays by Wu Yü"), p. 3.
[42] *Ibid.*, p. 15.
[43] *Ibid.*, p. 71.
[44] *La Jeunesse*, II, No. 3 (November, 1916), 4–5.
[45] *Ibid.*, No. 4 (December, 1916), 4–5.

good or bad government on the virtuous or evil character of the ruler. . . . Confucius regarded the distinction of the superior and the inferior or the noble and the lowly not only as an ethical standard and a political principle but accepted it as a fundamental law of the universe. . . . The basic principle of *The Spring and Autumn Annal* is the superiority of the king. . . . From all these, Confucianism inevitably leads to monarchism." [46] Hu Shih, writing on an anniversary of Confucius' birth, declares that "In the last two or three decades we have abolished three thousand years of the eunuch system, one thousand years of foot-binding, six hundred years of the eight-legged essay, four or five hundred years of male prostitution, and five thousand years of judicial torture. None of this revolution was aided by Confucianism." He enumerates five great achievements in recent years; namely, the overthrow of the monarchy, the modernization of education, the transformation of the family, the reform of social customs, and the experiment in political organization. None of these, he observes, has anything to do with Confucius. He maintains that "the six Confucian Classics are inadequate to provide leadership." [47]

These are strong statements based on solid facts. But they are one-sided arguments, for every one of them can be countered with an equally strong argument supported by equally solid facts. Nevertheless, Chinese intellectuals were in the mood to destroy Confucianism. Following the call of Ch'en and Hu, Chinese professors and students alike shouted, "Destroy the old curiosity shop of Confucius." They burned the effigy of Confucius in straw.[48] The upshot is that Confucian Classics are no longer studied in schools. Confucian

[46] *La Jeunesse*, III, No. 6 (February, 1917), 1–4.

[47] Hu Shih, *Hu Shih lun-hsueh chin-chu* ("Recent Academic Writings of Hu Shih"), pp. 508–10, 519–23.

[48] Arthur Christy, "Old Religions Made New," *Asia*, XXXV, No. 8 (August, 1935), 527.

temples in the different counties are no longer used to honor the sage. In my recent trip between Chungking and Chengtu, I found one temple used as a barracks, one used partly as a dormitory for civil servants and partly as a hospital, one used as a garbage dump, and one in complete ruin. On the religious side, only ancestor worship continues, chiefly in the rural areas. Even here, signs of decline are obvious and definite. Young students no longer participate in ceremonies before ancestral shrines. In modern homes there is not even provision for an ancestral shrine.

It appears, then, that the downfall of Confucianism has been complete. There is neither a Confucian organization nor a Confucian periodical. Save for the national holiday in his honor, there was nothing in 1949 to remind the Chinese people of the twenty-five hundredth anniversary of Confucius' birth. That anniversary was observed in silence. Because of the civil war, a symposium planned by Chinese scholars did not materialize, nor did the conference of the United Nations Educational, Scientific and Cultural Organization scheduled for Nanking. The only celebration, if it may be so called, was found in the publications by two non-Chinese scholars, an article entitled "The Date of Confucius' Birth" by Professor Homer H. Dubs and a book entitled *Confucius, the Man and the Myth* by Professor H. G. Creel.[49] So far as the Chinese people are concerned, except for a few articles by refugee scholars they seem to have forgotten Confucius.[50]

I wonder how Confucius would feel if he were alive today. It may sound fantastic, but there are several reasons to be-

[49] Homer H. Dubs, "The Dates of Confucius' Birth," *Asia Major*, n.s., I, Part II (April, 1949), 143–46; Creel, *Confucius, the Man and the Myth.*

[50] The magazine *Min-chu p'ing-lun* (*Democratic Review*), published in Hong Kong by refugee scholars, including T'ang Chün-i and Ch'ien Mu, issued a special number (Vol. I, No. 6) in September, 1949, and again (Vol. II, No. 5) in September, 1950, in celebration of the birth anniversary of Confucius.

lieve that he would not be disappointed but would be pleased instead. In the first place, the Chinese people have not really forsaken him. They have abandoned certain Confucian religious practices and are giving up many Confucian social, political, and educational institutions, but they have not discarded the fundamental doctrines of Confucianism. Respect for parents, for example, is not questioned, although parental authority in marriage is being challenged. The official sacrifice to Heaven has been terminated, but most Chinese still believe in Heaven. Secondly, what has fallen is *institutional* Confucianism. But since Confucianism has never been highly institutionalized, the loss of its institutions has never been a death blow. Because it was free from rigid organization, it could change from one school to another without any fatal effect. By virtue of this fact, Confucianism has changed from the Western Han Confucian School to the Eastern Han Confucian School, then to the Rationalistic Neo-Confucian School in the twelfth century, to the Idealistic Neo-Confucian School of the fifteenth century, and later to the Critical School of the last three centuries. Confucianism survived all these transitions. There is no reason to believe that what is happening today is not another transition. In the third place, paradoxically enough, while Confucianism was being renounced, there were new tendencies that in the long run will make it purer, more authentic, and perhaps stronger.

Four such tendencies deserve our attention; namely, the revaluation of Confucianism, the discovery of the true religious position of Confucius, the development of the Idealistic School of Confucianism, and the growth of the Rationalistic School of Confucianism. We shall now discuss these tendencies, centering on major developments as represented by outstanding writers, and see what elements of Confucianism are being perpetuated and developed.

THE REVALUATION OF CONFUCIANISM

The amazing thing about the revaluation is that it began at the very moment anti-Confucianism was reaching its climax in 1918. Even more amazing is the fact that one of the first to offer a revaluation was a person with no training in the Confucian Classics, a Christian, and a rebel—Sun Yat-sen (1866–1925). At the time when rebels of the Intellectual Renaissance were crying, "Take down the Confucian signboard," Sun Yat-sen had the courage to turn to Confucianism for a psychological basis for his political doctrines. Obviously impatient with Chinese inertia, he not only urged action but sought a theoretical basis for it. He therefore enunciated his own doctrine of knowledge and conduct to the effect that it was "easy to act but difficult to know." This question of the relation of knowledge and conduct had been a perennial problem among Confucianists, reaching its zenith in Wang Yang-ming's doctrine of the unity of knowledge and action. Although Wang (1472–1528), a very active man himself, advocated an ethics for active living, his theory of knowledge is Idealistic and contains a strong element of quietism. This clearly did not meet the demand of a revolutionist. Sun therefore pronounced his own doctrine that it was easier to act. His doctrine is logically weak because it does not have a clear definition of knowledge or action, and the ten evidences he gives,[51] such as that it is easier to eat than to know what one eats, that it is easier to live in the process of evolution than to evolve a theory of evolution, and so on, are inconclusive. At best, his doctrine has practical efficacy at a particular time but has no universal validity or necessary truth. However, the fact that he took up a traditional Confucian problem when other people avoided it

[51] Sun Yat-sen, *Sun Wen hsueh-shuo* ("Doctrine of Sun Yat-sen"), Chaps. 1–4.

deserves our admiration. In 1924, when searching for an ethical basis for his political reconstruction, he went directly to the traditional Confucian virtues. He insisted that to restore China as a nation it was necessary to recover and preserve her ancient virtues, especially loyalty, filial devotion, kindness, love, faithfulness, justice, harmony, and peace.[52] It is interesting to note that he put loyalty to the nation ahead of the traditional "first virtue," filial devotion. It cannot be said that he was motivated by politics, for he gained nothing politically by advocating an unpopular system. This fact makes his evaluation of Confucianism all the more significant. As a natural development of his tendency, his follower, Chiang Kai-shek used in 1934 the four Confucian Cardinal Virtues of *li i lien ch'ih* (regulated attitude, right conduct, clear discrimination, and real self-consciousness) as the four pillars for the New Life Movement which he and the Nationalist government sponsored in the middle 1930s.

Another person to revaluate Confucianism was Liang Sou-ming, who was originally a Buddhist. In 1921 in Peking, the center of the Intellectual Renaissance and anti-Confucianism, he championed the Confucian philosophy of life. In his lectures on Eastern and Western civilizations and their philosophies, he stimulated the Chinese to a degree seldom seen in the contemporary world. He rejected Buddhism in favor of Confucianism at the time when everyone else regarded Confucianism as decadent, outmoded, and doomed. After examining both Indian and Western philosophies, he boldly declared that the future civilization of the world will be a reconstructed Chinese civilization. He said that the West is forward looking and has therefore conquered nature, developed science, and produced democracy;

[52] *San Min Chu I: The Three Principles of the People,* trans. by Frank W. Price, p. 126.

but it lacks spirituality. It emphasizes struggle. In contrast, India is backward looking and is therefore strong in religion but inferior to the West and China in almost everything else. China, on the other hand, looks both to the past and the future and has consequently developed the Mean or Centrality (*chung*) [53] that has avoided the extremes of the West and India. He urged China to (1) reject the Indian attitude completely, (2) adopt the civilization of the West with certain modifications, and (3) revaluate critically and promote "the Chinese spirit." [54]

What is this Chinese spirit? According to Liang, it is the Confucian *jen*. He reminded us that Confucius always praised life, saying that "change is production and reproduction," and that "the great virtue of Heaven and Earth is life." For Confucius, he contended, the sharp intuition of this dynamic universal process is *jen*.[55] Now, the psychological state of *jen* is both calm and sensitive. In essence, *jen* is identical with Centrality. However, China has hitherto tended to the quietism and meekness of Lao Tzu and has neglected the Confucian saying that "the firm, the strong, the resolute, and the simple are near to *jen*." [56] The way

[53] Literally middle, mean, or center. In Confucianism this word denotes the central or proper principle of balance between activity and tranquillity, the Moral Law, the central self or moral being in which the passions such as joy, anger, grief, and pleasure have not awakened and which exist in a state of absolute tranquillity without being moved. To Confucianists, this is the "ultimate principle" of the universe and "the basis of existence."

[54] Liang Sou-ming, *Tung-hsi wen-hua chi ch'i che-hsueh* ("Eastern and Western Civilizations and Their Philosophies"), pp. 199, 545, 63, 55, 66, 202.

[55] Variously translated as goodness, love, benevolence, true manhood, human-heartedness, man at his best, etc. In particular it means love, but in general it means the sum total of virtues, the moral principle, man's character or nature, "that by which a man is to be a man." From this moral connotation the meaning is extended to signify the central principle of existence, the love of which is evidence in universal production and reproduction. For a detailed explanation of this word, see my article, "Jen" in *The Dictionary of Philosophy*, ed. by Runes, p. 153.

[56] *Analects*, XIII, 27.

out for China, he concluded, is to revive the dynamic Confucian concept of *jen* as a firm and strong way of life.[57]

It can readily be seen that Liang's views are an oversimplification of the several civilizations. He had no adequate understanding of either Western or Indian culture. His conclusion resembles that of the Confucianists several decades earlier who advocated "Chinese learning for substance and Western learning for function." But the important point for us is that he and Sun Yat-sen accentuated the trend to revaluate Confucianism. This trend was reinforced by the eventual shift of emphasis in the Intellectual Renaissance itself, which gradually turned from debunking to objective reexamination. The point was finally reached where even such a left-wing writer as Kuo Mo-jo goes so far as to say that Confucius and his pupils were always on the side of rebels and sympathetic to the liberation of the people, and that their fundamental standpoints were social progress and social welfare.[58] Hu Shih himself grants that "not only is it my opinion that Confucianism will furnish very fertile soil on which to cultivate modern scientific thinking but Confucianism has many traditions which are quite favorable to the spirit and attitude of modern science." He further says that "throughout the history of China you find Confucianism always the philosophy of political reform." [59] In the West, Professor Creel's *Confucius, the Man and the Myth* represents the turning point from denouncing Confucius as a conservative, unimaginative, dogmatic, and authoritarian

[57] Liang Sou-ming, *op. cit.*, pp. 121, 126, 128–29, 211–13. In his preface to the third edition, he discarded his original idea that in the West intuition operates on the rational faculty, in China the rational faculty operates on intuition, while in India the rational faculty operates on sensation. But his general thesis was retained.

[58] Kuo Mo-jo, *Shih p'i-p'an shu* ("Ten Critiques"), pp. 72, 75.

[59] In *Modern Trends in World-Religions*, ed. by A. Eustace Haydon, pp. 46, 83.

schoolman to praising him as a creative, human, liberal, democratic social reformer. All these revaluations have extreme significance for Confucianism.

THE DISCOVERY OF THE RELIGIOUS POSITION OF CONFUCIUS

The revaluation has not converted Confucian critics like Hu Shih to be pro-Confucianists, but it does indicate a trend of objective and constructive study. This trend has led to a number of discoveries about Confucius. Among these the discovery of his true religious position is of the most direct interest to us.

For centuries Confucius had been believed to have followed tradition in religion. "I transmit but do not create," he once said.[60] During the debate over the question of state religion, conflicting claims were made that he founded a religion, that he did not, that he was deeply religious, and that he was not. A number of efforts have been made to clarify the question. Of these, the most important and most fruitful were made by Hu Shih and Fu Ssu-nien. In his well-known essay entitled "*Shuo ju*" ("On the Literati"),[61] certainly an epoch-making and permanent contribution to Chinese scholarship, Hu Shih says that the word *ju*, which later denoted a Confucian scholar or literati, originally meant weakness, referring to people who wore ancient-style garments and whose expression indicated meekness. These people, according to him, were descendants of the Yin Shang Dynasty (c. 1523–c. 1028 B.C.) who retained their ancient garments and practiced traditional rites, including the custom of three-year mourning. As descendants of a conquered

[60] *Analects*, VII, 1.

[61] Hu Shih, *op. cit.*, pp. 3–81. For a German translation of the essay, see von Wolfgang Franke, trans., "Der Ursprung der Ju und ihre Beziehung zu Konfuzius und Lau-dsï," *Sinica Sonderausgabe*, 1935, pp. 141–71; 1936, pp. 1–42.

people, they were suppressed and despised, but because of their religious heritage they were able to make a living by advising on and performing religious rites.

Confucius, being a native of Lu, which was originally a part of Yin, belonged to this group of "weak" people. But two things made him an outstanding and a different *ju*. One was the fact that at his time there was a prophecy that a True King would arise every five hundred years, and, according to Mencius, Confucius was regarded as such a True King. This naturally strengthened his strong sense of social responsibility. The other was that Confucius was a farsighted person, who realized that the ancient Yin heritage had to be modified to suit the new culture of the Chou period (c. 1027–256 B.C.) in which he lived. The result was that he became a *ju* not of the weak but of the strong, and his school represented a new type of *ju*, firm, active, and progressive. Thus Confucius was not the founder of the *ju* school as Chinese historians have held, but he revived an old tradition, injected into it some new blood, and raised it to new heights. As the guiding star of this renaissance, Confucius followed certain Yin religious traditions but rejected the popular worship of spirits, and held an advanced and rather abstract and rational concept of Heaven. Eventually his religion became that of the Chinese literati.[62]

Hu's theory is by no means flawless. It has been challenged by Fung Yu-lan, Kuo Mo-jo, Creel, and others, who believe that the *ju* were not descendants of a conquered race but decayed aristocrats or descendants of such aristocrats who had degenerated into the priestly profession, and that they were weak because they were not warlike, according to one theory, or not economic laborers, according to another.[63] We

[62] *Ibid.*, pp. 9–10, 16–17, 19–22, 26–27, 33, 37, 42, 52, 66, 76, 80.
[63] Fung Yu-lan, *Chung-kuo che-hsueh shih pu* ("Supplement to A *History of Chinese Philosophy*"), pp. 28, 59; Kuo Mo-jo, *Ch'ing-t'ung shih-tai* ("The Bronze Age"), pp. 134–36; Creel, *op. cit.*, pp. 313–14.

are not concerned with the historical and linguistic questions involved. What is significant for us is that Hu's theory about Confucius' religious position, in its basic aspects, has not been contested.

In fact, his theory was reinforced by Professor Fu Ssu-nien (1896–1950), although Fu had his own new ideas. Hu Shih built his theory entirely on familiar literary sources. Fu, on the other hand, based his research on the inscriptions on recently discovered oracle bones. In his *Hsing-ming ku-hsun pien-cheng* ("A Critical Study of the Traditional Theories of Human Nature and Destiny"), generally praised as the outstanding work on Chinese studies in the last decade, he proves that the religion of the Shang Dynasty was basically ancestor worship. In the oracle bones, the word *ti* often means ancestors. The term *Shang-ti,* which appears only once in the oracle bones, refers to *Ti-k'u,* the High Ancestor of the Shang people. Gradually the term came to denote the Lord on High who controls all natural forces and human fortune. Thus the concept of Shang-ti had already been held in the Shang period and did not differ from the concept of T'ien or Heaven in the Chou times.[64] Although the word *t'ien* occurs only once in the oracle bones, the fact remains that the term existed. It is inconceivable, Fu believes, that the Shang people, who had both the term *t'ien* and the idea of an all-powerful Shang-ti, did not have the concept of T'ien as a general name for superior deities.[65] Professor Fu therefore rejects the theory that the concept of T'ien originated with the Chou people and contends that there was no cultural break between the Shang and the Chou. On the contrary, the cultural development was continuous.[66]

[64] In the history of Chinese thought the two terms T'ien and Shang-ti are sometimes interchangeable. But in general the latter means the anthropomorphic Supreme Lord who directs and governs the universe, whereas the former refers to the Lord in the sense of omnipresence and all-inclusiveness.
[65] Fu, *Hsing-ming ku-hsun pien-cheng,* II, 7B, 4A, 8A.
[66] *Ibid.,* II, 14A.

However, Fu points out that while there was no radical change in religion and other institutions between the two periods, there was one significant transition, and that was what he calls "the dawn of humanism." Take, for example, human sacrifice. This was a common practice in the Shang period, but by the time of Confucius, five or six hundred years later, there were only a few isolated cases, and Confucius condemned it as barbarous. The conclusion is that the break took place between the Shang and the Chou.[67] The Chou people followed the Shang in their great reverence for Heaven but at the same time laid increasing emphasis on human motivation and human activities. The result was an equal emphasis on Heaven and man.[68] This point is very important, because the balance between Heaven and man has been a dominant idea throughout the history of Chinese thought and occupies a central place in present Confucian tendencies.

According to Professor Fu, out of this equal emphasis on Heaven and man grew five theories of Heavenly Mandate which became prevalent in Confucius' time. The first was Fatalism,[69] that the Mandate of Heaven is fixed and unchangeable. Secondly, there was Moral Determinism,[70] to the effect that Heaven always encourages virtue and punishes evil; in other words, reward or punishment depends on man's behavior. Thirdly, there was the theory of Anti-Fatalism,[71] as later advocated by Mo Tzu of the fifth century B.C. Fourthly, there was the theory of Naturalistic Fatalism,[72] which differs from Fatalism in that, whereas in Fatalism mandates are considered as coming from an anthropomorphic Lord, in Naturalistic Fatalism they are regarded as following a mechanical law. Lastly, there was the theory of

[67] Fu, *op. cit.*, II, 14B, 15A.
[68] *Ibid.*, II, 19A.
[69] *Ting-ming lun.*
[70] *Ming-cheng lun.*
[71] *Fei-ming lun.*
[72] *Ming-yun lun.*

"Waiting for Heaven's Mandate," [73] meaning that, generally speaking, while the Will of Heaven is to reward good and punish evil, there are exceptional cases where virtuous men do not enjoy longevity and the wicked do not suffer poverty. As stated in the "Chao-kao" of *The Book of History*, "A gentleman takes virtue seriously and waits for the Mandate of Heaven." Or, as Mencius put it, "To wait by cultivating one's personal character is the way to fulfill or establish Heavenly Mandate." [74] As Fu points out, this last theory is a tendency away from traditional religion and inclines towards moralism. That was the position of Confucius, and that has been a leading tenet of Confucian thought throughout the ages.[75]

From the above, three things may be stressed. The first is that Confucius' idea of Heavenly Mandate was not original but was an idea prevalent at his time. Secondly, the Confucian theory was a combination of Fatalism and Moral Determinism. Fatalism means that human conduct can never influence Heavenly Mandates, and Moral Determinism means that human conduct can always influence Heavenly Mandates. Confucius rejected both as extremes and chose the middle ground, that of "Waiting for Heavenly Mandates." [76] This is why he said, "I do not murmur against Heaven," [77] (that is, one should bear one's own responsibility), and at the same time said, "I have prayed for a long time" [78] (that is, Heaven does intervene). This doctrine was greatly elaborated by Mencius, who said that "Death sustained in the course of carrying out one's duty to the fullest extent may correctly be ascribed to the Mandate of

[73] *Ssu-ming lun.*
[74] *Meng Tzu* (*The Works of Mencius*), Book VII, Part I, Chap. 1. For an English translation, see *The Works of Mencius*, trans. by James Legge, in *The Chinese Classics*, 2d ed.; also in *The Four Books.*
[75] Fu, *op. cit.*, II, 22A–24B.
[76] *Ibid.*, II, 37B.
[77] *Analects*, XIV, 37.
[78] *Ibid.*, VII, 34.

Heaven."[79] As Juan Yuan (1764–1849) has stated, this theory has been the essence of Confucianism.[80]

The third point to stress is that the Confucian transition from religious Fatalism to humanistic Waiting for Heaven's Mandate was the reason why Confucius seldom talked about the Way of Heaven. He still looked upon Heaven with great reverence, for, to him, the Way of Heaven was the foundation of rites, and governmental measures were the applications of those rites. But he did not talk much about the Way of Heaven, because there was always an element of uncertainty in its operation and because he chose to lay increasing emphasis on human affairs. In short, the major premise of Confucian ethics was still the Way of Heaven, but there was a growing attention to man.[81]

Fu's interpretation is quite convincing, having as it does both literary evidence and historical facts on his side. His general conclusion agrees with that of Hu Shih's; namely, that Confucius was neither a mere transmitter of an old religion nor the founder of a new one, but he raised the old religion to a higher level by establishing the balance between Heaven and man. Thus he paved the way for the development of the long Confucian tradition of the unity of man and Heaven. For two thousand years that tradition has never weakened.

Is this tradition alive today? For the answer to this question, we must proceed to discuss the third and fourth tendencies in contemporary Confucianism, the development of the Idealistic and the Rationalistic Neo-Confucian Schools.

THE DEVELOPMENT OF IDEALISTIC NEO-CONFUCIANISM

The Confucian tradition of the unity of Heaven and man, greatly developed in the Western Han period (202 B.C. to

[79] *Works of Mencius*, Book VII, Part I, Chap. 2.
[80] Fu, *op. cit.*, II, 37A–38A. [81] *Ibid.*, II, 38A–B.

A.D. 9), culminated in the Idealistic Neo-Confucianism of Lu Hsiang-shan (1139–92) and Wang Yang-ming (1472–1528) or the Lu-Wang School.[82] This school has been revived in modern China. Most writers on contemporary Chinese thought agree that it is one of the most remarkable intellectual developments in China in the last half century.[83]

One writer has traced the Lu-Wang movement in the twentieth century from K'ang Yu-wei through his pupil T'an Ssu-t'ung, and thence through Chang T'ai-yen, Ou-yang

[82] Lu Hsiang-shan was the founder of the Idealistic School of Neo-Confucianism. He declared that "The six [Confucian] Classics are my footnotes" and he said that "the universe is identical with my mind, and my mind is identical with the universe." To him both the mind and the universe are expressions of Tao. "There is no Tao beyond events, and there are no events beyond Tao."

Confucian Idealism reached its climax in Wang Yang-ming, to whom the mind and *Li* are the same thing. External objects are not really independent of the mind. The mind embraces all *Li*, Reason or Law. In order to discover *Li*, one needs to return to his own mind, which is originally good and clear. One has the native ability to know good and the native ability to do good. Not only is the knowledge of the good inborn, but practicing the good is also native, so that knowledge and conduct are identical. One's duty is to maintain tranquillity of mind, realize one's good nature, intuit good and put it into practice. One who does that is a man of *jen*, who loves all things as well as all people. In this way the common mind of all things is realized and "Heaven and Earth and I are a unity."

For a full treatment of Lu Hsiang-shan's philosophy, see Siu-chi Huang, *Lu Hsiang-shan, a Twelfth Century Chinese Idealist Philosopher*, and Cady, *The Philosophy of Lu Hsiang-shan, a Neo-Confucian Monistic Idealist*. For the philosophy of Wang Yang-ming, see *The Philosophy of Wang Yang Ming*, trans. by Frederick Goodrich Henke, and Wang Tch'ang-tche, *La Philosophie morale de Wang Yang-ming*. For a summary of the Lu-Wang philosophy, see my chapter, "Neo-Confucianism," in *China*, ed. by Harley Farnsworth MacNair, pp. 259–60.

[83] See Ho Lin, *Tang-tai Chung-kuo che-hsueh* ("Contemporary Chinese Philosophy"), p. 3; Hsieh Yu-wei, "Philosophy in the Seven Years of War of Resistance" (in Chinese), in Sun Pen-wen, *Chung-kuo chan-shih hsueh-shu* ("Scholarship in China during the War"), pp. 12–13; Kuo Chan-po, *Chin wu-shih-nien Chung-kuo ssu-hsiang shih* ("History of Chinese Thought in the Last Fifty Years"), pp. 17–34, 175–78. Kuo's book was written from the viewpoint of dialectic materialism and almost entirely neglects Idealistic Neo-Confucianism and Buddhism. Nevertheless, it does include modern interpreters of Neo-Confucian Idealism like T'an Ssu-t'ung and Liang Sou-ming.

Ching-wu, Liang Sou-ming, and Ma I-fu to Hsiung Shih-li.[84] Liang was the first strong advocate after the Intellectual Renaissance. As already noted, he interprets *jen* as the intuition of the dynamic process of "production and reproduction," which is identical with the *Li* (Law, Principle, Reason) of Heaven or the Law of Nature (*T'ien-li*). To realize this *Li* fully, one's mind must be both calm and alert. As Wang's pupil Nieh Shuang-chiang (1487–1563) said, only through calmness can one penetrate Reality and only through alertness can one respond to the total stimuli of the universe. To be calm means to be balanced or "central," which means *jen*. In effect, this means that Reality is to be discovered in the mind. To Liang, the chief contribution of Wang Yang-ming to Chinese thought has been to correct the tendency of Neo-Confucianists of the Sung period (960–1279) to look for *Li* externally, and to advocate its realization through the exercise of what Wang Yang-ming called our native knowledge of the good and our native ability to do good. This is understood by Liang as calm but keen and sharp intuition, *jen*. When *jen* is practiced, truth is revealed and virtue is realized, and one ultimately becomes one with the universe.[85]

Such philosophy sounds quietistic and has often been so misunderstood. Actually, it is a philosophy of sharp decision and vigorous action. As Liang points out, it was such philosophy that produced great men like Huang Tsung-hsi (1610–95) and Wang Ch'uan-shan (1619–92), who refused to submit to invaders, and many martyrs who opposed the Manchus. Liang himself finally gave up teaching and went into active rural reconstruction and political reform. In this

[84] Ho Lin, *op. cit.*, pp. 3–22. For a brief account of the revival of Idealistic Neo-Confucianism, see Brière, "Les Courants philosophiques en Chine depuis 50 ans (1898–1950)," *Bulletin de l'Université l'Aurore*, Série III, Tome X, No. 40 (October, 1949), 589–94.
[85] Liang Sou-ming, *op. cit.*, pp. 127–30, 149–50.

way he has translated the Lu-Wang Neo-Confucian philosophy into action. The development of this philosophy continued in Professor Hsiung Shih-li, to whom we must now turn.

Without going into the philosophy of the Lu-Wang School, we may simply say that Lu's philosophy is summed up in his famous aphorism, "The mind is the universe," and that Wang's system is condensed in his celebrated saying that "Heaven and Earth and the ten thousand things form one body." These two sentences represent the gist of Hsiung's philosophy.

Hsiung is important not only because he is the most outstanding contemporary representative of Neo-Confucian Idealism, but also because he exemplifies the tendency to Confucianize Buddhism. Reserving this second aspect for a later discussion, we shall concentrate now on his development of the Lu-Wang Neo-Confucian Idealistic philosophy.

Following both the Buddhist theory that things are impermanent and the Confucian doctrine that the universe is a Great Change as propounded in *The Book of Changes* [86] which formed the basis of Neo-Confucian philosophy, he emphasizes the fact of a "Running Current." [87] In fact, he glorifies it, in distinct contrast to Buddhism, which deplores

[86] *I ching*. Among several English translations, see the one by James Legge, *The Yi King*, in *The Sacred Books of the East*, Vol. XVI, and the version by Z. D. Zung, *The Text of Yi King*.

[87] Hsiung Shih-li, *Hsin wei-shih lun* ("New Idealism"), p. 49. Originally lectures at the National Peking University in 1923, the book was privately published in 1932. The present edition contains nine chapters in 358 pages, and is written in the colloquial style, or rather "translated" from the original edition in the classical style. Among other works by Hsiung are: *P'o p'o hsin wei-shih lun* ("Refuting the Refutation of New Idealism"), *Tu-ching shih-yao* ("Important Guides for the Study of Classics"), *Fo-chia ming-hsiang t'ung-lun* ("Buddhist Concepts Explained"), *Yin-ming ta-su shan-chu* ("Commentary on the Great Treatise on Buddhist Logic"), *Shih-li yü-yao* ("Important Sayings by Hsiung Shih-li"), all of which were published in the *Shih-li ts'ung-shu* ("Collection of Works by Hsiung") in 1947.

momentary existence.[88] I shall discuss in the third chapter in what sense Professor Hsiung is a Buddhist and in what sense he is not. Let us now treat him as a Neo-Confucianist, a label he himself and his pupils strongly prefer.

What is this Running Current that forms the center of his philosophy? To him, it is Reality in the ultimate sense. This Reality is self-existent and pure—self-existent in the sense of not having been created, and pure in the sense of being devoid of evil. It is absolute. It is "hidden," that is, without form. It is constant and eternal. It is whole, harmonious, and indivisible. It is changing because it manifests itself in countless phenomena, and yet it is unchanging because its self-nature remains unaltered in the process of change.[89] Such being its attributes, Reality may also be called Constant Transformation.[90]

As I have already mentioned, this concept of flux is derived from Buddhism and *The Book of Changes*. But whereas Buddhism rejects flux as illusory, Hsiung affirms it as the elementary fact of existence. How is this flux possible? It is possible, he says, because of the great principle of simultaneous negation and affirmation, which change implies. "Whenever we talk about change," he explains, "we imply that there must be an opposite, some sort of activity, an inner contradiction, and the reason why contradiction leads to development." [91] In this, Hsiung follows closely *The Book of Changes*, which expounds the idea that in every event or entity there are both the negative and positive elements which negate and at the same time affirm each other in a harmonious operation. He also draws support from the Taoist classic, the *Tao-te ching*,[92] which says in an often quoted

[88] Hsiung, *Hsin wei-shih lun*, p. 50.
[89] *Ibid.*, p. 54.
[90] *Ibid.*, p. 55. *Heng-chuan.*
[91] *Ibid.*, p. 55.
[92] For English translations of the *Tao-te ching*, see *The Way and Its Power*, trans. by Arthur Waley; "The Book of Tao," trans. by Lin Yutang, in his *The Wisdom of Laotse*, pp. 41–325; also in his *The Wisdom of India and China*, pp. 583–624.

passage: "The Way engenders the One. The One engenders the two. The two engender the three. The three engender all things. All things possess *yin* (the passive principle) and contain *yang* (the active principle), and the blending of the vital force produces harmony." [93] As Hsiung interprets this, the One produces the two which negate it, but the two produce the three which affirm both the One and the two.[94] Seen in this light, Hsiung believes, Taoism was really an offshoot of *The Book of Changes*, a novel theory that is difficult to maintain.[95]

Using the vocabulary of *The Book of Changes*, Hsiung calls these opposing principles Contraction and Expansion (*hsi p'i*), literally, "closing" and "opening." [96] There can be no change unless there is activity, and activity must be expressed in some direction. Contraction is activity tending in one direction and Expansion is activity tending in the other. Both are instantaneous, disappearing the very moment they arise.[97] "As soon as the function of activity begins," he says, "there is some sort of organizational concentration which takes the positive forms of collection and concretion. In this process, there is an infinite number of tendencies to take material form. It is from these tendencies that the material universe is born." [98] It is also because of these tendencies that the world is one of multiplicity, since organization and formation follow numerous principles and patterns, and each organization or formation involves many others.[99] In short, in manifesting itself as Contraction, Reality tends to assume definite, concrete, and stable material form, but in doing so it negates its original character of change.[100]

But at the very instant Contraction begins to act, there is another force called Expansion, which "operates within

[93] See *Tao-te ching*, 42.
[94] Hsiung, *Hsin wei-shih lun*, pp. 55–56.
[95] *Ibid.*, p. 68.
[96] *Book of Changes*, Appendix I, Chap. 6.
[97] Hsiung, *Hsin wei-shih lun*, pp. 56, 70–71.
[98] *Ibid.*, p. 57.
[99] *Ibid.*, p. 182.
[100] *Ibid.*, p. 57.

Contraction, acts as its own master, thereby demonstrates its strong power, and causes Contraction to follow it in the process of change." It is the power that opposes the tendency to take material form.[101] Thus as soon as there is Contraction, there is Expansion. The two forces work simultaneously but in opposite directions. Because of this opposition, there is change. In other words, there is always the tendency in Constant Transformation to manifest itself in material form and thereby to negate its self-nature of change, but there is at the same time always the tendency to retain its self-nature of change and oppose materialization.[102] This opposition obtains in the whole realm of existence as one. It also obtains in every single thing or event. In its tendency to retain its self-nature of change, Expansion combines the universe as One. In its tendency to assume material forms, Contraction differentiates the One into the Many. In either case, the opposition is at work.[103]

Obviously these two antagonistic forces are not to be interpreted as two different things. They are merely two different forces, functions, or aspects of the same Constant Transformation.[104] As Hsiung says, "Contraction and Expansion are not different Realities but are merely the different functionings of the same force or operation. Expansion necessarily depends on Contraction for its activity, and Contraction necessarily depends on Expansion for its evolution and direction." [105] If there were no Contraction, Expansion would have no channel to work through nor material to work with, and the universe would be empty. On the other hand, if there were no Expansion, there would be no motive force for change, and the universe would be static and dead.[106] But by the nature of change, they always operate simultane-

[101] Hsiung, *op. cit.*, p. 102.
[102] *Ibid.*, p. 57.
[103] *Ibid.*, p. 182.
[104] *Ibid.*, p. 59.
[105] *Ibid.*, p. 60.
[106] *Ibid.*, p. 66.

ously. Although they negate each other, they are also synthesized and harmonized.[107]

In conventional philosophical terms, Contraction is matter and Expansion is mind.[108] But matter and mind must not be sharply contrasted as two different Realities. Matter is not to be understood as an ordinary concrete and solid object, completely distinguished from what is ordinarily thought of as mind. Rather, it is but "a manifestation of Contraction in its activity to collect and congeal." [109] In "completing a thing," Contraction does not really produce a static, fixed, concrete object, but merely leaves a "trace" of its operation which "appears" to be a concrete, substantial entity.[110]

Here we have the explanation of why Professor Hsiung calls his philosophy Idealism, or *Wei-shih*, literally, "mere-ideation." He is insistent in making clear that his Idealism is not identical with Western Idealism, which denies matter as unreal. He uses the word *wei* not in the sense of *only* but in the sense of *especially*.[111] To him, the division of matter and mind into two different and parallel realms violates truth, for, to repeat, they are but two different forces or aspects of the same Reality. Nevertheless, Expansion is superior to Contraction, because it is "the master" in the whole process of Constant Transformation. It is the determining factor and the directing force in the Running Current. It is this master that converts the self-contradictory transformation into a "Grand Harmony," [112] to borrow a term made famous by the Sung Neo-Confucianist Chang Heng-ch'ü (1020–77).[113] It is this master that makes the fluctuating

[107] *Ibid.*, p. 59.
[108] *Ibid.*, p. 59.
[109] *Ibid.*, p. 67.
[110] *Ibid.*, p. 61.
[111] *Ibid.*, Preface, p. iii.
[112] *T'ai-ho*, Grand Harmony or Infinite Harmony, the state and totality of being.
[113] Chang was one of the Five Masters of early Neo-Confucianism. To him, the universe is the process of integration and disintegration of *ch'i* (material force, matter in the dynamic sense). Its integration and disintegration

transformation regular, the varying transformation uniform, the apparent transformation real, and the restricted transformation free.[114] Because of this "master," the universe is not a static equilibrium of equal and opposite tensions but an evolutionary development. By the same token, the universe is not a chaos but an order, and, to borrow again from *The Book of Changes* and Sung Neo-Confucianists, "All things are in their proper stations." [115]

It would be a serious mistake to view this "master" as the Creator who is the father of the cosmos. It is not a religious being; instead, it is the Cosmic Mind.[116] As such, it is an "absolute totality." [117] It is "*jen*, the source of all transformation and the foundation of all beings." [118] It is the Original Mind, different from the "mind of habits," [119] which is the mind studied in psychology and which expresses itself in thought, will, and the emotions. The mind of habits presupposes an object and in a certain sense is an object itself, an object without self-nature, whereas the Original Mind is the very nature by which things realize themselves but which does not itself become objectified.[120]

This Original Mind existed before the material universe, which is really its manifestation. It is the Mind of the entire universe. It is also the Mind of each and every thing. They are different and yet the same, like ocean and waves, one manifesting through the other.[121] In this unending process

---

follow *Li* or Law, thus resulting in a universe of order. In this scheme of things, nothing is isolated. Everything has its opposite. No two things are identical with one another. All things are in a state of change, and all change is cyclical. The universe forms one body, so that "Heaven is my father and Earth is my mother. . . . All people are my brothers and all things are my companions." For a good statement of his philosophy, see Fung Yu-lan, *A Short History of Chinese Philosophy*, pp. 278–80.

[114] Hsiung, *Hsin wei-shih lun*, pp. 113–14.

[115] *Ibid.*, p. 122.

[116] *Ibid.*, pp. 61–62.

[117] *Ibid.*, p. 282.

[118] *Ibid.*, p. 261.

[119] *Hsi-hsin.*

[120] Hsiung, *Hsin wei-shih lun*, p. 304.

[121] *Ibid.*, p. 65.

of manifestations, the Mind evolves, reaching a higher stage in organic life and an even higher level in consciousness.[122]

From the above, it is clear that Reality, as Constant Transformation, is but a process, and being a process constitutes its very reality. Professor Hsiung feels that only in discovering the identity of "reality" and "function" can we fathom the depth of truth.[123] "From the point of view of reality," he says, "function consists of reality. Reality is perfectly tranquil and yet exceedingly active. It is absolutely nonexistent and yet mysteriously existent. Tranquillity and nonexistence describe the original state of reality, while activity and existence describe its wonderful function. . . . Therefore, only in its function can reality be revealed. . . . From the point of view of function, reality lies in functioning. . . . Spoken of as reality, it is the One True that embraces countless transformations. Spoken of as function, it is countless transformations that are the One True. Therefore reality is no different from function." [124] "Function is the manifestation of reality, and reality is the reality of function. Without reality there will be no function, and separated from function there can be no reality." [125] "When we call function the mind," he warns us, "we must not forget that function cannot be divorced from reality. As soon as we talk about function, we already realize the self-nature of reality which is function itself. When we call reality the mind, we must remember that from the point of view of reality, function lies in reality. In the final analysis, reality and function cannot be cut into two pieces." [126]

In identifying function and reality, Hsiung draws heavily from Taoism and *The Book of Changes*, both of which were assimilated into Neo-Confucianism.[127] But Western philoso-

[122] *Ibid.*, p. 64.
[123] *T'i-yung.*
[124] Hsiung, *Hsin wei-shih lun*, p. 153.
[125] *Ibid.*, p. 45.
[126] *Ibid.*, p. 256.
[127] *Ibid.*, p. 58.

phy is not left out of his eclecticism.[128] Although he owes much of his philosophy to Buddhism, it is the identification of function and reality that turns him from Buddhism to Confucianism. "Because I criticize Buddhist schools for accepting only Being or Non-Being as real,[129] I found the harmonious synthesis in *The Book of Changes* on which both Confucianism and Taoism are based." [130] He considers, quite correctly, that Buddhism only appreciates the tranquil character of Reality,[131] believes that there can be no transformation in absolute tranquillity,[132] and fails to understand the Running Current.[133] This failure stems from the Buddhist doctrine of renunciation of the world, which leads to the denial of the world in action.[134] Confucianism, on the other hand, highly respects the virtue of "production and reproduction" [135] and therefore understands that "there is change in absolute passivity and transformation in absolute tranquillity." [136]

True to the Confucian tradition, Hsiung equates this virtue of production and reproduction with *jen,* which is "the first among all virtues from which no other virtue can be isolated." [137] He reminds us that Confucius not only said that the man of *jen* is tranquil, but also remarked that the four seasons run their course.[138] The sage paid equal regard to both reality and function. As a result, the mutual identification of reality and function has become a dominant feature in the entire history of Confucianism. The synthesis reached its peak in Wang Yang-ming, whose saying, "From the point of view of reality, function lies in reality," has become a

[128] Hsiung, *op. cit.*, p. 125. See Chou T'ung-tan's review of *Hsin wei-shih lun* in *T'u-shu chi-k'an* (*The Quarterly Bulletin of Chinese Bibliography*), V, No. 4 (December, 1944), p. 64.
[129] See below, pp. 131–32.
[130] Hsiung, *Hsin wei-shih lun*, Preface, p. i.
[131] *Ibid.*, p. 106.
[132] *Ibid.*, p. 120.
[133] *Ibid.*, p. 113.
[134] *Ibid.*, p. 126.
[135] *Ibid.*, p. 109.
[136] *Ibid.*, p. 107.
[137] *Ibid.*, p. 107.
[138] *Ibid.*, pp. 109–10. The references are to *Analects*, VI, 21, and XVII, 19.

proverb.[139] Hsiung says that his entire book is devoted to this single idea that reality and function are one.[140] Because of this conviction, he bitterly attacks those Buddhist schools that separate consciousness into mind and mental functions and divide activities and phenomena into parallel domains.[141] He even criticizes Neo-Confucianism for treating *Li* (Principle) and *ch'i* (matter) as two,[142] although in doing so he exaggerates the dualism of Neo-Confucianism. He does so, no doubt, because he wants to be emphatic in stating that Reality is one.

How is this Oneness to be realized for us? It can be realized if we practice *jen*, he says, for it is the Mind itself and it is the basic virtue common to all men and Heaven and Earth.[143] Following Wang Yang-ming, Hsiung says that if we discover the *jen* in us, we will clearly see that all things constitute the same Reality. As Ch'eng Ming-tao (1032–85) has expressed it in a celebrated saying, "A man of *jen* forms one body with all things." [144]

This process of realization is called by Neo-Confucianists *t'i-jen*, which, roughly, means personally witnessing, personally testing, and understanding through personal experience. To Hsiung, *t'i-jen*, which he regards as "the outstanding spirit of Chinese philosophy," is the highest form of knowledge, combining and surpassing both intuition and reasoning. It is an inward process of "returning to the mind" to discover Reality therein. One who witnesses Reality this way

[139] Hsiung, *Hsin wei-shih lun*, p. 114. The saying is found in *The Philosophy of Wang Yang-ming*, p. 122.

[140] Hsiung, *Hsin wei-shih lun*, Preface, p. ii. Also *idem, Shih-li yü-yao*, I, 1B; Chou T'ung-tan, in *Quarterly Bulletin of Chinese Bibliography*, V, No. 4 (December, 1944), 60.

[141] *Ibid.*, pp. 90, 159.

[142] Hsiung, *Hsin wei-shih lun*, p. 238. This dualism of Chu Hsi is exaggerated. See my chapter on Neo-Confucianism in *China*, ed. by MacNair.

[143] Hsiung, *Hsin wei-shih lun*, p. 260.

[144] *Ibid.*, pp. 160–61; Ch'eng I-ch'uan and Ch'eng Ming-tao, *Ch'eng-shih i-shu* ("Literary Remains of the Ch'eng Brothers"), Chap. 2, Part I.

will enter into enlightenment, in which everything forms one complete indivisible unity, with no distinction of the internal and external, the subjective and the objective, the One and the Many, or any other category of discrimination.[145] As a matter of fact, in *t'i-jen,* it is Reality illuminating and realizing itself.[146] This, according to him, is what Wang Yang-ming meant by "extending our native knowledge to the utmost," for Wang always combined the internal and the external as one.[147] In the end, all men and Heaven form one unity.

This is not the place to enter into a critical analysis of Professor Hsiung's philosophy. Certain defects are obvious. He overemphasizes the Mind and inward knowledge.[148] It is difficult to see how transformation is possible unless there is something definite and real to transform.[149] As it is also pointed out, change is unintelligible unless there is duration.[150] Nevertheless, in identifying reality and function and thus arriving at the unity of man and Heaven, he is a true Neo-Confucianist and has taken us to the summit of Neo-Confucianism.[151]

Ho Lin gives two reasons for the development of the Lu-Wang philosophy in Hsiung and others. One is that the emphasis on the Mind fits in with the modern emphasis on individual consciousness and national consciousness. Secondly, in a period of struggle and confusion of values, such as ours, it is natural to resort to consciousness.[152] I would add that modern science and philosophy have tended away

[145] Hsiung, *Shih-li yü-yao,* II, 21B.
[146] *Ibid.,* I, 9A.
[147] *Ibid.,* III, 45A.
[148] As pointed out by the editor of *The Quarterly Bulletin of Chinese Bibliography,* V, No. 4 (December, 1944), 64.
[149] Chou Ku-ch'eng, *Chung-kuo shih-hsueh chih chin-hua* ("The Development of Chinese Historiography"), p. 32.
[150] Hsieh yu-wei, *Hsien-tai che-hsueh ming-chu shu-p'ing* ("Critical Reviews of Modern Outstanding Works on Philosophy"), pp. 68–69.
[151] Hsiung, *Shih-li yü-yao,* I, 1A.
[152] Ho Lin, *op. cit.,* p. 19.

from the bifurcation of Nature and have encouraged the familiar trend of synthesis in Chinese thought.

THE DEVELOPMENT OF RATIONALISTIC NEO-CONFUCIANISM

The same spirit of the unity of Heaven and man characterizes the philosophy of Professor Fung Yu-lan, who represents the other wing of modern Confucianism. There is no doubt that Fung has been the most outstanding and the most creative of contemporary Chinese philosophers. He considers his New Rational Philosophy a "new tradition," [153] which, in his own words, "was considered as representing a revival of Chinese philosophy and also as a symbol of the revival of the Chinese nation." [154]

By a "new tradition" is meant a new development of Chinese traditional philosophy, more specifically the Neo-Confucian Rationalism of Ch'eng I-ch'uan (1033–1107) and Chu Hsi (1130–1200). Significantly, he calls his system new *li-hsueh* or Rational Philosophy, which is the name for the Neo-Confucian philosophical tradition of the Ch'eng-Chu School.[155] Accordingly he calls his most important book

[153] Fung Yu-lan, *Hsin yuan-tao* (*The Spirit of Chinese Philosophy*), Chap. 10. See English translation by E. R. Hughes, *The Spirit of Chinese Philosophy*.

[154] Fung Yu-lan, *A Short History of Chinese Philosophy*, p. 335.

[155] In the Ch'eng-Chu school, ultimate reality is the Great Ultimate (*T'ai-chi*) which generates the active principle, *yang*, and the passive principle, *yin*, which in their turn engender all multiplicity. Thus Reality is a progressively evolved and well-coordinated system. Everything has its own Great Ultimate, but the Great Ultimate for the entire universe is one. This is the case because all things have the same *Li* (Principle) in them, of which the Great Ultimate is the sum total. They all have *Li* because things must have their principles of being. As *Li* is the universal principle, "The *Li* of a thing is one with the *Li* of all things."

The agency through which *Li* operates is *ch'i*—material force—which, working through the principles of *yin* and *yang*, differentiates the One into the Many. *Li* and *ch'i* are supplementary but not separate, although logically *Li* is prior to *ch'i*. *Li* is "above form" whereas *ch'i* is "below form." Their cooperative functioning makes the universe a cosmos. The universe is thus characterized by "centrality" and harmony, and "the Great Ultimate is the *Li* of ultimate goodness." In short, the cosmos is a moral one.

Hsin li-hsueh, or "New Rational Philosophy." [156] What is new is that he incorporates into this rationalistic Neo-Confucianism the Western element of realism and Western

---

Man must comprehend *Li* through the "investigation of things" and "extension of knowledge" with sincerity (*ch'eng*) and seriousness (*ching*). When sufficient effort is made, understanding will be achieved; one's originally good nature will be realized, and one's destiny will be fulfilled, because "the complete realization of *Li* of things, the full development of one's nature, and the establishment of one's destiny are simultaneous."

For a brief summary of the philosophy of the Ch'eng-Chu School, see my chapter "Neo-Confucianism," in *China*, ed. by MacNair, pp. 256–59. For a fuller exposition, see Fung, *A Short History of Chinese Philosophy*, Chaps. 24–25.

See also: Chu Hsi, *The Philosophy of Human Nature by Chu Hsi*, trans. by J. Percy Bruce; P. C. Hsu, *Ethical Realism in Neo-Confucian Thought*; Bruce, *Chu Hsi and His Masters*; Fung Yu-lan, "The Philosophy of Chu Hsi," trans. by Derk Bodde, *Harvard Journal of Asiatic Studies*, VII, No. 1 (April, 1942), 1–51; Alfred Forke, *Geschichte der neueren chinesischen Philosophie*, pp. 69–104, 164–202.

[156] Fung Yu-lan, *Hsin li-hsueh* ("New Rational Philosophy"), pp. 1–2. This is the most important work by Fung. It is a work of 312 pages in ten chapters (*Li* and the Great Ultimate; *Ch'i* and the Two Modes; The Way—*Tao*—and the Way of Heaven; The Nature and the Mind; Morality and the Way of Man; Tendencies and History; Truth; Art; Past and Future Existences; and The Sage). For a summary of the doctrine set forth in this book, see my chapter "Philosophies of China," in *Twentieth Century Philosophy*, ed. by Runes, pp. 563–67; or my chapter "Trends in Contemporary Philosophy," in *China*, ed. by MacNair, pp. 326–29.

Following *Hsin li-hsueh*, there have been five books in which Fung attempted to complete his system in its various phases. *Hsin shih-lun* ("A New Treatise on Practical Affairs") (230 pp.) deals with social, political, and cultural reconstruction. *Hsin shih-hsun* ("A New Treatise on the Way of Life") (198 pp.) embodies Professor Fung's ethics. *Hsin yuan-jen* ("A New Treatise on the Nature of Man") (147 pp.) presents the theory of four different grades of existence, from the "natural man" to the sage. *Hsin yuan-tao* (*The Spirit of Chinese Philosophy*) (123 pp.), interprets the historical development of Chinese philosophy. In *Hsin chih-yen* ("A New Treatise on the Methodology of Metaphysics") (104 pp.) Fung develops his system of methodology. Before the publication of these works, his position as the leading Chinese philosopher was assured when he published his *Chung-kuo che-hsueh shih*. The first half of this work has been translated into English by Derk Bodde, under the title *A History of Chinese Philosophy, the Period of the Philosophers* (*from the Beginning to about* 100 B.C.). The translation of the second half is now in press. Among Fung's works in English, *A Short History of Chinese Philosophy* has already been mentioned.

logic, as well as the Taoist element of negativism and transcendentalism.[157]

According to Fung, there are four main concepts in his philosophy; namely, *Li* (Reason, Principle, or Law), *ch'i* (Matter), the Evolution of Tao, and the Great Whole.[158] Collectively, they are deduced from the statement that "something exists." [159] They all fall under the category of formal concepts, empty and without content. They are all logical implications.[160] As a matter of fact, not only these four, but all concepts are logically deducible. Take, for example, the idea of movement. To exist means activity, and activity means movement.[161]

Specifically, each of the four main concepts is derived from a proposition or a set of propositions.[162] The first concept, that of *Li*, is derived from the proposition in ancient Chinese philosophy which Ch'eng I-ch'uan greatly developed, that "if there are things, there must be laws," or *li*, as the Neo-Confucianists called them.[163] In order to be, a thing must be a certain particular thing and belong to a certain particular class. In other words, it has to follow certain *Li* by which a thing is what it is. Indeed, a thing has to follow an infinite number of *li*, for every quality and every relation follow *li*.[164]

Li as Principle is self-existent, absolute, and eternal. It is

[157] *The Spirit of Chinese Philosophy*, pp. 203–4.
[158] *Ibid.*, p. 205.
[159] *A Short History of Chinese Philosophy*, p. 335.
[160] *Ibid.*, p. 335; *The Spirit of Chinese Philosophy*, p. 205.
[161] *A Short History of Chinese Philosophy*, p. 335.
[162] *The Spirit of Chinese Philosophy*, p. 205.
[163] *Hsin li-hsueh*, p. 53. As we have noted, several times, *Li* is Reason, Law, the Rational Principle. It is the basic concept of Neo-Confucianism. The Rationalistic wing, that is, the Ch'eng-Chu School, understands it as the rational principle of existence, in contrast to *ch'i*, which is the material principle. The Idealistic wing, that is, the Lu-Wang School, identifies it with the mind. *Li* meaning propriety or rites and *li* meaning profit are represented by different Chinese characters and are therefore to be clearly distinguished from this philosophical term.
[164] *Ibid.*, p. 60.

a universal as understood in Kung-sun Lung (b. 380 B.C.?) and in Western philosophy.[165] It is neither in nor above the world, since it does not enter into temporal or spatial relations. A thing needs to follow *Li*, but *Li* need not necessarily be realized in a thing. It belongs to the realm of Reality but not to the realm of Actuality. Actuality implies Reality but not vice versa.[166] Hence there are more *Li* than are realized in the actual world. The sum total of all *Li* is the Great Ultimate.[167]

The second concept, that of *ch'i* or Matter,[168] is derived, as in the Ch'eng-Chu Neo-Confucianism, from the proposition that "if there is *Li*, there must be *ch'i*," which means that if there be actualization of a *li*, there must be the *ch'i* which actualizes it. For a thing to be able to exist, there must be the *ch'i* by which it can exist.

In a relative sense, *ch'i* is that by which a thing can exist, as, for example, blood in the human body. But blood itself requires that by which blood can exist. And so on until we arrive at that by which *all* things can exist. This is *ch'i* in the absolute sense. It is Matter, a logical concept, which Fung calls "the *ch'i* of the true prime unit," [169] using Ch'eng's term with a new meaning. Being that according to which actuality becomes possible, *ch'i* has the characteristic of existence. But itself does not exist, whether in *Li* or in the actual world. In this, Fung departs from Neo-Confucianists like Ch'eng I-ch'uan and Chang Heng-ch'ü who consider *ch'i* to be *in* the actual world.[170] In other words, *ch'i* is not a "what," but that which makes the "what" actual. As such, it is the Taoist

[165] Fung, *op. cit.*, p. 43.
[166] *Ibid.*, pp. 10, 27–28.
[167] *Ibid.*, pp. 38, 42, 47, 53–55, 61–62; *The Spirit of Chinese Philosophy*, pp. 205–7.
[168] *Hsin li-hsueh*, pp. 63–68; *The Spirit of Chinese Philosophy*, pp. 207–9. *Ch'i* is literally breath, force, power, and has been variously translated as ether, matter, vital force. See my article, "Ch'i," in *The Dictionary of Philosophy*, ed. by Runes, p. 50.
[169] *Chen-yuan chih ch'i.*
[170] See p. 37, n. 113.

non-being, an "unnamable," to use another Taoist term.[171]

The third proposition is that existence viewed as a whole is the process of the actualization of the Great Ultimate by means of the *ch'i* of the true prime unit.[172] This is the Evolution of Tao,[173] that is, the "great operation" or "great current," to use Confucian terms,[174] involving existence in its entirety and without cease.[175]

This is true because existence means a continuous process, for a thing cannot exist unless it continues to exist. All processes imply change and movement, and the change and movement implied in all processes is the First Mover. To borrow a Neo-Confucian dictum, "There is the Non-Ultimate and yet there is the Great Ultimate." [176]

This continuous process is Creation. It is characterized by "formation, development, decay, and dissolution," in terms of daily renewal by the cyclical process, by progress toward and retrogression from *Li*, by increase and decrease in the actualization of entities, and by the appearance of new classes. This process is dialectic, resulting in new and higher qualities.[177]

This movement of perpetual transformation involves all processes of change and movement, since each process, as an actualization of *Li*, implies a movement not only in one thing but in all things under that *Li*. In the end, all processes taken as a whole constitute the Evolution of Tao.

The fourth proposition is represented by the Buddhist saying that "One is All and All is One." This is the Great Whole,[178] the One,[179] Heaven.[180] This is a formal concept, because it is merely the general name for the All [181] and not

[171] *The Spirit of Chinese Philosophy*, p. 209.
[172] *Ibid.*
[173] *Tao-t'i.*
[174] *Hsin li-hsueh*, pp. 97, 99.
[175] *Ibid.*, p. 100.
[176] *The Spirit of Chinese Philosophy*, p. 209.
[177] *Hsin li-hsueh*, pp. 100, 109, 120.
[178] *Ta-ch'üan.*
[179] *Hsin li-hsueh*, p. 37.
[180] *Ibid.*, pp. 36, 38.
[181] *Ibid.*, p. 40.

an assertion about the actual world.[182] It is the Absolute in Western philosophy,[183] just as the concepts of *Li, ch'i,* and Tao may be compared to the concepts of being, non-being, and becoming, respectively.[184]

The Great Whole is the goal of life and is to be realized through "investigation of things" and "extension of knowledge." To Ch'eng I-ch'uan and Chu Hsi, these meant speculation. Chu Hsi believed that the mind was the embodiment of all the principles of *Li* and therefore could know the whole of *Li* by knowing a part of it. To Fung, on the other hand, the contents of *Li* can be known only by objective and systematic study. He therefore insists on the inductive method and experimental logic. By analyzing actual entities, one may know the realm of actuality, and from this one may know the realm of truth. When one understands *Li* perfectly, one will realize *Li* to the utmost. Investigation of things will lead to "knowing Heaven" and realization of *Li* will lead to the "full realization of one's nature" and "serving Heaven." [185] The person who knows Heaven and serves Heaven is a sage, a being transcending his own level of existence and becoming "one with all things." [186] This is *jen.* To quote Ch'eng Ming-tao again, "A man of *jen* forms one body with all things." [187]

In his *Hsin yuan-jen* ("A New Treatise on the Nature of Man") [188] Fung divides man's life into four spheres: the innocent, the utilitarian, the moral, and the transcendental. In the innocent sphere, man's conduct is conditioned by his natural endowment, personal habits, and social conditions.[189] On this level, he behaves without understanding what he is doing.[190] In the utilitarian sphere, man is aware

[182] *The Spirit of Chinese Philosophy,* p. 212.
[183] *Ibid.,* p. 213.
[184] *Ibid.*
[185] *Hsin li-hsueh,* pp. 295–305.
[186] *Ibid.,* p. 294.
[187] *Ibid.,* p. 304.
[188] See note 156, above.
[189] *Hsin yuan-jen,* p. 31.
[190] *Ibid.,* p. 42.

of his activities, but his actions are motivated by self-benefit. He may or may not do good to others. In the moral sphere, his activity is guided by righteousness. Here man becomes conscious of his moral nature and realizes that only in the Whole, that is, society, can he fully realize his individuality. He knows he is only part of a society.[191] In the transcendental sphere, or the Sphere of Heaven and Earth, life is dedicated to "serving Heaven." Man realizes that full development of his nature cannot stop with the wholeness of society but must be extended to the wholeness of the universe.[192] He becomes a citizen of Heaven.[193]

This state of complete enlightenment is the state of unity of Heaven and man. It is remarkable that while Hsiung, in developing the Idealistic wing of Neo-Confucianism, and Fung, in developing the Rationalistic wing, seem to be traveling in opposite directions, they arrive at the same destination of the unity of Heaven and man. This very fact of the revival of both wings of Neo-Confucianism ought to be a strong challenge to those who maintain that Confucianism is dead. We are not primarily concerned with the validity of their philosophies. These are by no means final or perfect. Questions have been raised, for example, how Fung's Reality can be real without existence[194] and how his *Li* can be equated with universals in Western philosophy.[195] The important fact for us is that Confucianism has been revived. What is more, this revival has religious implications. Both systems are obviously naturalistic. What, then, have they to do with religion?

Both Hsiung and Fung would be horrified if their philosophical systems were considered as religions. Hsiung rejects

[191] *Ibid.*, pp. 32–33.
[192] *Ibid.*, p. 33.
[193] *Ibid.*, p. 90.
[194] Chou Ku-ch'eng, *op. cit.*, pp. 8–9.
[195] Chang Shen-fu's review of *Hsin yuan-tao* and *Hsin yuan-jen* in *The Quarterly Bulletin of Chinese Bibliography*, VII, Nos. 1–2 (June, 1946), 5–6.

the ideas of a Creator, a universal architect, and the soul. To him, the belief in a Supreme God transcending all else violates the principle of equality. He insists again and again that his Reality cannot be interpreted as an anthropomorphic God.[196] He emphatically states that his system is philosophy, which he says is better and higher than religion, because religion like Buddhism distinguishes the realm of Nirvana and the realm of life and death, thus bifurcating Reality, whereas in philosophy the two realms are united and identified.[197] Fung believes that religion involves a superhuman power as an object of worship, a religious interpretation of ethics, a paradise where all things are perfect, and the doctrine of Creation. As such, religion belongs to the moral sphere, whereas the transcendental sphere is purely philosophical.[198]

In spite of all these protests, however, the philosophy of Hsiung and Fung, alike, is definitely religious, though not a religion. In the first place, even a naturalistic philosophy like theirs may contribute generously to religion, as the philosophy of Spinoza has clearly demonstrated. As one writer has pointed out, the Great Whole of Fung is, essentially, not different from Spinoza's God.[199] Secondly, while they oppose those religions having "dogmas and superstitions," [200] Heaven and Hell, and a personal Creator, they do not oppose religion as such. Hsiung confides that, although he scarcely believes in religion, he does not reject it, but holds an attitude of reservation toward it and does not talk about it.[201] Fung, however, positively believes in religion and has developed his own philosophy of religion in a special chapter in his *Hsin li-hsueh* (this will engage our attention later).[202]

[196] Hsiung, *Hsin wei-shih lun*, pp. 161, 231, 175, 192, 54, 226.
[197] Hsiung, *Tu-ching shih-yao*, II, 47; *Shih-li yü-yao*, II, 21A.
[198] Fung, *Hsin yuan-jen*, pp. 90–92.
[199] Kuo Chan-po, *op. cit.*, p. 201.
[200] Fung, *A Short History of Chinese Philosophy*, p. 340.
[201] Hsiung, *Tu-ching shih-yao*, p. 45B. [202] See below, pp. 247–48.

In the third place, when it comes to the way of attaining the highest state of being, both Hsiung and Fung offer methods that are basically religious. To Hsiung, the way to reach the state of pure unity is through *t'i-jen,* already described. The chief psychological requirement in the method is *ch'eng,* sincerity or truth.[203] "Sincerity is the way of Heaven," says the most religious of the ancient Confucian Classics, the *Chung-yung* (*The Doctrine of the Mean*), "and the attainment of sincerity is the way of man." [204]

Fung recommends the method of seriousness (*ching*) [205] as the way of life and the surest way to transcend the ordinary and to attain sagehood. He says that both religionists and philosophers believe that man can reach a realm in which the "I" and "the other," as well as the internal and the external, all disappear. This is the realm of sagehood. In ordinary religions, the way to this realm is spiritual endeavor and quietness. While quietness is a discipline outside daily activities, seriousness as a discipline can be followed any time and anywhere. In recommending this method, Fung faithfully follows the Sung Neo-Confucianists whose philosophy is undeniably religious. Lastly, and most important of all, both Hsiung and Fung arrive at the central Confucian concept of the unity of man and Heaven. Such a concept is basically religious. This was true in the Han and Sung times. It remains true today.

[203] Hsiung, *Tu-ching shih-yao,* p. 47A. *Ch'eng* means honesty, sincerity, absence of fault, actuality, being one's true self, being true to the nature of being. See my article, "Ch'eng," in *The Dictionary of Philosophy,* ed. by Runes, p. 49.

[204] XX, 18. For English translations of the Classic, see, among others, *The Doctrine of the Mean,* trans. by James Legge, in *The Chinese Classics,* Vol. I and *The Great Learning and the Mean-in-Action,* trans. by E. R. Hughes, pp. 105–44.

[205] *Ching* ordinarily means respect or reverence but philosophically means seriousness, the inner state of unity of mind, absolute equanimity, and absolute steadfastness. See my article, "Ching," in *The Dictionary of Philosophy,* ed. by Runes, p. 53.

It may be said, however, that the Confucian renaissance has already ended. With the Communist triumph in China, Hsiung has entered into voluntary silence, and Fung has repudiated himself. In a recent article reporting the results of his "new learning" and confessing his past mistakes, he says that his New Rational Philosophy is but a twilight of old Chinese philosophy, just as Neo-Thomism is a twilight of Western philosophy. He regrets that he has emphasized the eternal and neglected the concrete. He now realizes that Marxism-Leninism is comparable to modern medicine, whereas old Chinese philosophy is comparable to medieval medicine.[206] In a still later article he specifically rejects the main thesis of each of the five books on which his system is built. He says that the main point of his *Hsin yuan-jen,* to become a "citizen of Heaven," is, in the final analysis, escapism. As to his chief work, *Hsin li-hsueh,* he says his great mistake is to have emphasized the contrast of the particular and the universal instead of stressing their unity. According to his self-appraisal, the book is too strongly influenced by Taoism and Buddhism and reflects the crumbling old society.[207]

Let us grant that Fung has a genuine change of heart. Nevertheless the strong tendency of Confucian developments in the last three decades cannot be terminated by a personal declaration or even by government order. Moreover,

[206] Reprinted in *Hua-ch'iao jih-pao* (*China Daily News*), New York, February 21, 1950. For the English version, see "I Discovered Marxism-Leninism," *People's China,* I, No. 6 (March 6, 1950), 11. In "An Unsent Letter to Fung Yu-lan," Chang Chün-mai (Carsun Chang) says, "You maintain that you strengthen the spirit of Chinese philosophy. . . . The fundamental spirit of Chinese philosophy is the correspondence between words and deeds. . . . You now treat Chinese philosophy as a means of making a living." *Tzu-yu chen-hsien* (*Freedom Fortnightly*) (in Chinese), II, No. 8 (August 1, 1949), 21; also *Tsai-sheng* (*National Renaissance*), No. 23 (September, 1950).

[207] "Self-Appraisal about *Hsin li-hsueh*" (in Chinese), *Kuang-min jih-pao* ("The Bright Light Daily"), October 8, 1950; reprinted in *Hsin-hua yueh-pao* ("New China Monthly"), III, No. 1 (November, 1950), 193–97.

what the Chinese Communists will do to Confucianism is by no means sure. In his *China's New Democracy,* Mao Tse-tung attacks Confucianism as semifeudal,[208] but in his *Lun hsin chieh-tuan* ("On Entering the New Stage"),[209] he advises his party members to learn from Confucius and Sun Yat-sen as well as from Marx and Lenin. Finally, he concedes that "the new culture of China is developed from the old culture of China. Therefore we must respect our own history; we cannot cut off history." [210]

But the Communist government has abolished the national holiday for Confucius. It is a clear sign that Confucianism is approaching a crisis. However, this is not the first; Confucianism has gone through one crisis after another in the last fifty years. What is the situation after all these storms had passed? Much of Confucianism died, but much of it is and will be alive.

[208] Originally published in Chinese in 1940. See English edition, p. 48.
[209] P. 13. [210] Cf. *China's New Democracy,* Eng. ed., p. 62.

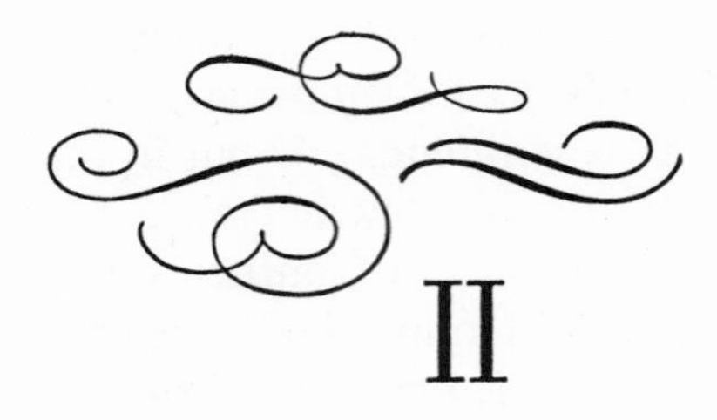

II

Modern Movements in Buddhism

To a superficial observer, modern Chinese Buddhism must present an ugly picture of superstition, magic, and idolatry. For several hundred years, no important scripture or commentary has been written. The clergy is notoriously ignorant and corrupt. Temples are either in poor state of preservation or saturated with an atmosphere of commercialism. Masterpieces of descriptions of this sad picture are to be found in the works of J. J. M. de Groot.[1]

But there is a brighter side even to a dark picture. Professor D. T. Suzuki, the eminent Zen Buddhist scholar, was certainly not unaware of the deplorable conditions of Chinese Buddhism. But in his trip to China in 1935, he also saw the more pleasant aspects. He visited magnificent temples like the Ling-yin in Hangchow and the T'ien-t'ung in Ningpo

[1] *The Religion of the Chinese*, pp. 177–78, 187–88, 191–92; *Religion in China*, pp. 285–319; *The Religious System of China, passim.*

and felt sure that these majestic edifices could not have been products of mere tradition but must have been concrete expressions of a deep faith, especially when they are fruits of the labor of the masses without support from the aristocracy. He was also impressed with the mellowness and serenity of Chinese monks, in sharp contrast to the hurried actions of Japanese priests. He noticed, too, that in China, clerics of all ranks wore the same type of cotton garments and received visitors in the same guest hall, an unmistakable indication of the democratic spirit, again in contrast to Japan, where high priests enjoy a special reception room. He remarked upon the perpetual light in the library, with a monk keeping watch at all hours. Such is the Buddhist respect for learning.[2] I may add that the perpetual light and the constant vigil symbolize the Buddhist conviction that not only must truth be discovered through study, but the discovery must be made by oneself.

All this is evidence of the fact that underlying the superficial ugliness there is something great and strong in Chinese Buddhism. In the last five decades it has suffered a long series of what the Buddhists call "catastrophes." Special taxes or "contributions" have been imposed on the Buddhist church. Temples have been converted by the government, warlords, or the community gentry into schools or barracks, without compensation. Other properties have been confiscated for sale to support schools, local defense corps, or provincial troops. Tenants of temple farms have refused to pay rentals. Images have been destroyed. And monks and nuns have been driven out. "In large cities, some thirty per cent of Buddhist properties have been appropriated for barracks and police stations, and some fifty per cent for schools." [3] But in spite

[2] Suzuki, "Impressions of Chinese Buddhism" (in Chinese), *Hai-ch'ao yin* ("The Sound of the Sea Tide"), XVI, No. 2 (June, 1935), 27–36.
[3] Ta-hsing, "Fifteen Years of Religious Catastrophes in Retrospect" (in Chinese), *ibid.*, XVI, No. 1 (January, 1935), 103.

of all these catastrophes, Buddhism has refused to succumb; instead, it has raised its head and taken a firm and bold stride forward.

MODERN REFORMS

The story of the advancing step in modern Chinese Buddhism is a story of modern reforms. These were chiefly brought about under the leadership of the great abbot T'ai-hsu (1889–1947), who has been called the St. Paul of Chinese Buddhism.[4] "Between 1908 and 1914," the Abbot recalled, "aroused by the destruction of temples . . . I launched the movement to defend the religion, propagate the faith, reform the order, and promote education." [5] He aimed at a threefold "revolution" in Buddhism, through the regeneration of the clergy, the rededication of Buddhist properties for the benefit of the people, and the reconstruction of Buddhist doctrines.[6] In 1929, he declared that new Buddhism must be (1) humanistic, (2) scientific, (3) demonstrative, and (4) world-wide.[7] Towards these ends, a number of projects were undertaken. We need not go into the details of these, some of which have been succinctly but revealingly summarized by Reichelt, Hamilton, Hodous, Latourette, Friess and Schneider, Braden, Haydon, Eliot, and others.[8] The endeavors at education, social service, and

[4] Y. Y. Tsu, "New Tendencies in Chinese Religions" (in Chinese), *Wen She* ("Literary Society Magazine"), II, No. 7 (May, 1927), 44.

[5] T'ai-hsu, *Fa-hsiang wei-shih hsueh* ("Dharma-Character Idealistic Philosophy"), p. 838.

[6] Fa-fang, "Present Conditions of Chinese Buddhism" (in Chinese), *Hai-ch'ao yin*, XV, No. 10 (October, 1934), 28.

[7] T'ai-hsu, "Developments and New Movements in Buddhism" (in Chinese), *ibid.*, X, No. 1 (March, 1929), 5–8. For T'ai-hsu's works, see Frank R. Millican, "T'ai Hsu and Modern Buddhism," *Chinese Recorder*, LIV, No. 6 (June, 1923), 326–33.

[8] Karl Ludvig Reichelt, *Truth and Tradition in Chinese Buddhism*, trans. by Kathrina van Wagenen Bugge, pp. 297–317; James Bissett Pratt, *The Pilgrimage of Buddhism*, pp. 379–92; Clarence H. Hamilton, *Buddhism in India, Ceylon, China and Japan*, pp. 79–83; also his "Buddhism," in *China,*

a new Buddhist philosophy will be discussed later. At this point we turn to the national, international, and intellectual aspects of the movement.

Although Buddhism has penetrated all parts of China for centuries, there never had been a national organization until 1912. At that time, when the question of a state religion arose in the Parliament, Buddhist laymen, led by Ou-yang Ching-wu (1871–1943), organized the China Buddhist Association for the sole purpose of fighting the proposal. Its pronouncements bitterly criticized the inability of the Buddhist clergy to uphold their religion. As a countermeasure, the clergy formed a national society of their own, the Buddhist Association of China. This was the first national organization of Chinese priests in Chinese history. Although it set education as the primary objective, actually its effort was mainly devoted to the very materialistic aim of protecting temple properties.

The two groups rivaled each other for some time, but eventually apathy and inefficiency so vitiated both that they fell into virtual oblivion. In 1929, a new national organization was established, called the Chinese Buddhist Society. It enjoyed steady growth, so that in 1936 there were 476

ed. by MacNair, pp. 295–300; Lewis Hodous, *Buddhism and Buddhists in China*, pp. 63–71; Kenneth Scott Latourette, *The Chinese, Their History and Culture*, pp. 657–58; Horace L. Friess and Herbert W. Schneider, *Religion in Various Cultures*, pp. 196–97; Charles Samuel Braden, *Modern Tendencies in World Religions*, pp. 122–28; A. Eustace Haydon, *Modern Trends in World-Religions*, pp. 75–80; Sir Charles Eliot, *Hinduism and Buddhism*, III, 335. The best articles in English on the conditions of modern Chinese Buddhism are those by Wei-huan, "Buddhism in Modern China," *T'ien Hsia Monthly*, IX, No. 2 (September, 1939), 140–55; by C. Yates McDaniel, "Buddhism Makes Its Peace in the New Order," *Asia*, XXXV, No. 9 (Sept., 1935), 536–41; and by Y. Y. Tsu, "Trends of Thought and Religion in China," *New Orient*, II (1933), 321–29. An earlier study and also excellent is Tsu's "Present Tendencies in Chinese Buddhism," *Journal of Religion*, I, No. 4 (July 2, 1921), 497–512. See also *China Christian Year Book*, 1928, pp. 41–46; 1929, pp. 122–141; 1931–32, pp. 102–6; 1932–33, pp. 100–112; 1936–37, pp. 101–4; *China Handbook*, 1937–1945, pp. 25–26.

branches in China, with 118 in the province of Szechuan alone.[9] Interrupted by war, the Society was revived by T'ai-hsu in 1939 in the wartime capital Chungking. Although it claimed 4,620,000 members in 1947,[10] the organization is loose and weak.

The fact that Chinese Buddhists have not been able to effect a strong national society is a clear reflection of Buddhist incompetence for organization. But it also betrays a lack of interest in a national church. Since Buddhism has not been broken up into competitive and antagonistic denominations and its division into schools is largely academic, there is no need for a centralized, national setup. Significantly, T'ai-hsu's proposal for a national church with a national monastery in the capital did not receive even lukewarm reception.[11]

If, however, he failed in forming a national church, he did succeed in making Chinese Buddhism more international. In 1925 he represented China in the East Asia Buddhist Conference in Japan. Three years later he toured the world and lectured on Buddhism. He instituted the annual World Conference on Buddhism in Kuling. He sent his pupils to study in various Buddhist countries and invited Buddhist lecturers from abroad. In all these efforts Buddhist laymen gave generous help. In 1935 the Chinese Buddhist Society at Nanking sent a group of four students to Siam. Another group went to America and Europe. In 1936 five went to Ceylon and three to Japan, besides those going to Tibet. Three years later the Buddhist Association of China and the Chinese Government sent a good-will mission of five, with T'ai-hsu as leader, to Burma, Ceylon, India, and Malaya. In 1940 Fa-fang became an exchange professor at Ceylon, where he died in 1951. In 1945 two more students

[9] *Chinese Year Book*, 1936–37, p. 1445.
[10] *China Handbook*, 1950, p. 25. [11] Haydon, *op. cit.*, p. 98.

went to Ceylon, and, a year later, Ceylon reciprocated by dispatching three scholars to China. In Shanghai Buddhist laymen established the World Buddhist Laymen Association. In the Wuchang Buddhist Institute an international Buddhist library was founded. In 1949 five priests proceeded to Siam for further study. These ventures, though limited in scope, cannot help but strengthen the international character of Chinese Buddhism which has been historically international for two thousand years.

In this connection it may be well to point out again that Chinese Buddhism is not, and never has been, nationalistic. It did not contrive to become a state religion. It did not identify itself with Chinese culture or the Chinese race. It was not a war issue. It is amazing that while modern China has become nationalistic in more ways than one, the Buddhist religion has remained aloof from nationalism. Here we have another contrast between Buddhism in China and Japan. Whereas Japan has produced a nationalistic sect, the Nichiren,[12] whose founder exclaimed, "I will be the pillar, the eyes, and the vessel of Japan" and proclaimed Japan the center of Buddhism, no such thought was ever entertained in China.

It will be seen that the international program of Chinese Buddhism has been almost exclusively intellectual in character. Indeed, the intellectual interest has dominated the reform movement as a whole, obviously under the influence of China's Intellectual Renaissance. It has been a movement of intellectual awakening most of all.

The story of intellectual resurgence goes back to the cele-

[12] Named after its founder, Nichiren (1222–82), the school is an offshoot of the T'ien-t'ai (Tendai, in Japanese) sect and follows the *Lotus Sutra* as its chief scripture. It is distinguished by a fighting attitude and a nationalistic spirit. There are at present eight branches in Japan, with some five thousand temples and seven million adherents. The Nichiren School proper and the Kenpon-Hokke (Elucidating the Original *Lotus*) branch are the most influential.

brated layman, Yang Wen-hui (1837–1911), who was chiefly responsible for the revival of Buddhist literature. He brought back many texts from Japan that had been lost and forgotten in China and introduced much material from both Japan and Korea. In the 1870s he initiated large-scale Buddhist publications. He published the Chinese Tripitaka, the Buddhist Canon, for the first time since 1738. He distributed upwards of a million Buddhist tracts. His Buddhist Scriptures Circulation Center in Nanking was no doubt the spring of a current that led to publication and circulation centers in Peking, Tientsin, Shanghai, and his native Yangchow. In the first years of the Republic a devout Buddhist in Shanghai reproduced the Japanese 卍 Tripitaka (Kyoto, 1902–5) of 8,534 *chüans* (parts) in forty volumes. In 1923 lay Buddhist intellectuals, notably Liang Ch'i-ch'ao, Chiang Wei-ch'iao, Wang I-t'ing, together with Ts'ai Yuan-p'ei and other scholars, published in 720 stitched volumes the *Hsu tsang-ching* ("Supplement to the Tripitaka"), consisting of some 1,750 commentaries and subcommentaries; this was first published in Kyoto in 1905–12.[13] In 1933–36 lay leaders Chu Ch'ing-lan and Yeh Kung-ch'o reproduced the 1238–1310 edition of the Tripitaka of 6,362 *chüans* in 570 stitched volumes. In 1934–35 many volumes of books in the Tripitaka were published by the Institute of Inner Learning under the series title *Tsang-yao* ("Important Works of the Tripitaka"). In 1935 forty-five works of the Sung Tripitaka were published in 120 stitched volumes by the San-shih Hsueh-hui of Peiping and the Sung Tripitaka Society of Shanghai under the title of *Sung-tsang i-chen*. A substantial part of the Ch'ing edition of 1735–38 was also republished.[14] At present, Buddhist laymen are bringing out

[13] Lü Ch'eng, *Fo-tien fan-lun* ("General Remarks on the Buddhist Canon"), pp. 31A–33B.

[14] Fa-fang, "Chinese Buddhism in 1936" (in Chinese), *Hai-ch'ao yin*, XVIII, No. 4 (April, 1937), 18–19.

the *Min-kuo ta tsang-ching* ("The Chinese Republic Tripitaka") which includes Pali literature, untranslated and not easily available works, and new treatises. Some eighty volumes have come off the press. What a far cry from several decades earlier, when Yang Wen-hui could not even find a copy of the much recited *Amitabhasutra!* [15]

Aside from these large-scale publications, a number of research projects were carried on. Many institutes for research and study opened their doors in Peking, Shanghai, Chengtu, Chungking, Fukien, and Chaochow. One of the two most famous, most productive, most lasting, and most influential is the Institute of Inner Learning (Nei-hsueh Yuan) founded by Yang Wen-hui's pupil Ou-yang Ching-wu, in Nanking in 1922. There Liang Ch'i-ch'ao and other equally prominent authorities lectured and such brilliant scholars as Hsiung Shih-li were fostered. The Wuchang Buddhist Institute, founded by T'ai-hsu, is famous for lectures by the abbot himself and other scholars, as well as for its library of some forty thousand volumes, no small quantity for a private collection in China. Outside these institutes, much has been accomplished in research and publication by Buddhist laymen or critics such as Liang Ch'i-ch'ao, Chang T'ai-yen, Chiang Wei-ch'iao, Hsiung Shih-li, Hu Shih, and T'ang Yung-t'ung, whose *Han Wei Liang-Chin Nan-Pei-ch'ao Fo-chiao shih* ("History of Buddhism from the Third Century B.C. to the Sixth Century A.D.") is a classic.

In both quantity and quality, publications by Buddhist organizations have been gratifying. There was no Buddhist periodical before 1912. But during the period of 1920–35, no fewer than 537 works, including a Buddhist dictionary of 3,302 pages, and 58 periodicals were published.[16] Most

[15] See note 30, below.

[16] Ch'en-k'ung, "Buddhist Publications in the Last Fifteen Years" (in Chinese), *Hai-ch'ao yin*, XVI, No. 1 (January, 1935), 180–97. The periodicals included 2 annuals, 4 quarterlies, 17 monthlies, 7 semimonthlies, 5 pub-

of the periodicals had a small circulation and lived a short life. The most outstanding, however, the *Hai-ch'ao yin* ("The Sound of Sea Tide"), founded in 1920, still continues to command a high respect among Chinese scholars, Buddhist and non-Buddhist alike. Among current periodicals, the *Chueh yu-ch'ing* ("Waking All Living Beings"), published in Shanghai, and the *Jen-chien-shih* ("The Human World"), published in Peking, are also well known.

These intellectual accomplishments and other achievements in the New Buddhism make it perfectly clear that the renaissance in Buddhism did not stem from "disillusionment and negative influence of Western philosophy," as has been surmised.[17] They are unmistakable indications that Buddhism is gaining a new life.

This new life expresses itself in seven different tendencies: (1) in understanding, from the T'ien-t'ai and Hua-yen philosophy to Wei-shih Idealism, (2) in experience, from Pure Land formalism to pietism, (3) in practice, from the Disciplinary and Meditation Schools to the Mystical School, (4) in literature, from Chinese to Pali and Tibetan, (5) in attitude, from ritualistic performance to religious demonstration, (6) in leadership, from the clergy to the layman, and (7) in objective, from the other world to this world. The tendency toward Idealism will constitute a later section. We shall now discuss the second tendency, from formalism to pietism.

IN EXPERIENCE, FROM PURE LAND FORMALISM TO PIETISM

Chinese Buddhism in the last several hundred years may be said to have been reduced to the Pure Land School. Of the

---

lished thrice a month, 6 weeklies, 3 dailies, and 15 published irregularly. They were published in all parts of China, with 17 in Kiangsu Province. See also Wei-huan, "Buddhism in Modern China," *T'ien Hsia Monthly*, IX, No. 2 (September, 1939), 150–51.

[17] Braden, *op. cit.*, p. 126.

ten schools that were introduced into or developed in China, the Realistic (Chü-she, Abhidharmakosa) School, the Nihilistic (Ch'eng-shih, Satyasiddhi) School, the Middle Doctrine (San-lun, Madhyamaka) School, the Idealistic (Wei-shih, Vijnanavada) School, and the Mystical (True Word, Chen-yen) School all disappeared after the ninth century.[18] In the past millennium, Chinese Buddhism has not extended beyond the T'ien-t'ai, the Hua-yen (Avatansaka), the Meditation (Ch'an, Dhyana), the Pure Land (Ching-t'u, Sukhavati), and the Disciplinary (Lü, Vinaya) Schools. As the last-named has scarcely existed as an independent sect but has been largely incorporated into the other schools, Chinese Buddhism may be said to consist of no more than four schools. Although distinguished from one another academically, actually they are not independent, much less mutually exclusive. Every large temple, regardless of the school to which it claims to belong, has a meditation hall, follows the Pure Land School in practice, and adheres to the T'ien-t'ai and Hua-yen Schools in doctrines; hence the common saying that Chinese Buddhism is "T'ien-t'ai and Hua-yen in doctrines and Meditation and Pure Land in practice." This is to say that, generally speaking, a Chinese Buddhist believes in the T'ien-t'ai principle of the Perfectly Harmonious Threefold Truth to the effect that the Realm of the Void, or noumenon, and the Realm of Temporariness, or phenomenon, are combined in the Realm of the Mean in which facts and principles are interwoven, interpenetrating, and interrelated, so that "the three thousand worlds arise in every moment of thought." [19] The Chinese Buddhist also

[18] For elementary information on these five schools, see below, pp. 102–5.

[19] According to T'ien-t'ai, the Threefold Truth is established in this way: All things are Void because they are dependent on causes and therefore have no self-nature. But they do enjoy temporary existence. Being both Void and Temporary is the nature of dharmas and is the Mean. The three—Void, Temporariness, and the Mean—are Three-in-One and One-in-Three. In the world of Temporariness, that is, the phenomenal world, there are ten realms

believes in the Hua-yen doctrine that the World of Facts, the World of Principles, the World of Principles Realized in Facts, and the World of the Harmony of these Facts are synthesized through "inter-identification" and "inter-penetration" into the Universe of One-Truth.[20] In actual practice, he meditates according to the traditions of the Ch'an School and follows the Pure Land custom of reciting the holy name of the Buddha.

But the All-in-One and One-in-All philosophy of T'ien-t'ai and Hua-yen is intelligible to only a minority of Chinese Buddhists, and Ch'an, originally a powerful concentration

---

of existence (those of the Buddhas, Would-be-Buddhas, Buddhas-for-Themselves, Direct Disciples of the Buddha, heavenly beings, spirits, human beings, departed beings, beasts, and depraved men). Each of these is characterized by ten features ("thus-characterized, thus-natured, thus-substantiated, thus-caused, thus-forced, thus-activated, thus-conditioned, thus-effected, thus-remunerated, and thus-completed-from-beginning-to-end"), in all, one thousand realms. In turn, each realm consists of the three divisions of living beings, of space, and of the aggregates which constitute beings, or a total of three thousand realms. Each realm involves all other realms. Their totality is the True State, Absolute Reality, Ultimate Void, Thusness, or Nirvana.

Since everything involves everything else, it follows that "Buddha-nature is everywhere over the world," and every being can be saved. Hence the doctrine of "salvation for all."

The school, also called the Lotus School, was founded in China by Chih-i (531–97) in the T'ien-t'ai (Heavenly Terrace) Mountain on the authority of the *Lotus Sutra*. In Japan it was founded by Dengyo Daishi (Saicho, 767–822) in 804. The school there has three branches (Sammon, Jimon, and Shinsei) with several thousand temples and over two million followers. See below, pp. 94–97.

20 The Hua-yen (Avatansaka in Sanskrit and Kegon in Japanese, all meaning "Flowery Splendor") School never existed in India. But its name and doctrine are both traced to the *Avatansakasutra* from India. The school in China was nominally founded by Tu-shun (557–640), but Fa-tsang, the Great Master of Hsien-shou (643–712), is considered the real founder. The main tenet of the school is the Universal Causation by the Dharmadhatu, that is, the Realm of All Elements. It is the mutual causation of all elements, as expalined by its Ten Profound Propositions and its doctrine of the Sixfold Character of Dharmas (see below, p. 97).

The Hua-yen doctrine was brought to Japan by Shinsho (Shen-hsiang) in 740, where it owns several scores of temples and has some twenty thousand adherents.

of the mind to intuit truth, has degenerated into habitual quiet sitting. Only the recitation of Buddha's name expresses some degree of devotion. It is not much to say, therefore, that Chinese Buddhism has been finally reduced to the Pure Land. This is the reason why most Chinese Buddhists, if not all, are considered followers of the Pure Land School.[21] To some of them, the recitation of "*Nan mo a mi t'o fo*" ("I honor Thee and resort to Thee, Amitabha Buddha") may well express profound pietism. But to many of them, such vocal exercise, as well as the fingering of rosaries, the murmuring of scriptures, the chanting of verses, the bowing and offering before images, the setting free of living creatures, and the praying for long life and immortality have become pure formalism without meaning or vitality. It was high time for a revival.

The revival came about gradually and through the sincerity and devotion of a countless number of literate and illiterate Buddhists. Before 1921 signs of awakening were already evident in the then Pure Land center at Hung-lo Mountain near Peking.[22] But the man who provided much of the inspiration and central point of crystallization was Abbot Yin-kuang (1861–1940). He renounced society at the age of

[21] The school was founded by Hui-yuan (334–416) and follows the three scriptures: the larger and smaller *Sukhavativyuhasutras* and the *Amitayurdhyanasutra* (all translated in *The Sacred Books of the East*, Vol. XLIX). It teaches absolute faith in Amitabha and salvation through "Other's Power" as the "Easy Way" or the "Pure Land Path," instead of salvation through "One's Own Power" as taught by other Buddhist schools, which is the "Difficult Way" or the "Holy Path." It advocates the recitation of the forty-eight vows of the Buddha described in the larger *Sukhavati*, especially the three fundamental ones; namely, the eighteenth, which promises birth in the Pure Land to the faithful, the nineteenth, which promises a personal welcome by Amitabha to all people at their death, and the twentieth, which assures birth in the Pure Land as the result of the repetition of Buddha's name. In Japan, where it was founded by Honen (1133–1212), it is divided into four sects (Jodo, Shin, Yuzunembutsu, and Ji) with almost twenty million followers.

[22] Fa-fang, *Wei-shih shih-kuan chi ch'i che-hsueh* ("History of Vijnaptimatrata System and Its Philosophy"), p. 3.

twenty-one and embraced Buddhism in Puto Island, center of Pure Land Pietism. Eleven years later he was elected head of the Hua-yü Temple. Primarily interested in a religious life rather than philosophy,[23] he preached with tireless effort in the general triangular area of Shanghai, Hangchow, and Nanking, especially the former, where he was later a resident priest, in the T'ai-p'ing Temple. His activities were particularly vigorous from 1919, undoubtedly in reaction to the Great War, to 1931, when he moved to the Pao-kuo Temple in Soochow, which became the new center of Pure Land worship. By that time he had had, in the words of Karl Reichelt, "numerous followers and disciples all over China, more especially the provinces of Kiangsu and Chekiang." [24] Reichelt, who knew Yin-kuang personally, speaks of the abbot as "old dear pious Yin-kuang" [25] who was an "old and highly beloved master" to his followers with whom he stood in "sacred and deeply affectionate relation." [26]

A man of great compassion, Yin-kuang would publicly lecture or privately advise his disciples, in stern and straightforward manner, but never without warmth and affection, about the all-importance of piety, holiness, and faith in realizing one's Buddha-nature and in combating evil. To him, salvation comes only by faith, which alone can provide the seeker after truth with the vitality and re-creative dynamic force necessary to the crossing of the troubled sea to the Other Shore. He was living faith itself. "To read Yin-kuang's popular tracts, advocating faith in Amitabha," said Reichelt, "and still more, to listen to him when he expounds the mysteries of the living faith, that is something one never forgets." [27] In the 1920s he distributed numerous pamphlets giving inspiration and guidance for a good, religious life. For

[23] "A Short History of Great Master Yin-kuang" (in Chinese), *Chung-kuo Fo-chiao chi-k'an* ("Chinese Buddhist Quarterly"), Fall, 1943, p. 17.
[24] Reichelt, *op. cit.*, p. 311.
[25] *Ibid.*, p. 320.
[26] *Ibid.*, p. 311.
[27] *Ibid.*, p. 314.

his wisdom he drew freely from the treasures of Confucianism and Taoism, in which he was well versed and which he considered essentially harmonious with Buddhism.[28]

The result of Yin-kuang's uplifting efforts, and also those of Ti-hsien (1858–1932) of the Kuan-tsung Temple at Ningpo, whose lectures in Peking immediately following the First World War attracted national attention, has been an extensive revival in Pure Land Pietism. These two priests, and a large number of clerics and laymen, gave new meaning to traditional practices, injected new life into daily observances, and elevated themselves and their followers to new levels of religious experience. Pure Land laymen organized, for both men and women, some four hundred Lotus Societies, Associations for the Study and Cultivation of Buddhism, Pure Karma (action-influence) Societies, Halls for the Recitation of Buddha's Name, Buddha Halls, Vegetarian Halls, and similar institutions all over China, especially along the Yangtze and the coast. The members come together not to engage in superstitious practices or to request earthly blessings, but to satisfy their spiritual longings. They study the holy scriptures, particularly the *Heart Sutra,*[29] the *Amitabhasutra,*[30] the *Diamond Sutra,*[31] and the *Surangama-*

[28] Although Yin-kuang was definitely a conservative, I did not get the impression from reading his works that he opposed the harmonization of Buddhism with Confucianism and Taoism, as is suggested in the *China Christian Year Book,* 1929, p. 128. Fa-fang (*Wei-shih shih-kuan chi ch'i che-hsueh,* p. 3), perhaps the most scholarly Buddhist priest in China lately, said definitely that Yin-kuang "attached equal importance to Confucian mores."

[29] *Hsin ching.* See English translation by F. Max Müller, "The Smaller Pragna-paramita-hridaya-sutra," in *The Sacred Books of the East,* Vol. XLIX, Part II, pp. 153–54. Other English versions include: Daisetz Taitaro Suzuki, "The Prajnaparimitahridaya," in his *Manual of Zen Buddhism,* pp. 27–32; Shao Chang Lee, "Essence of the Wisdom Sutra," in his *Popular Buddhism in China,* pp. 23–26.

[30] *A-mi-t'o ching.* Among English translations, see the version by Müller, "The Smaller Sukhavati-vyuha," in *The Sacred Books of the East,* Vol. XLIX, Part II, pp. 89–103.

[31] *Chin-kang ching.* Among several English translations, see those by Müller,

sutra,[32] recite the holy name of the Buddha, and experience Reality in the realm of the Boundless and Infinite Buddha. Just how many Chinese Buddhists may be included in these groups it is difficult to estimate. But it has been stated on good authority that 60 or 70 percent of the four million Chinese lay devotees count themselves as followers of Pure Land.[33]

IN PRACTICE, FROM THE DISCIPLINARY AND MEDITATION SCHOOLS TO THE MYSTICAL SCHOOL

While many Chinese Buddhists were searching for new religious experience in the Pure Land tradition, others looked for it in Mysticism, which was introduced into modern China essentially because the practices in both the Disciplinary and Meditation Schools had lost spirituality. As has already been pointed out, the Disciplinary School has hardly existed as an independent sect in China. Although a number of temples along the coast claim to belong to it, actually it has been practically absorbed into other schools. In the twentieth century, only Abbots Hung-i and Ching-yen of Honan were known as Masters of the Disciplinary School. The so-called center of the school in the Paohua Mountain near Nanking enjoys high prestige as the most coveted place for ordination. It conducts a semiannual ceremony for ordina-

"The Vagrakkhedika or Diamond-Cutter," in *The Sacred Books of the East,* Vol. XLIX, Part II, pp. 109–49; Lee, "The Diamond Sutra," in his *Popular Buddhism in China,* pp. 27–52; Suzuki, "Vajracchedika" (first half and selections), in his *Manual of Zen Buddhism,* pp. 43–56.

[32] *Leng-yen ching.* For a résumé of this very philosophical text, see Suzuki, *Manual of Zen Buddhism,* pp. 74–84. For selections, see translation by Wei-tao and Dwight Goddard, in Lin Yutang's *The Wisdom of China and India,* pp. 491–549. Samuel Beal's rendering in his *A Catena of Buddhist Scriptures* is unintelligible.

[33] Chiang Wei-ch'iao, "Chinese Buddhism in the Last Ten Years" (in Chinese), *Kuang-hua pan-yueh k'an* ("Kuang Hua University Semi-Monthly"), III, Nos. 9–10 (June, 1935), 141; Pao-ming, "Present Tendencies in Chinese Buddhism" (in Chinese), *Hai-ch'ao yin,* VII, No. 3 (March, 1926), 1.

tion, a very impressive affair. But so far as the meaning of religious discipline goes, the School has long since forgotten the "four aspects" of discipline; namely, its "rules"; its "substance," or moral consciousness aroused by taking vows and ever active in directing meritorious deeds; its "action," expressed in words and thoughts as well as in deeds; and its "character," which should be so good as to be exemplary. Discipline has come to mean only initiation and ordination. Much of this has been devoid of spiritual value and no longer capable of leading to genuine religious experience.[34]

Similarly, the glorious tradition of the Meditation School has lost its religious power. Not that there are no more Ch'an Masters or Ch'an centers. The two most prominent and most representative Ch'an abbots in China today, the elderly Hsu-yun in South China and Lai-kuo, Master of the Kao-min Temple in Yangchow, are generally revered for their magnificent personalities and their exemplary work. The Chiang-t'ien Temple in Chinkiang and the Kao-min Temple are still the citadels of Ch'an and lend high prestige to any priest who has been resident there. Besides, there is a meditation hall in all large temples, regardless of school affiliation. Contrary to the Japanese Meditation School (Zen), which has remained a distinct and independent sect, Chinese Ch'an has penetrated all schools and has practically lost its own identity. What is understood by Ch'an today is nothing but performance of ceremonies, stripped of the original meaning of instantaneous intuition of truth. Originally, Ch'an meant "directly pointing to the human mind and to become a Buddha by seeing one's own Buddha-nature." This was to be achieved either through Tathagata Meditation, that is,

[34] The school is called Vinaya (Discipline) in Sanskrit, because it is based on the *Vinaya* section of the Buddhist Canon. Its doctrine was elaborated and completed by Tao-hsuan (596–667) in the South Mountain. Its Discipline includes 250 "prohibitive precepts" for monks and 348 for nuns. It is called Shin Ritsu (New Discipline) in Japan.

meditation involving keen deliberations and a clear understanding of the identity of the Buddha and the originally undefiled mind, or through Patriarchal Meditation requiring no intellectual effort but sharp imagination and sensitive consciousness. But today Meditation means nothing more than a sheer convention of quiet sitting.[35]

The deterioration of Ch'an in Chinese history was caused by many factors, historical as well as philosophical. One reason is that Ch'an in China has shifted from Ch'an as religious enlightenment to Ch'an as wit. In India, Meditation requires asceticism. In China, asceticism is not taken seriously. Of the Buddhist "three learnings," Indian Meditation stresses discipline and concentration. Chinese Meditation, on the other hand, emphasizes wisdom. As Hu Shih

[35] The Meditation doctrine is "not founded on words or scriptures" but on "a special transmission outside of the Sacred Teaching." It is based on the doctrine of the Buddha Mind, that is, the "Store of the All-Seeing True Law and the Profound Mind of Nirvana." Interpretations of the Buddha Mind among Meditation Masters vary, but in general it is conceived as the Void which is "neither holy nor unholy, neither cause nor effect, neither good nor evil, neither form nor characteristic." The world of multiplicity, with all its specific characters and distinctions, is the result of our ignorance and attachment, and as such is but a dream. Consequently, to penetrate the Buddha Mind some Masters urged *wu-nien* or absence of thought in the sense that the mind is not in any way to be attached to or influenced by objects. Others advocated *wang-ch'ing* or "ignoring our feelings." Still others, contending that the phenomenal world was after all the manifestation of the Buddha-nature, recommended *jen-hsin,* that is, letting the mind take its own course.

The Meditation School attributes its mystic beginning to the Buddha himself. In China it was founded by Bodhidharma in the Liu Sung period (420–479). The doctrine was ultimately transmitted to its sixth patriarch, Hui-neng (638–713). Then the school split into the Southern School of Abrupt Enlightenment and the Northern School of Gradual Enlightenment. The Northern School, founded by Shen-hsiu (605–706), soon disappeared, but the Southern School, founded by Hui-neng, developed into seven sects. Since the eleventh century, however, only the Lin-chi and the Ts'ao-tung Sects have continued in China. In Japan, Zen was introduced several times from the seventh to the ninth century. Eisai founded the Rinzai Sect there in 1191, and Dogen founded the Soto Sect in 1227. The Fuke Sect was founded by Kakushin in 1255 and was abolished in 1868. The Obaku Sect was founded by Ingen in 1654. Japanese Zen, including all its sects, has some ten million followers.

characterizes it, "Indian Meditation demands concentration and the ability to stay unperturbed by outside influence, whereas Chinese Meditation demands wisdom and the ability to find a way out of a seemingly hopeless situation." [36] He tells two stories to bring the contrast into sharp focus. According to a third-century Chinese version of an Indian story, an Indian prince would appoint as his prime minister the person who could hold a tray full of oil and go from the north city gate to the south gate without spilling it, on the penalty of death for failure. One aspirant accepted the dangerous challenge. On his way, he successively saw his parents, wife, and children crying; met the most beautiful women; encountered a mad elephant which frightened people away; saw the palace on fire, from which came wasps to attack him; and encountered storm and lightning. None of these disturbed him, and he succeeded in becoming the prime minister. This is Indian dhyana or Meditation.

The Chinese story is one told by the Ch'an Master Fa-yen (d. 1104). A successful thief was getting on in years. His son asked him about his method of making a living. The thief led the boy to a rich man's mansion, broke through the wall, opened a large wardrobe, told the boy to get in, locked him there, loudly gave alarm, and fled home. The residents searched the house but decided that the thief had escaped through the hole in the wall. All this time the son inside the wardrobe was worried and angry. Suddenly a brilliant idea flashed upon him. He imitated the sound of a rat gnawing in the wardrobe. The family told the maid to light a lamp and examine the wardrobe. Thereupon, the boy leaped out, blew out the lamp, and quickly made his way out. To mislead his pursuers, he threw a rock into the well. When he got home, he found the old thief waiting. As

[36] Hu Shih, "The Development of Chinese Ch'an" (in Chinese), *Shih-ta yueh-k'an* ("Normal College Monthly"), No. 18 (April, 1935), p. 9.

he protested to his father about what had happened, the old man said, "From now on, my son, you need not worry about having enough rice to eat." [37]

The choice of a thief as the key character in the Chinese story is typical of the rebellious Ch'an spirit against conventional morality. But the real moral of the story is that Ch'an means sharpness of mind to solve practical problems. Thus Ch'an is no longer a religious discipline as in India, but the quickness of mind to handle critical situations. It has become the play of exciting wit, penetrating wisdom, lightning decision, and creative intelligence. As such Ch'an has vastly enriched Chinese art and poetry and has made the Chinese character fascinating. But all this has been at the expense of religious values. Like the devitalized tradition of Discipline, Ch'an has ceased to be a spiritual force. At best, it is the flash of a brilliant mind. At worst, it is stolid "quiet sitting." It no longer satisfied the religious yearnings of Chinese Buddhists. For this, they had to turn elsewhere. Many have found satisfaction in Pure Land Pietism. Others sought it in the Mystical School.[38]

Buddhist Mysticism as developed in the True Word School never had much attraction for the Chinese. While

[37] With slight variation in details, the story is quoted in Suzuki, *Essays in Zen Buddhism,* 1st series, pp. 296–97.

[38] The Mystical School considers the universe itself to be the Great Sun Buddha, who comprises the two Realms of Buddha's Law-Body of Wisdom and of Buddha's Law-Body of Principle. These are respectively the realms of effect and cause, Great Enlightenment and Great Compassion, the Buddha and sentient beings, and so on, but the two realms constitute one universe. They are but two aspects of the same Law-Body. The nature of the universe consists of the Six Great Elements of Earth, Water, Fire, Air, Space, and Consciousness, all of which are mutually dependent and penetrating. None can exist without the others, as, for example, no Buddha exists outside of sentient beings and no sentient being exists outside of Buddha.

The school is the second largest Buddhist sect in Japan. It has nine million followers, and its center is the famous Koya Mountain. The doctrine was brought from China by several Great Masters, among whom was Kobo Daishi (Kukai, 774–835), who organized and systematized the school and became its founder.

several other schools enjoyed centuries of long life, it disappeared from the Chinese scene within a hundred years after it was transmitted in China by three Indian teachers, Subhakarasimha (637–735), Vajrabodhi (663–723), and Amoghavajra (705–774). Since the ninth century, it has persisted not as a distinct sect but merely in such mystical rituals as finger-intertwining and incantation in masses for the dead and similar occasions. As it declined in China, it was introduced into Japan by Keikwa (746–805), where it is now the second largest Buddhist denomination. Here we have another contrast between Japanese and Chinese Buddhism. Whereas the Chinese cared little for mystical experience, this has become to the Japanese a major attraction. It has been in Japan that the True Word (Shingon) traditions have been perpetuated. These are the "Three Mysteries" of Action, Speech, and Thought, meaning that all phenomena are the action, speech, and thought of the Great Sun Buddha, and that the exercise of these mysteries by human beings, through finger-intertwining and other activities, the incantation of True Words, and the concentration of thought, will lead to communion and identification with the Buddha, resulting in "Buddha-in-me and I-in-Buddha." In China all this was forgotten, so much so that Chinese students studying in Japan at the turn of the century found in Japanese Shingon an intriguing element of novelty.

This interest was promptly intensified by both study and translations. The first to go to Japan particularly to explore Mysticism was Kuei Nien-tsu (1869–1916), pupil of the famous Yang Wen-hui. Unfortunately he died before he completed his studies.[39] But others continued the search. The man principally instrumental in the reintroduction of Mysticism was the layman Wang Hung-yuan, who studied

[39] T'ai-hsu, "The Present Tendency of the Revival of Mysticism in China" (in Chinese), *Hai-ch'ao yin*, VI, No. 8 (August, 1925), 12–14.

the mysteries under the renowned Japanese Master Gonda Raifu. He translated books on Mysticism into Chinese and outlined the essentials of the doctrine in *Hai-chao yin* in 1918 (a special number on Mysticism was issued in the following year).[40] Following this, Japanese preachers came to lecture in China, and a number of Chinese priests went east to Japan for further light. Of these seekers after truth, only Ta-yung, Ch'ih-sung, and Hsien-yin seriously delved into the system. The latter died upon his return to China. Ch'ih-sung, who went in 1920 to Koya Mountain, center of Japanese Mysticism, and was ordained there, in time returned to preach in the Pao-t'ung Temple in Hankow and in Chang-shu. He was enthusiastically received, especially in Central China.

The influence of Ta-yung was even greater. He was a judge advocate in the army before following T'ai-hsu in 1922. After he returned from Koya in 1923 he spread the Mystical doctrine in Hangchow, Peking, Hupei, and Shanghai, attracting a sizable following. In the meantime, Wang Hung-yuan, through his Association for the Renaissance of Mysticism and his publications, propagated the Mystical teachings far and wide from his native Chaochow in South China; Monk Mandju (Man-shu, Su Yuan-ying), brilliant, romantic pupil of Yang Wen-hui, was spreading the gospel around Canton;[41] and a Buddhist lay woman, Miss Ch'eng Chai-an, of interior Szechuan, having been indoctrinated in Japan, was transmitting the secrets in Chungking and Soochow.[42] In the 1920s and early 1930s Mysticism prevailed not only in the places already mentioned but also in Hunan and East China.

[40] Fa-fang, *op. cit.*, p. 5.
[41] *Ibid.*; Yu Sun, "Contemporary Buddhism and Confucianism in China" (in Chinese), *Wen-hua yü chiao-yü* ("Culture and Education"), No. 85 (March, 1930), p. 26.
[42] Chiang Wei-ch'iao, in *Kuang-hua pan-yueh k'an*, III, Nos. 9–10 (June, 1935), 141.

Abbot Ta-yü, originally a Master of Pure Land Pietism, was said to have been suddenly invested by Buddha Manjusri [43] with mystical power. His fame traveled rapidly in all directions, and he converted several thousand people in Peking and Shanghai.[44]

Various reasons may be offered for this phenomenal growth of Mysticism. Exoteric Buddhism emphasizes theory, while esoteric Buddhism emphasizes practice. Mysticism, one of the esoteric systems, naturally had a certain appeal to the practical Chinese. The two chief practical systems of Chinese Buddhism, Discipline and Meditation, having lost their vitality, Mysticism could naturally and logically take their place. Furthermore, as has already been indicated, the history of Chinese Buddhism is one of persistent reduction to the simplest way of salvation. Discipline and Meditation, though simple enough, still required self-mastery. They belong to the "self-power" tradition of Buddhism. In Mysticism, however, the secret powers of the Buddha work directly, generously, and indiscriminately. It requires no mental concentration as in Ch'an or even the recitation of Buddha's name as in Pietism. It belongs to the "other-power" tradition. In Ch'an, Buddahood may be discovered in one's own mind. In the Disciplinary School, it is realizable in one's body. But in Mysticism, one's self *is* the Buddha. The Law-body of the Great Sun Buddha, the personification of the Secret Truth, pervades the entire universe, resulting in the identification of the I and the Buddha. This idea was derived from the Hindu concept of the identity of Brahma and the Self. It is entirely in agreement with the Chinese concept of the unity of Heaven and man.

The movement did not continue for long, however. After

[43] Buddha as the embodiment of Wisdom.

[44] Ta-yuan, "The Changing Phenomenon of Buddhist Developments in China in the Last Fifteen Years" (in Chinese), *Hai-ch'ao yin*, XVI, No. 1 (January, 1935), 52–53.

a heartening start, Ch'ih-sung met many difficulties and became discouraged. Ta-yung passed away in Tibet. China's relation with Japan was now becoming hostile, and Wang Hung-yuan, with his close Japanese connections, was politically implicated. Gradually Chinese Buddhists turned away from Japanese or Eastern Mysticism to Tibetan or Western Mysticism.

Long before this (in the early 1920s), Mongolian lamas of the only lama temple in China proper, located in Peking, had gone out to preach along the Yangtze. In 1926, Mongolian lamaist representatives were invited to perform their services in many chief cities in North and Central China. From 1925 to 1929, a scholarly lama from Sikang lectured in Peking, Hankow, and Szechuan. But it was the combination of the presence of the Panchan Lama in China and the development of the international situation that gave the movement of Tibetan Mysticism an impetus. The Panchan Lama was now, in the 1930s, residing in the Chinese capital. Naturally, such an eminent personage created profound interest in his religion. Japan had invaded Manchuria and was definitely threatening North China. For national defense, the Chinese faced the West as far as Tibet, whose religion assumed tremendous importance. Moreover, the government itself took active steps to promote Tibetan Mysticism.[45] High officials participated in masses officiated by the Panchan Lama. The Ta-lin Temple in Kuling was repaired at government expense as a place of worship for top officials.[46] In 1936, the government granted scholarships to monks to study in Tibet and for Tibetan lamas to study in China. In 1937, the Tibetan scholar, Hsi-jao-chia-tso, was in-

[45] Fa-fang, "The Present Conditions of Chinese Buddhism" (in Chinese), *Hai-ch'ao yin*, XVIII, No. 4 (April, 1937), 24.

[46] Wang I-ch'ang, "The Buddhist Transformation of China and the Chinese Transformation of Buddhism" (in Chinese), *Wen-hua p'i-p'an* ("Cultural Critique"), II, No. 1 (November, 1934), 60–64.

vited by the government to lecture in five national universities.

Another reason for the rise of Tibetan Mysticism is that while Mysticism, being esoteric, inclines to practice rather than theory (as has already been pointed out), Tibetan Mysticism emphasizes practice even more strongly than Japanese Mysticism, and has therefore greater appeal to the Chinese. Thirdly, the situation in China, torn by civil war, by government corruption, and by social chaos, brought many Chinese into a repentant mood. It was not easy to accumulate merits or pure karma as required in the Pure Land School, or to penetrate philosophy as required in Wei-shih Idealism, to achieve salvation. It was far easier to embrace Mysticism, which excuses and sometimes even accepts sin as an "expedient way" to Paradise.

In spite of these enticing qualities, however, Tibetan Mysticism, like Japanese Mysticism, did not endure for long. After the initial mystical charm wore off, it soon lost its power of captivation. After all, Mysticism does not really suit the Chinese temperament. The educated Chinese did not look upon asceticism with favor; much less did they care for such absurd practices as recalling the soul and causing spirits to descend from Heaven. Of course, the uprooting effects of the war with Japan accentuated the decline. But Mysticism contained in itself the seed of its own destruction. Besides, there was hardly any literature to satisfy the intellectual Chinese, with the consequence that few educated laymen were attracted. And the unusually rigid regulations governing ordination did not help the movement. Mysticism did offer the Chinese some spiritual solace in times of internal turmoil and international war. As a constructive religious force, however, it failed miserably. The only aspect of the movement that is still alive today is the interest in Tibetan literature aroused by it. We shall now turn to this trend.

IN LITERATURE, FROM CHINESE TO PALI AND TIBETAN

As is well known, Chinese Buddhist literature has been almost entirely confined to the Sanskrit tradition and has neglected both the Pali and Tibetan traditions. The movement of Tibetan Mysticism has convinced the Chinese that Chinese Buddhist literature must be enriched from these two sources. Among the first to study Tibetan Buddhism were Lü Ch'eng and T'ang Chu-hsin. Since 1921, they and other scholars have translated a number of Tibetan texts into Chinese.[47] From 1922 on, the Institute of Inner Learning offered in its curriculum courses on the Tibetan language and grammar, and started the compilation of a Tibetan-Chinese dictionary. In 1924, a Tibetan Institute was established in Peking by Ta-yung. In the following year, a group of twenty-nine students, mostly pupils of T'ai-hsu, set off to study in Tibet. For political reasons, the Tibetan authorities permitted only a few to enter.[48] In 1932, the World Buddhist Institute was founded in Chungking, followed by the Institute of Chinese and Tibetan Buddhism in 1933. A year later, the Institute of Mysticism in Peking and the Bodhi Society in Shanghai came into being. They were all engaged, partly or exclusively, in the study and translation of Tibetan literature, and sometimes Pali literature also. In 1932 the Bodhi Society in Peking published a Tibetan-Chinese dictionary. About that time the translation department of the Bodhi Society in Shanghai published several translations of Tibetan texts.[49] Today Fa-chou is especially devoted to the study and translation of Pali literature, as was the late Fa-fang.[50] Although no startling result has been obtained, the trend is extremely important. It is impossible to predict how it will be

[47] Fa-fang, *Wei-shih shih-kuan chi ch'i che-hsueh*, p. 6.
[48] *China Year Book*, 1936–37, p. 1446.
[49] For a list of these books, see *ibid.*, p. 1448.
[50] Fa-fang, *op. cit.*

affected by Communist control of Tibet. The Institute of Chinese and Tibetan Buddhism, now outside Chungking, is maintaining a precarious existence. Nevertheless, intellectual curiosity about a vast uncultivated field of Buddhism has been aroused. Sooner or later it will lead to new information, now interpretation, and perhaps even new developments. Pali studies will surely alter Chinese ideas about the Buddha, for example. Chinese Buddhism, being largely based on the Sanskrit Canon, follows it in treating the Buddha as a supramundane deity. In the Pali Canon, on the other hand, the Buddha is presented as a humane and earthly teacher; if this is accepted, Chinese concepts of the Buddha are bound to be changed. The study of Tibetan is likely to correct many Chinese translations and revise Chinese interpretations. For example, from a study of the Tibetan translation of the *Mahayanasamparigraha*, it is found that the version agrees with the three earlier Chinese translations and differs in some important interpretations from Hsuan-tsang's version. This raises an important question, whether Hsuan-tsang's presentation of the Idealistic philosophy of Asanga and Vasubandhu, which the Chinese have accepted as the correct version, may not be open to challenge after all.[51] Unless the trend is terminated by unforeseen circumstances, it may open a new stage for Chinese Buddhism.

However, before this stage is set, there must be competent dramatic personnel. That is to say, there must be a new type

[51] Lü Ch'eng, "The Tibetan Version of the *Mahayanasamparigraha*" (in Chinese), *Nei-hsueh*, No. 2 (1925), pp. 99–128. As an example of what the study of Tibetan may contribute, Professor Kenneth K. S. Ch'en of Harvard wrote me: "Scholars have often wondered why the Cullavagga in the *Vinayapitaka* should suddenly start with the story of the Rajagaha Council in Chap. 11. A study by Obermiller of the Tibetan Vinayaksudraka indicates that in the Tibetan version, the *Mahaparinirvanasutra* and the portions of the Cullavagga (Chaps. 11–12) which deal with the first two councils were originally connected together in one continuous account. Later Pali theologians cut off the portions dealing with the councils and placed them in the Vinaya."

of monks and nuns, a new order or sangha, to whom religion means actual religious living instead of ritualistic gymnastics. This leads us to the trend in modern Chinese Buddhism from ritualistic performance to a meaningful demonstration of faith.

IN ATTITUDE, FROM RITUALISTIC PERFORMANCE TO RELIGIOUS DEMONSTRATION

The main occupation of Chinese monks and nuns has been performance of rituals for funerals and other occasions, usually for a consideration. There can be no escape from the unpleasant fact that the sangha (Buddhist order) is a congregation of ignorant and selfish people to whom religious observance has no spiritual significance. T'ai-hsu complained that "the entire Chinese clergy is interested in self-benefit." [52] Even if we liberally discount the statement of the reformer, it still points to an undeniably intolerable situation.

The main reason for this sad state of affairs is the type of people who join the order. Of the half million monks and one hundred thousand nuns, or five clerics for every two temples,[53] it is safe to say that the large majority has no sound

[52] *T'ai-hsu Ta-shih wen-ch'ao* ("Selected Works of T'ao-hsu"), p. 224.

[53] There has never been a census of Chinese Buddhist monks and nuns. Chinese Buddhists themselves, following T'ai-hsu, often quote the figure of 800,000, of whom 60 percent are monks and 40 percent nuns. The *China Handbook*, 1937–1945, a Chinese Government official publication, says that "there are in China more than 267,000 Buddhist temples and 738,000 monks and nuns" (p. 26). The *Hai-ch'ao yin* once cited one million monks and nuns in China, with a great number along the coast, especially in Chekiang and Kiangsu (Reichelt, *Truth and Tradition in Chinese Buddhism*, p. 296). Hodous (*op. cit.*, p. 66) said that a conservative estimate, based upon partial returns, put the total number at half a million, with 20 percent nuns. Pratt (*op. cit.*, p. 336) accepted this estimate. Grace Goodrich also said that there were about 100,000 nuns, and added that they were mostly in the South and along the coast ("The Nuns of North China," *Asia*, XXXVII, No. 2, February, 1937, 90). Both Hodous (*op. cit.*, p. 66) and McDaniel (*op. cit.*, p. 536) said that the number of monks was increasing in the 1920s. They gave no source for their statements and I have found no evidence to support them, although the fact may well have been true.

conception of their religion. Few "shaved their heads" because of their own faith. Most of them "escaped to the Gate of the Void" because of disappointment of one sort or another—poverty, sickness, the parents' devotion or their promise to present the child in return for healing illness or other blessings, broken homes, or even crime.[54] One nun gave these eight reasons for Chinese women to don the Buddhist robe: (1) genuine and deep faith; (2) presentation by parents because of devotion, sickness, lack of support, lack of people to take care of the child, or an astrologer's advice; (3) hopelessness after husband's death; (4) unhappy marriage; (5) poverty; (6) family troubles or other disappointments; (7) influence of sisters, close relatives, or friends who have become nuns; (8) in cases of servants, running away from the cruelty of their mistresses. Of these, "unhappy marriage accounts for a great number," and "60 or 70 percent made the choice because there was no other way out." Of the

The best report on the number of Chinese monks and nuns is Hui-chu's "Miscellany of Statistics on Buddhist Monks and Nuns" (in Chinese), which is based on government figures of 1931, in *Hai-ch'ao yin*, XVI, No. 3 (March, 1935), 27–28. According to this, there were 45,229 monks and 12,824 nuns in the province of Kiangsu. This means one monk for every 470 males and one nun for every 1,250 females. There were 42,501 monks and 11,517 nuns in Hunan, and 38,548 monks and 12,028 nuns in Hupei. The total for Anhwei, Kiangsi, and Hopei was about 21,000 for each province. Of the two thousand-odd counties in China, more than a hundred did not have a single monk or nun. In Kiangsu Province, the highest ratio for monks was found in Tungtai County, where there was a monk for every 196 males, and the highest ratio for nuns was in the Chiangtu County, where there was a nun for every 556 females. In all counties in the province, monks outnumbered nuns, except in Nanhui and Fenghsien, where there was a total of 599 nuns but only 402 monks. The writer concluded that the total for the entire country, excluding lamas, could not have exceeded 500,000 for monks and 100,000 for nuns, "far from T'ai-hsu's estimate of 800,000." These figures, he added, include those who lived the celibate and ascetic life in monasteries and nunneries but did not shave their heads, that is, they were not really monks and nuns but lay people who "cultivated a religious life while keeping their hair."

[54] Reichelt, *Truth and Tradition in Chinese Buddhism*, pp. 231–34. See also Pratt, *op. cit.*, pp. 336–37; Grace Goodrich, in *Asia*, XXXVII, No. 2 (February, 1937), 90.

fifteen initiates the nun had seen, seven cried bitterly during the ceremony.[55]

Such being the constituency of the sangha, it is obvious that a thorough reform is overdue. As early as 1915, T'ai-hsu saw the need of a "new sangha,"[56] which would be a society of men and women well selected, who would not officiate in masses and funerals for money but would do productive work and demonstrate a truly religious life.[57] With this in mind, T'ai-hsu vigorously pushed a threefold program—to restrict and regulate the selection of clerics, to provide education for them, and to promote social service.[58] But the reformer was not able to translate many of his ideals into reality. From 1929 to 1933, the government announced several regulations for temples and for the clergy but they remained on paper. All in all, little has been done in this direction.[59]

In the field of social service, the showing has been more encouraging. There have been lectures, study groups, scripture classes, libraries, museums, evangelistic meetings, Young Men's Buddhist Associations, Red Cross work, first aid during the war, hospitals, orphanages, famine and flood relief, collection and distribution of clothing, visits to prisons, caring for and liberating living creatures, and so forth.[60] Much of this has been stimulated by Christian churches, and the Buddhist program has faithfully followed the Christian pattern. In terms of monks and nuns available and in terms

[55] Miao-t'an, "My Views on the Reforms of Nuns" (in Chinese), *Hai-ch'ao yin*, I, No. 11 (November, 1920), 78–80.
[56] T'ai-hsu, *T'ai-hsu Ta-shih wen-ch'ao*, pp. 219–38.
[57] Ta-wu, "New Tendencies in Chinese Buddhism in the Last Fifteen Years" (in Chinese), *Hai-ch'ao yin*, XVI, No. 1 (January, 1935), 78–79. Cf. Haydon, *op. cit.*, p. 78.
[58] *China Christian Year Book*, 1928, pp. 43–44.
[59] Ta-hsing, "The Movement to Reform the Clerical System in the Last Fifteen Years" (in Chinese), *Hai-ch'ao yin*, XVI, No. 1 (January, 1935), 105–10.
[60] Ta-hsing, "An Examination of Buddhist Activities in the Last Fifteen Years" (in Chinese), *ibid.*, pp. 81–98.

of real need, the actual service has been meagre. The important point, however, is that Chinese Buddhism has gained a strangely new conviction and has assumed a noble social responsibility. It is worth recording that when the Chinese Buddhist Society met in Nanking in May, 1947, in which some seventy delegates from China Proper, Tibet, and Sinkiang participated, one of the four projects decided upon was the realization of a program of public welfare and social relief.[61]

In the field of education, some really ambitious undertakings have been attempted. Strange to say, the first Buddhist school in China was founded by a Japanese.[62] Because the government confiscated Buddhist properties to support education in 1907, Buddhists initiated a program of their own. Eventually there was a Buddhist college in Shanghai in 1914, which closed in three years. Following the Intellectual Renaissance of 1917, a number of Buddhist schools were established, including a few colleges, notably the Hua-yen College in 1921, the Wuchang Buddhist Institute in 1922, and the Fa-hsiang College in 1925.[63] Some of the Buddhist institutes were in reality colleges, especially the Institute of Inner Learning. From 1922 to 1933, there were twenty-two colleges, academies, and institutes, besides a number of schools, and in 1937 there were forty-five Buddhist seminaries.[64] Only four schools were for women. Few educational institutions of any grade had more than thirty or forty students. No enrollment ever exceeded sixty. Most of the schools lasted for only a few years.[65] They faced the insurmountable obstacles of financial stringency, govern-

[61] *China Handbook*, 1950, p. 26.
[62] Y. Y. Tsu, in *Wen She*, II, No. 7 (May, 1929), 46.
[63] *Nei-hsueh*, No. 4 (1928), p. 271.
[64] *China Year Book*, 1936–37, p. 1445; Wei-huan, "Buddhism in Modern China," *T'ien Hsia Monthly*, IX, No. 2 (September, 1939), 146–50.
[65] Wei-fang, "Education for the Sangha in the Last Fifteen Years" (in Chinese), *Hai-ch'ao yin*, XVI, No. 1 (January, 1935), 111–30.

ment confiscation of properties, inefficiency, conservatism, preoccupation with temple affairs and subordination of school interests to those of the temple, and elderly priests' reluctance to allow their younger followers to be exposed to dangerous modern ideas.[66] At present, the Institute of Inner Learning, now located in Szechuan with layman Lü Ch'eng as dean, is struggling for survival. The condition of the Wuchang Buddhist Institute is no happier. The Oriental Institute at Chengtu is making a heroic effort to carry on.

What effects have these social and educational programs had on the sangha? It must be conceded that the total effect has been disappointing. Nevertheless, there is a consoling factor, and that is that in a small way, a new sangha is emerging. For example, Chü-tsan, a Buddhist delegate to the People's Political Consultative Conference in the new government in China, is a monk well versed in Buddhist history and philosophy, was a college student before joining the order, knows several languages, and is modern and progressive in outlook. During the Second World War he founded the Hua-yen Academy in Central China with thirty students. He organized the Buddhist Youth Service Corps to help citizens of Changsha, as well as the Buddhist Youth War-Time Committee, Buddhist training classes, the Hunan Buddhist Association for the Support of the War of Resistance, and other groups. In 1942, he started a monthly, *Shih-tzu hou* ("Lion's Roar"), in Kweilin. He is now dean of the Wulin Buddhist Institute at Hangchow. A former girl student of mine attended college before she was baptized. When I called on her in 1949 in a small "vegetarian abode" where she was a resident nun, she was lecturing on the highly philosophical *Surangamasutra* to a group of women, including a college freshman. Buddhists like her and Chü-tsan did not

[66] Wei-fang, "Reflections on the Education for the Sangha in the Last Fifteen Years" (in Chinese), *ibid.*, pp. 131–39.

resort to the religion as an escape but chose it as a way of life. They represent a new type of Buddhist. Their number is pitifully small. In terms of quantity, the new crop is not impressive. In terms of quality, however, the Buddhist religion may yet be concretely demonstrated in spirituality and social worth. In the meantime, Buddhist laymen have been surging ahead, rapidly assuming leadership in the religion.

IN LEADERSHIP, FROM THE CLERGY TO THE LAYMAN

The shift from the Buddhist clergy to the layman was inevitable. Long ago China transformed Hinayana Buddhism centering on the monastic order to Mahayana Buddhism centering on lay society. The development of the tradition of salvation by self-effort has relegated the priest to secondary importance. The transition was hastened by the growth of Ch'an, which advocates salvation through "looking into one's own Buddha-nature." The weakness and degeneration of the sangha encouraged the transition; modern Buddhist developments have made it complete.

I have already mentioned the role of pioneering and leadership played by Yang Wen-hui in promoting Buddhist literature and by other laymen in Buddhist publications. I have also mentioned Wang Hung-yuan's share in the importation of Mysticism. I shall discuss later the dominant role played by Ou-yang Ching-wu and Hsiung Shih-li in the evolution of modern Buddhist thought.[67] Most of modern Buddhist activity, be it meditation, study, retreat, or charity, has been carried on in lay institutions such as Lotus Societies, Pure Karma Societies, Buddha Halls, and the like, rather than in temples. I am not forgetting the substantial part played by T'ai-hsu in Buddhist reforms. But even his projects have been largely financed by laymen. A Japanese scholar

[67] See below, pp. 105–18, 126–35.

once said that Chinese Buddhism could be represented by five people: Yin-kuang, T'ai-hsu, Wang I-t'ing, Wang Hung-yuan, and Ou-yang Ching-wu. Three of the five were laymen.[68] In the last several decades, the role of famous laymen has been far more impressive than that of monks. Many names have already been mentioned.[69] We could cite others. All of them have been intellectual and political leaders. They, and others like them, have provided Buddhism with leadership and money. They have promoted Buddhist thought and they have carried on most of the modern Buddhist program. Besides engaging in private and group worship, in studies and discussions, in publications and social work, and in the Buddhist international program, they even officiate in religious services. In this, they are taking over the prerogatives of the priest. They also take certain vows which were formerly restricted to the clergy. Thus the layman is increasingly taking over the function of the monk. For two thousand years, Chinese Buddhism has been traveling along this direction. The center of gravity of Buddhism has been gradually shifting from the monastery to society. This tendency is stronger and stronger today, not only in Buddhism, but in other religions as well.[70]

IN OUTLOOK, FROM THE OTHER WORLD TO THIS WORLD

The growing importance of the layman practically implies the growing importance of this world. This tendency from

[68] Hua-sheng, "Tendencies of Buddhist Thought in the Last Fifteen Years" (in Chinese), *ibid.*, p. 43.

[69] Chih-tsang, in his "Buddhist Laymen in the Last Fifteen Years" (in Chinese), *Hai-ch'ao yin,* XVI, No. 1 (January, 1935), 140–85, lists 71 prominent names including Chang T'ai-yen, Liang Ch'i-ch'ao, Wang Hung-yuan, Ting Fu-pao, Lü Ch'eng, Tai Chi-t'ao, Wang I-t'ing, Yeh Kung-ch'o. Some of these men were Confucian as much as they were Buddhist, if not more so. But they promoted Buddhism, especially its philosophy and literature. Others are included in T'an Yun-shan's "Present Conditions of Chinese Buddhism" (in Chinese), *Hai-ch'ao yin,* XV, No. 9 (September, 1934), 15–22.

[70] See below, pp. 176–78, 190, 194.

other-worldliness to this-worldliness also has a long historical background. One of the chief transformations of Buddhism in Chinese history has been the change from the other-worldly outlook to the this-worldly outlook. In all the schools that prevail to this day, this world is emphasized as much as, or even more than, the other world. In the Hua-yen School, both the World of Principles and the World of Facts are to be synthesized in a Harmonious Whole. In the T'ien-t'ai School, "every color and every fragrance is none other than the Middle Way." In these schools, and more particularly in the Ch'an, Mystical, and Disciplinary Schools, salvation is to be achieved "in this very body," and one can, and should, "become Buddha where you are." Only in the Pure Land School is the Other Shore or Paradise glorified. It may be argued that since most Chinese Buddhists are Pure Land devotees, it follows that Chinese Buddhism is other-worldly. It is true that the Chinese masses sincerely pray for rebirth in the Pure Land and make generous offerings for the salvation of the departed. It is also true that Heaven and Hell loom large in the eyes of most of the common people. Compared with Confucianism and Taoism, Buddhism is certainly much less this-worldly. But with the masses, praying for rebirth is very often purely an expression of piety, at least with no deprecation for the present world. Indeed, they pray for long life on this earth as much as "crossing the sea" to the Other Shore. As to educated devotees, they are seldom concerned with the future life. We shall return to this earthly tendency when we discuss the religion of the masses.[71] The trend is even stronger in other religions.

The tendency can be clearly shown by another contrast between Chinese and Japanese Buddhism. The most widely revered bodhisattva—Buddha-to-be—in the Far East, especially in the T'ien-t'ai, Mystical, and Meditation Schools,

[71] See below, pp. 172–73.

is Avalokitesvara.[72] Significantly, in Japan, this saint, called Kwannon, remains transcendental and heavenly. In China, on the contrary, the deity has assumed female form and has become "mother" to millions of devout Chinese. Certainly that is what Kuan-yin, as the Chinese call the Buddhist saint, means to them. As Kuan-yin, that is, "Seer of the Sound" (of suffering), the deity is generally the embodiment of mercy and compassion and particularly a guardian of children and protector of womanhood. In short, the deity represents mother love, which is certainly very, very close to earth, right in the midst of our homes. Even in the Pure Land School, in Japan the object of worship is Amitabha, the Buddha of the Western Paradise, whereas in China it is still Kuan-yin. When devout Chinese murmur "*A-mi-t'o-fo*," they are not referring to Amitabha in particular, but to Buddhas and bodhisattvas in general. More often than not, they refer to Kuan-yin.

It may be questioned whether Buddhism, essentially a transcendental religion, can go very far in the this-worldly direction in an era of science. To put it differently, will Buddhism be able to get along in this scientific era? In this respect, Buddhism is actually more fortunate than most other religions, wherein a major scientific discovery often creates a theological crisis; to Buddhism, it may easily mean confirmation. Ou-yang Ching-wu made famous the dictum that "Buddhism is neither religion nor philosophy" but a unique system that includes all branches of human discipline, including science.[73] T'ai-hsu claimed that modern astronomy agreed with the Buddhist theory of vast and many universes,[74] that Buddhism is entirely harmonious with sci-

[72] For an account, see my article, "Avalokitesvara," in *An Encyclopedia of Religion*, ed. by Ferm, pp. 92–93.
[73] Ou-yang Ching-wu, "Buddhism Is Neither Religion nor Philosophy" (in Chinese), *Min-Toh*, III, No. 3 (March, 1922), 1–13.
[74] T'ai-hsu, "New Physics and New Buddhism" (in Chinese), *Hai-ch'ao yin*, XVIII, No. 4 (April, 1937), 1–7.

ence,[75] and that Einstein's theory of relativity confirms the Buddhist philosophy of Wei-shih.[76] T'ai-hsu did not know much about science or Einstein. It is true that Th. Stcherbatsky interprets the Buddhist concept of the Void (*Sunya*) [77] as Relativity, but he uses the terms in the generalized sense of "non-reality," meaning that "a thing can be identified only by mentioning its relations to something else." [78]

However, T'ai-hsu's claim about the scientific character of Buddhism is not unfounded. Pratt has pointed out many parallels between Buddhist concepts and some of the dominant ideas of contemporary science: the great Void embracing numerous universes, time in terms of millions of years, things as aggregates of elements, elements being analyzable into ultimate Reality, which is not hard matter but energy, existence as events, theory of cause and effect, no substance, no permanence, no duration, no externality, and so on.[79] "This reduction of reality to a collection of dynamic point-instants," says Pratt, "is a rather striking anticipation of thinkers like Alexander, Russell, Whitehead, and Jeans." [80] Pratt further points out that the Buddha himself had an essentially scientific attitude of mind in asking what the symptoms were, their causes, and what could be done about them.[81] Whitehead acknowledges that Buddhist thought antedated Aristotle's idea of the unmoved mover.[82]

[75] T'ai-hsu, *Fa-hsiang wei-shih hsueh*, p. 56.
[76] *Ibid.*, p. 491.
[77] For an account, see my article, "Sunya," in *An Encyclopedia of Religion*, ed. by Ferm, p. 107.
[78] Th. Stcherbatsky, *The Conception of Buddhist Nirvana*, p. 42.
[79] Haydon, *op. cit.*, pp. 35–45.
[80] *Ibid.*, p. 41. See also H. J. J. Winter, "Science, Buddhism and Taoism," *The Aryan Path*, XXI, No. 5 (May, 1950), 206–8.
[81] *Ibid.*, p. 44.
[82] Alfred North Whitehead, *Process and Reality*, p. 520. Although Whitehead's own philosophy has points in common with Buddhist philosophy, such as the idea of events, he thinks that Buddhism overemphasizes the "sheer infinity of the divine principle" and thereby undermines the finite,

Pratt contends that the Buddhist attitude toward science is, after all, negative. He gives, as one reason that, since the world of multiplicity is not considered ultimate by Buddhists, scientific studies cannot be really important to them.[83] But if Buddhism develops in the direction of this-worldliness, as it unmistakably does, then the doctrine that "every color and every fragrance is the Middle Way" will assume increasing importance, and each component of the world of multiplicity will have an ultimate character of its own. As a matter of fact, in the All-in-One and One-in-All philosophy of Hua-yen and T'ien-t'ai, the world of multiplicity is strongly affirmed.

Will the scientific character save Buddhism under the new regime in China that claims to do everything according to science? It is impossible to predict what will happen to Buddhism.[84] Some five hundred monks have fled Communist China and are congregating in Hong Kong. If we believe some of these refugees, four hundred thousand out of a total of seven hundred thousand monks and nuns have been forced by the government to return to lay life, and two hundred thousand younger monks have been drafted to

---

with consequence that its followers lack energy and impulse. Whitehead's God is somewhere between "the God of the learned tradition of Christian theology" and "the diffused God of the Hindu Buddhistic tradition." He says that God must exhibit the immortal side of many persons and at the same time be the unification of personality. "He is the intangible fact at the base of finite existence." See Whitehead's "Immortality," in Paul Arthur Schilpp, ed., *The Philosophy of Alfred North Whitehead*, pp. 675, 694. I am grateful to Professor Charles Hartshorne of the University of Chicago for these references. I may add that in essence Whitehead's concept of God bears striking resemblance to the Buddhist idea of the Harmony of One and Many, especially as developed in the Hua-yen and T'ien-t'ai Schools. See Chu Pao-ch'ang, "A New Interpretation of Buddhist Idealism" (in Chinese), *Yen-ching hsueh-pao* (*Yenching Journal of Chinese Studies*), No. 23 (June, 1938), in which the author relates Whitehead's concepts to Buddhist philosophy.

[83] Haydon, *op. cit.*, p. 36.

[84] See below, pp. 168, 261–64, for further discussion on Chinese Communism and religion.

"fight for the New Democracy." [85] Although the figures are gross exaggerations, they signify the plight Chinese Buddhists are in. In the meantime, Buddhist priests themselves may be deserting their own religion. In Shanghai, monks of the Yü-fo Temple have opened a vegetarian restaurant. Both Ching-an and Ch'ing-liang Temples have been converted by the priests themselves into small handicraft factories producing towels and socks. Monks from the Fa-tsang Temple are cultivating farms near by. In South China, the two hundred-odd monks in the Ta-chien Temple at Kukong have taken up weaving and farming.[86] In Hangchow, 1,800 monks and nuns from 292 monasteries and 267 nunneries opened restaurants, are working in mills or on farms, and have organized a Hangchow Buddhist Association to coordinate their enterprises.[87] These reports certainly suggest that the Chinese Buddhist religion is disintegrating.

On the other hand, there are at least three things that make the future seem hopeful. First of all, the new government in China still recognizes Buddhism. This is shown by the fact that of the 585 delegates to the People's Political Consultative Conference, two Buddhists (one of them Chü-tsan) were accepted by the government. Secondly, throughout Chinese history, Buddhism has been able to get along with all kinds of regimes because it has seldom interfered with the state. "We monks will not salute kings." Declared many centuries ago, this is the most famous and most faithfully followed manifesto of Chinese Buddhism. It not only means total indifference to earthly honor and power, but also complete noninterference with the government. Perhaps this persisting aloofness will win for Buddhism a new lease on life.

[85] New York *Times*, April 16, 1950.
[86] *Wah Kiu Yat Po* (*Overseas News*), Hong Kong, May 15, 1950.
[87] *Hua-ch'iao jih-pao* (*China Daily News*) (in Chinese), New York, April 13, 1950.

Finally, no matter what objections the new government may have to the religion, few can deny that it has given the Chinese people spiritual comfort. There is no reason to believe that under the "New Democracy" spiritual comfort is unnecessary. It is certain that temple land will be restricted and, as such, will be devoted to better use, that superstitious practices will be suppressed, that only few people, if any, will be allowed to enter monasteries and nunneries, that they will be required to do economically productive work, and that they must dedicate their lives for the service of the people. If these are the only new conditions, Chü-tsan has assured me that Chinese Buddhists will welcome them with open arms.

III

The Development of Buddhist Thought

The development of Buddhist thought in the twentieth century has been exclusively the story of Buddhist Idealism. It constitutes a single current in three waves: the Idealism revived by Ou-yang Ching-wu, the Dharma-Character Idealism of T'ai-hsu, and the New Idealism of Hsiung Shih-li. Very little of these systems is known in the West.[1]

This single current is in sharp contrast to the mounting

[1] See my brief summary of the three movements in *China*, ed. by MacNair, pp. 320–25, or in *Twentieth Century Philosophy*, ed. by Runes, pp. 557–61. For a brief summary of the three Buddhist thinkers, see O. Brière, "Les Courants philosophiques en Chine depuis 50 ans (1898–1950)," *Bulletin de l'Université l'Aurore*, Série II, Tome X, No. 40 (October, 1949), 582–89. There is a good chapter on Buddhist thought in China in James Bissett Pratt, *The Pilgrimage of Buddhism*, pp. 393–416, although the chapter deals only with Buddhist thought in the early 1920s and only with certain aspects. For reviews of Hsiung's books by Clarence H. Hamilton, see the *Far Eastern Quarterly*, IX, No. 2 (February, 1950), 214–16; IX, No. 4 (August, 1950), 397–98.

waves and crosscurrents of Buddhist thought between the fifth and ninth centuries when many and various streams flowed in all possible directions. The gradual recession and the final disappearance of these currents were chiefly due to the persecutions of the year 845, which destroyed forty-six hundred large monasteries and over forty thousand smaller ones, drove more than two hundred and sixty thousand monks and nuns back to lay society, and confiscated hundreds of millions of acres of temple land. This was followed by the rise of Neo-Confucianism, which in the twelfth century finally dominated Chinese thought to the virtual exclusion of non-Confucian systems. But Buddhism contained in itself the cause of intellectual suicide. The Meditation School, Ch'an, was growing and expanding to overshadow other Buddhist schools. It was the Buddhist school that greatly influenced Neo-Confucianism. Since it taught salvation through abrupt enlightenment by calmly looking into one's own mind to discover Buddha-nature and instantly intuit the Void, neither a system of philosophy nor a body of literature was necessary. Consequently, the school concentrated on the development of techniques of concentration and intuition. It "refuses to build up a literature" and "transmits only from mind to mind," this transmission to be done in silence. For these reasons, Ch'an has been intellectually destructive and has been chiefly responsible for the conspicuous absence of epoch-making Buddhist philosophical works as well as the embarrassingly small number of great Buddhist masters in the last millennium. As a result, Chinese Buddhism in the last several centuries has been extremely weak in thought though strong in practice.

This does not mean, however, that Buddhism has been devoid of a philosophy. As has already been stated more than once, Chinese Buddhism has followed the Ch'an and Pure Land Schools in practice and has adhered to the T'ien-t'ai and Hua-yen Schools in doctrine. In other words, its philosophical teachings are found in the metaphysics and epistemology of the T'ien-t'ai and Hua-yen Schools. Their teachings are embodied in two basic doctrines—the harmony of the Void and the transitory world, on the one hand, and, on the other, that all dharmas,[2] that is, elements of existence, rise from the mind. That is to say, (1) synthesis of phenomenon and noumenon, and (2) Idealism.

These two doctrines were "completed" in the teachings of the T'ien-t'ai and Hua-yen Schools (regarded as the peak of Buddhist philosophical development) and are called the "final" and "round" doctrines of Buddhism: final, because they synthesize all extreme and one-sided philosophies of other Buddhist schools, especially the irreconcilable Schools of Being (that dharmas and the self are real) and Schools of Non-Being (that they are unreal),[3] and the conflicting Schools of Dharma-Nature (reality) and Schools of Dharma-Character (appearance);[4] round, because they assure Uni-

[2] In explanation of the word *dharma*, Junjiro Takakusu, the eminent Japanese Buddhist scholar, says: "It is derived from the verb *dhri* (to hold, or to bear), and its noun form, *dharma*, would mean 'that which is held to,' or 'the ideal,' if we limit its meaning to mental affairs only. This ideal will be different in scope as conceived by different individuals. In the case of the Buddha it will be Perfect Enlightenment or Perfect Wisdom (*Bodhi*). Secondly, the ideal as expressed in words will be his Sermon, Dialogue, Teaching, Doctrine. Thirdly, the ideal as set forth for his pupils is the Rule, Discipline, Precept, Morality. Fourthly, the ideal to be realized will be the Principle, Theory, Truth, Reason, Nature, Law, Condition. Fifthly, the ideal as realized in a general sense will be Reality, Fact, Thing, Element (created and not created), Mind-and-Matter, Idea-and-Phenomenon." See Takakusu's *The Essentials of Buddhist Philosophy*, ed. by Wing-tsit Chan and Charles A. Moore, p. 57. The word is used here in the fifth sense.

[3] Buddhist schools are generally divided into two categories, Schools of Being and Schools of Non-Being, depending on whether they affirm or deny the self-nature of dharmas and the ego. Schools of Being include the Chü-she in the Hinayana and the Wei-shih in the Mahayana, and Schools of Non-Being include the Ch'eng-shih in the Hinayana and the Middle Doctrine School in the Mahayana.

[4] The Hua-yen School classifies all Mahayana schools into these branches. The Schools of Dharma-Character affirm that dharmas issued from con-

versal Salvation by affirming Buddha-nature in all sentient beings, not just in certain groups as believed in several other schools, because they employ all possible means for salvation and because their "vehicle" for salvation is the One Vehicle [5] which includes the various vehicles of the different schools.

The two doctrines may be summed up in one word, Thusness, *Tathata* in Sanskrit and *Chen-ju* in Chinese, which literally means "true such." [6] It is the true nature of all dharmas, and, as such, transcends all appearance and specific characters. It is absolute, eternal; it is not being or nonbeing, nor both or neither. It is Dharma-Nature, Self-Nature, Buddha-Nature, the Void, the One Who Has Thus Come or Gone (Tathagata, referring to the Buddha), Truth, the True State, Nirvana. It is called Thusness or Suchness because all dharmas are "thus caused," "thus formed," "thusnatured," "thus substantiated," "thus activated," "thus circumstanced," and so on. In other words, all elements of existence are in these states of Thusness. When static, Thusness is timeless, spaceless, formless, and characterless, a thing-in-itself without manifestation; it is the noumenon, the Realm of Principles, the Void. When dynamic, it is manifested in specific forms and specific characters and in

---

sciousness as real, whereas the Schools of Dharma-Nature insist that the true nature of dharmas is Void. The former group is represented by the Idealistic School and the latter by the Middle Doctrine School.

[5] The Hua-yen School classifies Buddhist sects according to "five vehicles": (1) The "Small Vehicle," or Hinayana, which includes the Chü-she School and advocates individual salvation. (2) The Elementary Great Vehicle (Mahayana), which teaches universal salvation, assuring human beings that, with certain exceptions, all will be saved and will cross the troubled sea of suffering in a Great Vehicle to the Other Shore. The Idealistic and Middle Doctrine Schools belong to this Vehicle. (3) The Final Great Vehicle, that of T'ien-t'ai, which makes no exception but insists that all people, even the depraved, will be saved. (4) The Abrupt Doctrine of the Great Vehicle, represented by Ch'an, which teaches that one can attain salvation by abrupt enlightenment. And (5) the Round Doctrine of the Great Vehicle, the Hua-yen, which combines all the other Vehicles.

[6] *Chen-ju* is pronounced *jun-roo.*

an unceasing process of transformation involving all dharmas; it is phenomenon, the Realm of Facts, the world of Temporariness.

These two Realms are not to be bifurcated or contrasted. Since, according to the Ten Profound Propositions of the Hua-yen School, all things are coexistent, interwoven, interrelated, interpenetrating, mutually inclusive, reflecting one another, and so on, and, according to its doctrine of the Sixfold Character of Dharmas to the effect that each dharma has the six characteristics of universality, speciality, similarity, diversity, integration, and differentiation, therefore everything involves everything else and the world is in reality a Harmonious Whole. The two Realms are so interpenetrating that they are, in the standard phrase of the T'ien-t'ai School, "immanent in a single instant of consciousness." This does not mean that they are produced by the thoughts of man or the Buddha. Rather, it means that in every thought-moment, all the possible worlds are involved.

The Realms exist by virtue of their own dharma-nature; they are "immanent in principle." As they come into being through causes and conditions, they are "immanent in fact." "Immanence in principle" and "immanence in fact," however, are identical. The dharmas of beings, the dharma of the Buddha, and the dharmas of consciousness are, in the final analysis, the same. This being the case, every dharma is the embodiment of the real essence of Thusness. Conversely, Thusness pervades all, and its manifestation therefore gives rise to all. "The entire universe rises simultaneously," as the Buddhists say.

Since All is in One and One is in All, it follows that even the nature of the Buddha is not free from evil, and the nature of the depraved man is also essentially good. "Buddha-nature is everywhere over the world." Since everyone shares Buddha-nature, all people can and will eventually achieve Buddhahood.[7] This is the final doctrine of Universal Salvation in the Great Vehicle, that is, Mahayana Buddhism.[8] The time will come when all sentient beings will cross the sea of suffering to the Other Shore in this Great Vehicle together.

It is hardly necessary to point out that in this philosophy, Thusness is not the Void in the sense of emptiness, but is Reality with an infinite number of potentialities from which all determinate and differentiated elements are manifested. It is the Universe One and True, "Round and Harmonious without Obstacle."

To repeat, Buddhist philosophy is the philosophy of Thusness, which involves two basic concepts: the harmony of the Realm of Principles and the Realm of Facts or the synthesis of phenomenon and noumenon, and the immanence of the "three thousand worlds" in a single instant of consciousness, or Idealism. These two concepts constitute the quintessence of Buddhist thought, penetrate all schools, and form the backbone of their teachings. They represent the fundamental convictions of Chinese Buddhists in their metaphysi-

[7] The term *buddha* is interpreted in the two senses of awareness and awakening, the former denoting perfect wisdom and the latter denoting self-awakening, awakening others, and the perfect unity of awakening and ultimate truth. A Buddha is therefore One Who Is Enlightened. He is supermundane, omnipotent, and "immensely benevolent" and "immensely merciful."

[8] Mahayana, meaning Great Vehicle, teaches universal salvation and is distinguished from the Hinayana, which teaches individual salvation. The former is embodied in Sanskrit literature and flourishes in China (including Tibet), Korea, Japan, and Mongolia; hence the names Sanskrit Buddhism and Northern Buddhism. The latter is chiefly embodied in Pali literature and prevails in India, Ceylon, Burma, Indo-China, Siam, and Java; hence the names Pali Buddhism and Southern Buddhism. Many doctrinal differences separate the two schools. Among the distinctive features of the Mahayana are Idealism, Negativism, Thusness, Void, *alaya*-consciousness, Twofold Truth, Three Vehicles, *paramitas* (perfections), Transcendental Wisdom, Fourfold Nirvana, the universality of Buddha-nature, salvation for all, salvation by faith, vows, abrupt enlightenment, the transfer of merits, "expediency," mass for the dead, the emphasis on positive ethical ideals such as compassion, charity, benefiting others, loving words, effort, tolerance, and the absolute prohibition of meat-eating.

cal outlook. Whether Chinese Buddhists study scriptures or recite the holy name of the Buddha, these concepts are very much in their minds.

However, while Chinese Buddhists entertain these convictions, the chief concern in their religious life has not been philosophical understanding, much less philosophical development, but the practical problem of salvation. Since most Chinese Buddhists follow the Pure Land School of Pietism, faith has become to them the most important thing. This was the position of Yin-kuang, and this has been the position of millions of Chinese Buddhists. For this reason, they find *The Awakening of Faith* especially endearing: it is philosophically based on the fundamental Buddhist tenets but emphasizes faith.[9]

Ascribed to Asvaghosha,[10] the treatise is one of the most studied in the Far East. It restates the basic Buddhist philosophy that Thusness is, first of all, noumenon and phenomenon synthesized, and secondly, the Cosmic Mind. But its chief gospel is salvation by faith. It calls for the awaken-

[9] There are two English translations, a very poor one by Timothy Richard and Yang Wen Hwui (Yang Wen-hui), *The Awakening of Faith in the Mahayana Doctrine;* and a good but not easily accessible one by Teitaro Suzuki, *Asvaghosa's Discourse on the Awakening of Faith in the Mahayana.*

[10] Ascribed to Asvaghosha. There are two Chinese texts. According to tradition, they are Chinese translations from Sanskrit, one by Paramartha in 553 and the other by Siksananda in 700. Scholars are generally agreed that the author could not have been the Asvaghosha (c. A.D. 100) who wrote the *Buddhacarita.* Some Chinese scholars are of the opinion that the work is almost certainly of Chinese origin. According to Liang Ch'i-ch'ao, the treatise is a Chinese product and represents an attempt to reconcile the contesting philosophies of the Middle Doctrine, Ti-lun, and She-lun Schools that flourished in China in the sixth century. He further contends that the work could not have been written later than 582 because it was quoted by Hui-yuan, who died in that year, and it could not have been written earlier than 563 because it bears traces of utilizing the *Mahayanasamparigraha,* which was translated into Chinese in 563. See his *Ta-ch'eng ch'i-hsin lun k'ao-cheng* ("A Critical Examination of *The Awakening of Faith*"), pp. 48, 82, 84. Chang T'ai-yen, however, regards such arguments as speculative. See his *T'ai-yen wen-lu pieh-lu* ("Supplementary Essays by Chang T'ai-yen"), III, 104B–108A.

ing of "three aspirations; namely, aspiration through the perfection of faith, aspiration through the practice of all perfections, and aspiration through witnessing Thusness." [11] The perfection of faith will create in the mind three qualities: rightness, such as the right comprehension of Thusness; profundity, such as the accumulation of good deeds; and great compassion, that is, the desire to save all living beings.[12]

By faith is meant "(1) the belief in the fundamental, or to think joyfully of Thusness; (2) the belief in the Buddha as possessing an infinite number of merits and virtues, or to rejoice in worshiping Him, in paying homage to Him, in making offerings to Him, in listening to the correct doctrine, in disciplining oneself according to the doctrine, and in looking forward to perfect wisdom; (3) the belief in the great benefit of the Law, or always to rejoice in practicing all forms of perfections; and (4) the belief in the Sangha [Buddhist Order] [13] as observing true morality, or always to make offerings to the bodhisattvas [beings of enlightenment] and to practice truthfully all those deeds that benefit others as well as oneself." [14]

These ideas have been most prominent in the minds of the great multitude of devout Chinese Buddhists. The two basic philosophical doctrines were vaguely held. Their moving inspiration was faith rather than intellectual enlightenment. This was the philosophical situation in Chinese Buddhism at the turn of the century. *The Awakening of Faith* was then *the* Buddhist bible, and Abbot Yin-kuang's untiring and extensive citation of it for authority and inspiration lent it much weight. No one would deny that faith was necessary for a good religious life. But the emphasis on faith over phi-

[11] Cf. Suzuki's translation, p. 113. [12] Cf. *ibid.*, p. 116.

[13] Buddha, Dharma (Doctrine), and Sangha (Order) are called the Three Treasures of Buddhism. [14] Cf. Suzuki, p. 128.

losophy ran against the intellectual tide that was flooding China. China in the early years of the Republic was a China of intellectual fervor. The Intellectual Renaissance of 1917 created in the Chinese, even Buddhists, an intellectual mood. To young Chinese intellectuals, faith without intellectual content was blind, empty, and dangerous. While Yin-kuang was adored by all who came in contact with him, young Buddhist intellectuals considered him too conservative, out of harmony with the temper of the age. They rejected *The Awakening of Faith.* They not only emphasized philosophy but also looked for a new philosophy which, in their own minds, would surpass the philosophical position of the treatise. They turned to the Sui (590–618) and T'ang (618–906) Dynasties, when Buddhist philosophical currents had reached their highest peaks.

One would expect that young Buddhist intellectuals would explore the possibilities of all ten schools that flourished at that time. If they had done so, there would have been a greater variety of Buddhist thought in China in the twentieth century and probably greater philosophical creativity. Unfortunately, that is not the case. Their interest has been confined to one school only.

The intellectual situation of the ten schools in our own time is briefly this: Since the Disciplinary, Meditation, Pure Land, and Mystical Schools are primary schools of religious practice, their followers have very little interest in thought.[15] Although both Hung-i and Ching-yen are outstanding Disciplinary scholars, philosophically they have written little and have created less. Ch'an masters are better known for their religious influence than for their scholarship. Creative writing on Ch'an has been done by non-Buddhists like Hu Shih,

[15] For basic information about these schools, see notes 34, 35, 21, and 38, on pp. 69, 70, 65, and 72, respectively.

Liang Ch'i-ch'ao, and T'ang Yung-t'ung, and these chiefly on Ch'an history and literature.[16] In the Pure Land School, there is no leader equal to the Three Masters of the seventeenth century—Lien-ch'ih (1535–1651), Han-shan (1545–1623), and Ou-i (1598–1646), who contributed greatly to the philosophical synthesis of the Hua-yen and T'ien-t'ai philosophies with Pure Land pietism. Much study has been devoted to Mysticism, but it was practically limited to the introduction and elucidation of forgotten doctrines.

Of the more philosophical schools, neither the Nihilistic Ch'eng-shih (Satyasiddhi) School[17] nor the Negativistic Middle Doctrine (San-lun, Madhyamaka) School[18] has in-

[16] Liang may be considered a Buddhist layman, but he was, rather, a typical Chinese scholar interested in all religions and partisan toward none.

[17] The school is called Ch'eng shih (Satyasiddhi, "Completion of Truth"), because it is based on the *Satyasiddhisastra* by Harivarman (c. A.D. 250–350) of Central India, which purports to "complete" the Buddhist doctrine by showing that both the ego and the eighty-four dharmas recognized by the school are nonexistent. They are only "temporary names" because they are causally produced and have no permanence. Only Nirvana, the Supreme Truth, is real; hence the Twofold Truth, the Worldly Truth of dharmas and the ego, and the Higher Truth of the Void.

It is not certain whether the school ever existed in India as such. The *sastra* was translated into Chinese by Kumarajiva (344–413) in A.D. 411. Thus the school was one of the earliest in China and was very popular in the fifth and sixth centuries. Since the eighth century, it has been absorbed into the Middle Doctrine School. In Japan (where it is called Jojitsu), it always existed as a branch of the Middle Doctrine School since the Korean priest Ekwan introduced it into Japan in A.D. 625. The school is no longer active anywhere today.

[18] This is the Madhayamaka (Middle Doctrine) School of Nagarjuna (c. A.D. 100–200), one of the two wings of Mahayana Buddhism in India. It was introduced into China by Kumarajiva, who translated Nagarjuna's two treatises into Chinese; namely, the *Madhyamikasastra* (German translation by Max Walleser, *Die mittlere Lehre;* partial English translation by Th. Stcherbatsky, *The Conception of Buddhist Nirvana*) and the *Dvadasanikayasastra* ("Twelve Gates Treatise"). He also translated Aryadeva's *Satasastra* (English translation by Giuseppe Tucci, in *Pre-Dinnaga Buddhist Texts on Logic from Chinese Sources*). Consequently, the school is also called the Three-Treatise School (San-lun in Chinese, and Sanron in Japanese).

The ideal of the school is the Absolute or Ultimate Void. It distinguishes "common truth" from which point of view dharmas may be said to be

spired any new intellectual tide. Probably their extreme philosophies did not suit the climate of the time. The Nihilistic philosophy, to the effect that both the ego and dharmas are nonexistent, has been completely ignored in the last several decades except for a single elementary essay by T'ai-hsu in the *Hai-ch'ao yin*.[19] The Middle Doctrine School postulates an Absolute Void through the "eightfold negation" of production, extinction, annihilation, permanence, unity, diversity, coming, and departure. It disappeared soon after the ninth century. In the last forty years, lectures on the Negativism of the school were given in the Wuchang Buddhist Institute. Laymen Liu Yü-tzu and Chang Hua-sheng and the Reverend Yin-shun have written briefly on the Middle Doctrine philosophy. Fa-tsun has translated some Middle Doctrine texts from Tibetan and has lectured on them in Chengtu and Chungking. But these efforts have not led to a revival of Middle Doctrine philosophy.

Since the two living ideas of Chinese Buddhism—Idealism and the harmony of Principles and Facts—were developed in the T'ien-t'ai and Hua-yen Schools, naturally their philosophy has engaged the serious attention of some Buddhists.[20] More than forty years ago, Ti-hsien began to promote the

---

real, and "higher truth" from which point of view only the Absolute is real. Dharmas are only relatively real because they are produced through causation and therefore have only dependent existence but no self-nature. Production, permanence, unity, etc., are proved by the school to be unreal by the use of its "Four Points of Argument," that is, by refuting an idea as being, as non-being, as both being and non-being, and as neither being nor non-being. The belief in any of the four is an extreme and must be transcended by a higher synthesis through the dialectic method so that at the end only the Absolute is real.

The doctrines of the school were transmitted in China through Seng-chao (384–414) and were greatly elaborated and systematized by Chi-tsang (549–623). It rapidly declined after the ninth century and soon disappeared.

[19] Fa-fang, *Wei-shih shih-kuan chi ch'i che-hsueh* ("Idealism and Its Philosophy"), p. 2.

[20] For basic information about the T'ien-t'ai and Hua-yen Schools, see notes 19 and 20, on pp. 63 and 64, respectively.

study of T'ien-t'ai doctrines. Among later learned T'ien-t'ai priests may be mentioned Mo-an and K'ung-yeh of the Nanyo Mountain in Hunan and Tao-chieh of the Fa-yuan Temple in Peking. Today Ti-hsien's learned pupils are found in many parts of China, notably Ching-ch'üan of the T'ien-t'ai Mountain, Hsien-tz'u and Hai-jen of Kwangtung, Hsing-tz'u of the Fa-tsang Temple in Shanghai, Jen-shan of the Chin-shan Temple in Chinkiang, and T'an-yun in North China. Chih-feng of the Wuchang Buddhist Institute has also been attracted to the T'ien-t'ai philosophy.

Similarly, a certain amount of intellectual activity has been evident in the Hua-yen School. Yang Wen-hui was the first to promote the study of its doctrines along with his revival of Buddhist literature. In the early years of the Republic, Yueh-hsia established the Hua-yen College in Shanghai to teach Hua-yen literature and thought.[21] Unfortunately, the intellectual efforts in the T'ien-t'ai and Hua-yen Schools have not contributed much to the philosophical current in contemporary Buddhism. Ti-hsien was after all more interested in piety than philosophy. The Hua-yen College lasted for only three years, and Yueh-hsia's most promising pupil, Ch'ih-sung, was soon attracted to Mysticism. Besides, as Fa-fang has pointed out, their method of study was old-fashioned,[22] and consequently did not produce constructive results.

Compared to the schools just surveyed, the Realistic Chü-she (Abhidharmakosa) School attracted more serious attention. Around 1920, layman Hsi-sheng began to study Abhidharmakosa texts. He was soon joined by Chang Hua-sheng and others, and both the Wuchang Buddhist Institute and the Institute of Inner Learning included Realism in their curriculum. Fa-fang was perhaps the most persistent and most influential in this philosophy, having lectured on it in

[21] *Chinese Year Book*, 1935–36, 1513. [22] Fa-fang, *op. cit.*, p. 6.

Wuchang in 1921, in the World Buddhist Institute in Peking in 1931, and in the Institute of Chinese and Tibetan Buddhism in Chungking in 1938.

The reason for the comparatively greater development in Realism is definitely due to the fact that it is more harmonious with the modern scientific temper. According to the two chief propositions of the school, "All dharmas are real" and "All the past, the present and the future exist." Such a realistic outlook was popular with the Chinese. But somehow even this school did not form a new current in modern Chinese Buddhist thought. Of all the ten schools, it was the Idealistic School that became the greatest and strongest philosophical current. We shall first review its revival by Ou-yang Ching-wu and then relate its development in T'ai-hsu and Hsiung Shih-li.

OU-YANG CHING-WU'S REVIVAL OF IDEALISM

The Idealistic School was founded by Hsuan-tsang (596–664),[23] who visited India and studied all Buddhist philosophies there for seventeen years and translated seventy-five Buddhist works into Chinese. He transmitted the Idealistic doctrines of Asanga (c. 410–500) and Vasubandhu (c. 420–500) into China. He translated, summarized, and selected the important works of ten Indian Idealists, especially Dharmapala (439–507), in his *Ch'eng wei-shih lun*[24] ("Completing the Idealistic Doctrine") in which he developed and "completed" the Idealistic system of Asanga and Vasubandhu in China.[25] From this all-important work has come

[23] The name is variously spelled: Hsuan Chuang, Hiuen-tsang, Hiuan-Tsang, Hiouen-tsang, Yuan-tsang, Yuan-chwang, etc.

[24] French translation by Louis de La Vallée Poussin, *Vijnaptimatratasiddhi, le siddhi de Hiuan-Tsang.*

[25] The Idealistic School was one of the two wings (with the Middle Doctrine School) of Mahayana Buddhism in India. Called there the Yogacara, it was founded by Asanga, author of *Yogacarabhumisastra* and the verses of both the *Mahayanasamparigraha* and the *Madhyantavibhanga*. The Yoga-

another name of the school, Wei-shih (Vijnanavada), that is, the Mere-Ideation or Consciousness-Only School.[26]

The school reduces existence to one hundred dharmas in five divisions [27] and divides the mind into eight consciousnesses. Instead of treating the mind as one dharma as in other schools, it analyzes it into eight consciousnesses: the five sense-consciousnesses; the sixth consciousness or the sense-center which forms conceptions; the seventh consciousness or the mind-consciousness which wills and reasons on a self-centered basis; and the eighth consciousness, which is called the *alaya*-consciousness, meaning "store-consciousness." The last is so called because it stores the "seeds" or effects of good and evil deeds which exist from time immemorial and become the energy to produce manifestation. This store-consciousness is ever in a state of instantaneous change, perpetually "perfumed" (influenced) by incoming perceptions and cognitions from external manifestations. At the same time, it endows perceptions and cognitions with the energy of the "seeds," which in turn produce manifestations. According to the stock saying of the school:

---

cara doctrine was elaborated by his brother Vasubandhu, who wrote the *Vimsatika* (English translation by Clarence H. Hamilton, *Wei Shih Er Shih Lun, or the Treatise in twenty stanzas on Representation-only*), the *Trimsika* (French translation by Sylvain Lévi, *Matériaux pour l'étude du système vijnaptimatra*), and the commentaries on both the *Mahayanasamparagraha* (French translation by Étienne Lamotte, *La Somme du grand véhicule*), and the *Madhyantavibhanga* (Chap. 1, English translation by Th. Stcherbatsky, *Discourse on Discrimination between Middle and Extremes;* also English translation by D. L. Friedmann, *Analysis of the Middle Path and the Extremes*). With the translation of the *Mahayanasamparigraha* by Paramartha (499–569) into Chinese, the She-lun School came into existence. Eventually it was absorbed by the Fa-hsiang (Dharma-Character) School founded by Hsuan-tsang. For critical studies of this school, see A. Berriedale Keith, *Buddhist Philosophy in India and Ceylon*, Chap. 14; Edward J. Thomas, *The History of Buddhist Thought,* Chap. 18; Hsuan-tsang, trans., *Vijnaptimatratasiddhi*, Chap. 7.

[26] Also translated as "Representation-Only."

[27] The five categories are: (1) Mind, 8 dharmas, (2) Mental Functions, 51 dharmas, (3) Form, 11 dharmas, (4) Things Not Associated with Mind, 24 dharmas, (5) Non-Created Elements, 6 dharmas.

A seed produces a manifestation;
A manifestation perfumes a seed;
The three elements (seed, manifestation,
and perfume) turn on and on;
The cause and the effect occur at one and
the same time.

The process of perfuming and manifestation is called by the school Threefold Transformation. The ideation-store consciousness, *alaya,* is the "first transformation," which is always in the state of constant flux in which the seeds perpetually influence external manifestations, and manifestations perpetually "perfume" seeds. Seeds, perfuming, and manifestations keep on evolving and influencing one another without ceasing, acting at once as cause and effect. The mind-consciousness is the "second transformation," which depends on the *alaya,* but in turn conditions it. The nature and characteristics of mind-consciousness consist of intellection, and it is always accompanied by the evils of self-interest. The six sense-consciousnesses constitute the "third transformation." They are characterized by discrimination and differentiation, and it is these activities that give rise to the world of externality and multiplicity.

Since the phenomenal world is a result of manifestations, it is one of specific characters. It is to these dharma-characters that the school has directed its attention. Hence another name for the school; namely, Fa-hsiang, or Dharma-Character School.

These characters are manifestations because they are results of "perfuming," and the *alaya*-consciousness is susceptible to "perfuming" because it contains impure elements accumulated in the past and being accumulated from time to time. But there is also in it the pure "seed," which by discipline and enlightenment can be cultivated to overcome the impure or tainted aspect of *alaya.* When that stage is reached, all manifestations will be seen as ideation and therefore illusory, and the true nature of dharmas will be revealed. That is to say, the thought of *alaya,* itself a manifestation and subject to causal conditions, is transcended, and Thusness, which is beyond manifestation and causal conditions, will be realized. In short, the Realm of Dharma-Characters or the world of manifestations will be replaced by the Realm of Dharma-Nature or Thusness.

Such, as briefly outlined, is the Wei-shih philosophy. It reached full bloom in the seventh century, and soon afterward its rapid decline started. In 819 the Confucianist Han Yü (768–824) vehemently attacked Buddhism. There followed the persecution of 845, which reduced all the Buddhist sects to near death. Like other Buddhist schools, the Idealistic School came close to extinction. Since that time, only traces of it have continued. Moreover, within Buddhism itself forces were at work to bring about the decline of the Idealistic School. The Hua-yen School, growing in influence in the seventh and eighth centuries, had been passing judgment on the different Buddhist schools. It classified them into five grades, and included the Idealistic School in the second grade as the "elementary doctrine" in the Mahayana. In this category, it ranks higher than the Hinayana schools, which teach individual salvation, but falls below the Meditation School, T'ien-t'ai, and Hua-yen which claims to be the "Round Doctrine." According to Hua-yen, two defects in the Idealistic School cause its low rating. One is its advocation of the idea that not all people can attain Buddhahood, but that some people, devoid of Buddha-nature, are forever beyond redemption. This clearly falls short of the basic Mahayana belief in universal salvation. Secondly, in its theory of the distinction of dharma-character and dharma-nature, it does not recognize the harmony and unity of phenomenon and noumenon and is therefore inferior to the

Round and Harmonious Doctrine of the identity of the Realms of Principles and Facts. Although the Hua-yen School possessed no authority over the life and future of rival schools, its characterization of the Wei-shih School inevitably did much damage to the latter. At the same time, the Ch'an School was surging ahead. Its emphasis on intuition did not encourage philosophical speculation. Its effect on the Wei-shih philosophy, as on other Buddhist schools, requires no comment.

Even without these external causes, certain elements in the Idealistic system itself would eventually lead to its oblivion. Its philosophy was too abstract and abstruse for the practical Chinese mind. Its subtle epistemology and psychology did not suit the Chinese, who were primarily interested in social and ethical problems. Its terminology was too difficult, even for the Buddhists themselves. Above all, its hair-splitting analysis was not attractive to the Chinese, including Buddhists, who usually preferred synthesis.

On top of all this, the Idealistic School had the misfortune of having its most important texts lost and forgotten. That occurred in the Yuan period (1206–1368), the era of mystical Mongolian Lamaism, when the religious climate was not favorable to Mahayana Buddhism, particularly to the type of Buddhism having a strong intellectual flavor. With these basic works gone, both knowledge and interest evaporated. Although Neo-Confucianist Wang Ch'uan-shan (1619–92) exhibited keen interest in the Wei-shih philosophy and although in the past ten or twelve hundred years prominent Buddhist scholars have written on the subject, nothing profound has been produced because the fountain of scholarship was inaccessible.

For these reasons, Buddhist Idealism has been almost entirely forgotten in China. In Japan, however, it has continued. It was introduced into that country by Dosho (628–

700), a Japanese who had studied under Hsuan-tsang for more than ten years. Ever since its inception, it has carried on the Idealistic tradition without interruption, although the sect has been small. In 1880, the renowned Japanese Buddhist scholar Bunyu Nanjio presented to Yang Wen-hui a number of Buddhist texts on logic and philosophy, which had been lost to China. Layman Yang brought these back to China and published them, along with his revival of Buddhist literature. The most important of the hitherto lost Buddhist texts was the *Ch'eng wei-shih lun shu-chi* ("Notes on the Completion of the Idealistic Doctrine"), a monumental work of sixty *chüans*, written by Hsuan-tsang's pupil K'uei-chi (632–82). It contains the fundamental doctrines of the school, Hsuan-tsang's interpretations, and K'uei-chi's own elaboration. It is indispensable to the understanding of the Wei-shih philosophy. Yang published it in 1901 in sixty stitched volumes.

It was inevitable that the publication of such a great Buddhist classic, plus the glamor of the return of a lost treasure, should arouse immediate and strong interest. The leading authority on Chinese studies, Chang T'ai-yen, was attracted to it and wrote a commentary on the second chapter of *Chuang Tzu* in which he interprets Taoist epistemology in Buddhist Idealistic terms.[28] China was now on the eve of the Intellectual Renaissance. The time was ripe for the revival of any system of thought, however extreme. Moreover, European Idealism was at this time being introduced into China. What more natural than that the Chinese should be enthusiastic about a philosophy that has so much in common with the new ideas being imported from the West? Besides, the scientific method of analysis was rapidly gaining favor

[28] *Ch'i-wu lun shih* ("Commentary on the *Ch'i-wu lun*"), in *Chang-shih ts'ung-shu.* ("Works by Chang T'ai-yen"), Vols. XI–XII.

with the Chinese, and such exceedingly analytical philosophy as the Wei-shih system could not fail to appeal to them.[29] As Hamilton says, "Since the arguments of the Wei-shih philosophy are dialectically keen, well organized, and well articulated, it has always been regarded as a mountain peak in the development of Buddhist rationalism. In times of reflective ferment, as under the present impact of Western systems of thought, the Wei-shih literature tends to attract the more strongly speculative minds." [30]

It may be said that Chinese Buddhists were merely chauvinistic in returning to the past. But as the basic concepts of the Hua-yen and T'ien-t'ai Schools form the foundation of present-day Chinese Buddhism, it was a logical development to go back to Idealism, which forms the basis of Hua-yen and T'ien-t'ai philosophy. It also happened that *The Awakening of Faith* was now discovered to be (or at least judged to be) a forgery. It was natural for young Chinese Buddhist intellectuals to swing to a system directly opposed to *The Awakening of Faith.*

These young intellectuals were inspired, trained, and led by Ou-yang Ching-wu. His original sympathy was with the Hua-yen philosophy of dharma-nature. He became interested in the Idealistic philosophy of dharma-character in 1914 when a number of Wei-shih texts were published.[31] Thereafter, he devoted his whole life to the study and propagation of the system. He founded the Institute of Inner Learning in Nanking and gathered in this top-ranking academy an imposing array of Buddhist scholars to study and lecture on the Idealistic philosophy. He himself tirelessly lectured on

[29] Wei-huan, "Buddhism in Modern China," *T'ien Hsia Monthly*, IX, No. 2 (September, 1939), 143–44.
[30] Clarence H. Hamilton, "Buddhism," in *China*, ed. by MacNair, p. 298.
[31] T'ai-hsu, *Fa-hsiang wei-shih hsueh* ("Dharma-Character Idealistic Philosophy"), p. 838.

the subject, to audiences which included Liang Ch'i-ch'ao. He became the guiding spirit, and his Institute the center, of the Idealistic movement.

Ou-yang had no new philosophy of his own. Nor did he reconstruct traditional Idealism. He did not even write any lengthy treatise. His contributions to the Wei-shih School are found elsewhere. They are found, first of all, in the many prefaces which he wrote for classical Buddhist works published by the Circulation Center of the Institute of Inner Learning. The fruits of his elucidation, investigations, and systematization, they are of permanent value.[32] His contributions are also found in his lectures and pamphlets. In these ways, he revived the Idealistic philosophy.

The far more dramatic way in which he revived the Wei-shih philosophy, however, is his attack on *The Awakening of Faith,* in which he brought the fundamental doctrines of the Wei-shih School into bold relief.

Since the controversy between Ou-yang and his followers on the one side and the followers of *The Awakening of Faith* on the other, is both historically and philosophically important, we must examine the issues at least briefly. Ou-yang and members of the Institute of Inner Learning attacked the *Awakening* on two main grounds, that Thusness can be "perfumed" and that there can be causation without "seeds." As already stated, the Wei-shih holds that the external world is nothing but manifestations of consciousness. Consciousness goes through a threefold transformation. In this threefold process, Thusness is not involved. It remains always in the state of immobility, "eternal, blessed, ever self-preserving, and pure." It is above and beyond the three transformations of consciousness, and it is not in the dynamic process of dharmas. As the true nature of dharmas, it is free from

[32] Yu-sun, "Buddhism and Confucianism in Modern China" (in Chinese), *Wen-hua yü chiao-yü* ("Culture and Education"), No. 85 (March 30, 1936), p. 25.

all restricting characteristics. It is no-birth, no-substance, no-quality, no-existence, no-reality in the highest sense. It is in no way connected with the specific nature of dharmas. It is the thing-in-itself, forever separate from the thing as it appears to the imaginative and discriminative mind.

So far as the absolute attributes of Thusness are concerned, the *Awakening* is in agreement with Idealism. According to the *Awakening,* Thusness "was not produced in the past, nor will it be annihilated in the future. It is everlasting, permanent, and absolute. From time immemorial, its nature has been self-sufficient in all possible merits. This means that it is Great Wisdom and Enlightenment; that it illuminates the entire Realm of Dharmas; that it is real and omniscient; that it is the mind pure and perfect in its self-nature; that it is eternal, blessed, self-preserving, and pure; and that it is tranquil, unchanging, and free." [33] In all this characterization, the *Awakening* would have no quarrel with the Idealists.

But while the *Awakening* says that Thusness is eternal and unchanging, it also says that it is intimately connected with the world of multiplicity and specific characters: "The Mind has two aspects: the Mind of Thusness and the Mind as the Process of Production and Annihilation. Both of these two phases 'apprehend' [*she,* literally collect, combine, include, grasp, lay hold of] all dharmas, and because of this, one involves and cannot be separated from the other." [34] This means that while the Mind of Thusness "represents the totality of things and the all-inclusive whole of the realm of dharmas . . . and is neither produced nor annihilated . . . the Mind as the Process of Production and Annihilation manifests itself [as the law of causation] in accordance with the Realm of Principle, giving rise to the transformation of

[33] Cf. *Asvaghosha's Discourse on the Awakening of Faith in the Mahayana,* trans. by Suzuki, p. 95.

[34] Cf. *ibid.,* p. 55.

consciousness. The two minds are harmonious and identified, neither a unity nor a duality. . . . It apprehends all things [as One] and creates all things [as Many]." [35]

In short, Thusness is both tranquil and aroused. It is not just reality (*t'i*) but also activity (*yung*).[36] Put differently, "Thusness is, on the one hand, the True Void, because its true reality is shown in its complete detachment from all unreal characters, but, on the other hand, a True Non-Void, because it possesses self-reality since in its original nature it possesses all possible merits. . . . We should understand that Thusness does not have the character of being or non-being, nor that of both or neither; it does not have the character of unity or plurality, nor that of both or neither." [37]

It is clear that the main point is that Thusness is both tranquil and aroused. But such an idea was utterly unacceptable to Ou-yang. In his *Wei-shih chueh-tse t'an* ("A Decisive Analysis of Idealism"),[38] he mercilessly attacks the *Awakening* position that Thusness can be "perfumed." He argues that reality and activity are mutually exclusive and Thusness, being perfect, cannot be liable to external influence. "Thusness is purity, while perfuming is due to impurity. The two are incompatible. How can there be perfuming of Thusness?" [39] To be perfumed means to be moved. But Thusness, by its very nature, is unmoved. It therefore cannot be perfumed.[40]

The basis of Ou-yang's criticism lies in the assumption that there are two separate worlds, the world of higher or "real" truth versus the world of inferior or "worldly" truth,

[35] Cf. *ibid.*, pp. 56–60. [36] Cf. *ibid.*, pp. 95, 98.
[37] Cf. *ibid.*, p. 59.
[38] Published by the Institute of Inner Learning, 1922.
[39] Wang En-yang, "Doubts on the Idealistic Interpretation of the *Awakening*" (in Chinese), *Nei-hsueh* ("Journal of the Institute of Inner Learning"), No. 2 (1925), p. 130.
[40] Ta-yuan, "Comments on *A Decisive Analysis of Idealism*" (in Chinese), *H'ai-ch'ao yin*, IV, No. 5 (November, 1924), 11–12.

or the world of dharma-nature versus the world of dharma-character. To the Wei-shih School, only Thusness is absolute truth, whereas the world of multiplicity, being the effect of imaginary and dependent causes, possesses only relative or inferior truth. In contrast, the *Awakening*, as in the T'ien-t'ai and Hua-yen Schools, identifies the two levels of truth as merely the two aspects of the same thing, one involving the other. Phenomenon and noumenon are the two sides of Thusness and unity and multiplicity are but two modes of its being.

The position of the *Awakening* is clearly one of monism, or totality, as Takakusu prefers to call it.[41] But this position is objectionable to Ou-yang and his group. It is objectionable for both philosophical and ethical reasons. Philosophically, to the Wei-shih School, each consciousness is complete in itself, going through the threefold process of transformation. It is a mental state, strictly private and individual. Its nature is that of a monad, a world unto itself. Each subject dreams his own dreams, with a separate universe as his arena. If the universe seems to be one, that is because of our common past experiences. The universe is not monistic, nor dualistic, but pluralistic.

Ethically, since each consciousness is private and independent and since a self is but a stream of consciousnesses, it follows that the self is independent and free. Each individual possesses distinct qualities. Pratt has noted that nowhere else in Chinese Buddhism has the idea of independence been so vigorously put forth. Although he is wrong in saying that the Buddhist tendency towards multiplicity betrays Western influence,[42] he is certainly right in pointing out this Buddhist emphasis on individuality. In an age when freedom and individuality rated high in the scale of values, it is easy to see why members of the Institute of Inner Learn-

[41] Takakusu, *op. cit.*, pp. 47–48. [42] Pratt, *op. cit.*, p. 37.

ing rejected a philosophy of monism and preferred a pluralistic philosophy.

The whole problem is tied up with the problem of causation. Being monistic, *The Awakening of Faith* explains causation by Thusness itself. As has been said, Thusness can be both static and aroused. When aroused, it sees an external world, reflects it as does a mirror, discriminates and makes distinctions among things, and so goes on in endless succession. "Although Thusness abundantly embraces all merits," the treatise says, "it is free from all characters of distinction. In it all dharmas are of one taste and one reality, with no character of distinction nor dualistic nature. . . . All these characters of distinction are the results of the process of production and annihilation due to karma and consciousness. . . . When the discriminative mind is aroused and sees an objective world, it is Ignorance. But when Ignorance is not aroused because of the original purity of the mind, Thusness is then Great Wisdom and Enlightenment." [43] This is what the Hua-yen School calls "causation by Thusness," that Thusness, through Ignorance, is aroused and creates the external world.

In so far as considering the external world the result of Ignorance, Wei-shih and the *Awakening* are in agreement. Furthermore, both agree that the external world issues from the mind. As the *Awakening* says, "Separated from the mind, there would be no such things as objects of perception and conception. Why? Because all dharmas are based on ideation. All distinctions issue from the subjectivity of the mind." [44] But Ou-yang cannot accept the *Awakening* position that Thusness involves Ignorance, that it can be aroused, and that it can create. To the Wei-shih School, Thusness transcends Ignorance, is not aroused, and does not create. In

[43] Cf. *Asvaghosha's Discourse on the Awakening of Faith in the Mahayana*, trans. by Suzuki, pp. 76, 96–97. [44] Cf. *ibid.*, pp. 76–78.

a word, Thusness has nothing to do with causation at all.

According to Ou-yang's arguments and those of his pupils, if things need to be explained by the creation of Thusness, then Thusness itself needs to be created. Besides, "Thusness is One, whereas dharmas are many. For One to produce Many would be gross inequality." Similarly, "Thusness is pure, whereas dharmas are impure. It is illogical that the pure and the impure can produce each other." Again, "If Thusness can create, its attribute of neither production nor annihilation would be lost. This is a serious violation of the doctrines of the Mahayana." [45]

Furthermore, if Thusness can be perfumed and can create, "it will be like the One in Taoism which produces the two, or the Great Ultimate in Neo-Confucianism which produces the modes of *yin* and *yang,* or Jehovah in Christianity who created the universe. This is a most un-Buddhistic concept.[46] The theory is similar to the Sankhya theory that Matter and *purusha* (soul) produced the other twenty-three categories of existence. Since the Sankyha School and the Buddhist School have always opposed each other, to adopt such a Sankhya-like doctrine of the *Awakening* would amount to betrayal of Buddhism.[47]

In Ou-yang's way of thinking, causation can only be explained by the theory of "seeds" in the ideation-store, *alaya.* This store itself is an existence of causal combination, and in it the pure and the impure elements are causally combined and mixed. These are "seeds" which sprout in time when a cause occasions them. The store is the consciousness center and the objective world thus manifested is its environment. Thusness is entirely above all this.

[45] Wang En-yang, in *Nei-hsueh,* No. 2 (1925), p. 132.
[46] Ta-yuan, "The Changing Phenomenon of Buddhist Developments in China in the Last Fifteen Years" (in Chinese), *Hai-ch'ao yin,* XVI, No. 1 (January, 1935), 50.
[47] T'ai-hsu, *Fa-hsiang wei-shih hsueh,* p. 823.

Ou-yang deserves credit for raising the intellectual level of modern Chinese Buddhism. But his movement runs in the wrong direction. Aside from the fact that he looks to the past and defends the past, in modern Chinese religions his is the only movement toward particularization. All other schools, whether Buddhist or not, aim at synthesis. As has already been pointed out, the spirit of synthesis reaches the highest degree in the Hua-yen and T'ien-t'ai Schools where the Realms of Principles and Facts are harmonized and identified. But Ou-yang rejects this and insists on the complete separation of phenomenon and noumenon. He was radical enough to depart from his teacher, Yang Wen-hui, who declared that there was no essential difference between the Schools of Dharma-Nature and the Schools of Dharma-Character.[48] But he was conservative enough to adhere strictly and rigidly to a past system. Ultimately he sought first to harmonize Confucianism and Buddhism and later to harmonize the Schools of Being and the Schools of Non-Being. In the long run he could not resist the tendency to synthesize. But basically he adhered to his Idealistic philosophy.[49] In the meantime the Idealistic tide was being reverted toward the glorious spirit of synthesis in Buddhism. This was the work of Abbot T'ai-hsu.

T'AI-HSU'S DHARMA-CHARACTER IDEALISM

T'ai-hsu became interested in Idealism in 1909 when a Buddhist layman presented him with a copy of the *Ch'eng wei-*

[48] Preface to K'uei-chi, *Ch'eng wei-shih lun shu-chi,* p. i.

[49] See Ou-yang's pamphlet, *Shih chiao* ("Explaining the Doctrine"). Mr. James Shien, a former pupil of Ou-yang's, informs me that "the essay aims at removing the opposition between the Schools of Being and the Schools of Non-Being. But his basic idea is still the Character of Ultimate Truth of the Idealistic School, which combines the Being of Temporary Existence and the Non-Being of False Existence. . . . So far as ultimate salvation is concerned, he sees no difference between this Character of Ultimate Truth and the Nirvana of the Schools of Non-Being."

shih lun shu-chi. As a young monk, T'ai-hsu studied the *Surangama*, the *Lotus*, and similar classics.[50] He also studied the T'ien-t'ai and Hua-yen doctrines with Yang Wen-hui and Abbot Ti-hsien and others. But as to the works of the Wei-shih School, he "was always afraid that they would be difficult." [51] From 1908 to 1914, he was primarily occupied with the revival and reform of Buddhism. In 1914, however, when he was having a quiet sojourn in Puto Island, he began to study Idealism seriously and came to the conclusion that "to combine together and transform the various philosophies, the world needs the Idealistic doctrine." [52] Thereafter, for more than two decades he lectured and wrote on the subject, along with his continued activities for Buddhist reform. His lectures and essays have been gathered and published under the title *Fa-hsiang wei-shih hsueh* ("Dharma-Character Idealistic Philosophy") in 1938.

Being faithful to the orthodox tradition of the Wei-shih School, he holds that all dharmas are manifested out of ideation. The objective or external world is to be interpreted in terms of the "three object-domains." There is, first of all, the "object-domain of nature," which includes all objects of the outer world which are immediately apprehended. They have their "original substance" and present themselves as they are. The five sense-consciousnesses and the eighth consciousness perceive an object in this way. Secondly, there is the "object-domain of mere-shadow or illusion," including objects of imagination, memory, and all mental perceptions of things which have no real existence. Objects of this nature are produced by the sixth consciousness. Finally, there is the "object-domain with the original substance," that is, the subjective interpretation of the original substance, such as the

[50] For the *Surangama*, see above, 68, n. 32. For the *Lotus*, see partial translation by W. E. Soothill, *The Lotus of the Wonderful Law.*
[51] T'ai-hsu, *Fa-hsiang wei-shih hsueh*, p. 838.
[52] *Ibid.*

whiteness of an object. The object has original substance but is not perceived as it is because in the seventh consciousness it is seen from the subjective point of view.[53]

All these objects are ideations.[54] As ideations, they are devoid of self-nature but are merely aggregates conditioned by many causes. In this, T'ai-hsu remains faithful to the Wei-shih philosophy. But, according to his own statement, he tries to avoid one-sidedness. He says that his philosophy should not be likened to Western Subjective Idealism which denies the existence of "original substance" and reduces Reality to individual consciousness. Nor should it be identified with Western Objective Idealism which recognizes a Universal Mind.[55] He attempts to combine them both by holding that in the transformations of the eight consciousnesses, they transform both individually and collectively.[56]

Take the matter of substantiality and non-substantiality, for example. According to T'ai-hsu, there are two kinds of sense-center consciousness, isolated and simultaneous. When the sense-center consciousness is isolated from sense data and imagines an object, there is no "original substance" in that object. But when the five sense-consciousnesses which provide the sense data and the sense-center which combines them function simultaneously, the object is apprehended as a unity, together with its original substance. Both kinds of experience are real, relatively speaking.[57]

Similarly, the problem of the substantiality of the object-domain can be solved in this light. As the *alaya*-consciousness is the general store where all perceptions are collected and evolved, that consciousness in each mind takes the entire universe as object-domain. But at the same time, that consciousness is all one's own, individual and private.[58] In the

[53] T'ai-hsu, *op. cit.*, p. 89.
[54] *Ibid.*, p. 427.
[55] *Ibid.*, pp. 19–20.
[56] *Ibid.*, pp. ii, iv.
[57] *Ibid.*, pp. 24–27.
[58] *Ibid.*, pp. 27–28.

same way, the universal and the particular can be reconciled. As mentioned above, in the processes of transformation, consciousnesses function both individually and collectively. Where transformation takes place individually, there is a particular, and where transformations take place collectively, there is a universal. All other dichotomies—self and the other, general and specific characters, the mind and its object-domain, cause and effect, existence and annihilation, similarity and difference, life and death, being and non-being, reality and illusion, and so forth—are to be resolved in the principle of Relativity.[59]

According to this principle of Relativity, the world of dharma-nature and the world of dharma-character are not to be sharply contrasted. Here T'ai-hsu differs with Ou-yang Ching-wu, although both adhere to the theory that all dharmas are ideations. Instead of following Ou-yang in considering ideation as belonging only to the world of dharma-character, T'ai-hsu says that it has to do with both dharma-nature and dharma-character.

With regard to the doctrine that all dharmas are ideations, he remains within the framework of traditional Wei-shih. He says that all "names and characters" are manifestations of ideation, for they are but aggregates or successions of sensations and conceptions. The ego is such a succession. The entire universe, including all natural laws, is such a succession.[60] However, T'ai-hsu offers a theory of the threefold transformation of his own. He says there is, first of all, the "consciousness of life and evolution." It is somewhat similar to the blind life impulse, which, pushed by the "energy of seeds" stored up from time to time, manifests itself in various forms of life.[61] Secondly, there is the "consciousness of subjective will," which views and interprets all transformations

[59] *Ibid.*, pp. 15, 31–38.
[60] *Ibid.*, pp. 58–61.
[61] *Ibid.*, pp. 67–68.

from the subjective point of view.[62] Finally, there is the "consciousness of discriminated object-domain." This is the consciousness that, because of the effects of previous "seeds," discriminates and sees the external world. The result of individual "perfuming" and transformation is the individual object, such as the body, and that of collective "perfuming" and transformation is the collective object, such as the universe.[63]

In essence, this theory is not different from the orthodox doctrine of the threefold transformation of the eight consciousnesses, although the Abbot gives them new names. But he also applies ideation to the nature of dharmas and here directly opposes Ou-yang. To T'ai-hsu, the nature of dharmas is not above ideation but is in ideation itself. "By ideation as dharma-nature," he says, "is meant that the Universe of One True and the world of dharmas are equally Thusness." [64] "From the point of view of reality," he goes on, "there is illusion. Hence the mind rises and disappears. From the point of view of illusion, there is reality. Hence the mind is Thusness." [65] In other words, there is only one mind. As reality, it remains Thusness, and as function, it rises and disappears.

Being both reality and function, Thusness is neither real nor unreal, neither Void nor Non-Void, neither One nor Many.[66] When the Mind is aroused, Reality is discriminated into multiplicity. But all dharmas obey the same laws and possess the same nature, and are therefore One.[67] In this way, T'ai-hsu not only synthesizes dharma-nature and dharma-character but also synthesizes Wei-shih and Hua-yen.[68] This synthesis makes T'ai-hsu's system different from

[62] T'ai-hsu, *op. cit.*, pp. 63–67. [63] *Ibid.*, pp. 67–69. [64] *Ibid.*, p. 425.
[65] *Ibid.*, p. 428. [66] *Ibid.*, pp. 412, 465. [67] *Ibid.*, p. 464.
[68] Wang I-ch'ang, "The Buddhist Transformation of China and the Chinese Transformation of Buddhism" (in Chinese), *Wen-hua p'i-p'ing* ("Cultural Critique"), II, No. 1 (November, 1934), 60.

the traditional Wei-shih philosophy in a very important way.

We have then two Idealistic systems opposing each other, the orthodox Idealism centering around the Institute of Inner Learning under the leadership of Ou-yang Ching-wu, and the Dharma-Character Idealism of the Wuchang Buddhist Institute under the leadership of T'ai-hsu. For years the two Institutes rivaled each other, primarily on the issue of the nature of Thusness. The rivalry was partly professional, for there is such thing as "professional jealousy" even among Buddhists, and partly philosophical. Ou-yang and his circle have been compared to the orthodox Confucianists of the Han period and T'ai-hsu and his followers to the Neo-Confucianists of the Sung era.

The chief differences between Ou-yang and T'ai-hsu may now be briefly outlined. First of all, T'ai-hsu does not distinguish Idealism and Dharma-Character as two different schools, as does Ou-yang.[69] To T'ai-hsu, "Mere-ideation refers to the origination and dharma-character refers to products. One is cause and the other effect. They are merely two phases of the same process and should not be too sharply divided." [70] This is the reason why he chose to call his system Dharma-Character Idealism.[71]

Secondly, T'ai-hsu does not separate dharma-character and dharma-nature, as does Ou-yang. As his pupil Ta-yuan says, "As principle, Reality is not created, but as facts and functions, it is created." [72] The difference between nature and character is relative. Thirdly, instead of criticizing the *Awakening*, T'ai-hsu and his group defend it, saying that the apparent contradiction between the Wei-shih School and the *Awakening* is due to the fact that the Wei-shih literature deals with dharmas of imaginary nature, whereas the *Awak-*

[69] T'ai-hsu, *Fa-hsiang wei-shih hsueh*, p. 16.
[70] *Ibid.*, pp. 2, 10, 425. [71] *Ibid.*, p. 16.
[72] Ta-yuan, "Fundamentals of Idealism" (in Chinese), *Hai-ch'ao yin*, V, No. 8 (August, 1923), 24.

ening deals with dharmas of true self-nature, but that their ultimate teachings are the same.[73] T'ai-hsu considers Ou-yang's criticisms of the *Awakening* to be on weak grounds. For instance, there is no reason why the Wei-shih School should attack the *Awakening* for describing Thusness as both reality and function instead of as function alone, so long as the treatise defines it.[74] Furthermore, to attack the *Awakening* as illogical for treating Thusness both as unmoved and active is to ignore the fact that the *Awakening* describes Thusness as a trinity of reality, character, and function. They need not be mutually exclusive.[75] Again, Ou-yang attacks the *Awakening* because it implies that Thusness can create. But if Thusness cannot create, says Ta-yuan, it would be meaningless because it would then be unrelated to the world of dharmas. It is absurd to say that Thusness is the totality of dharmas and yet has nothing to do with them.[76]

In the fourth place, whereas Ou-yang considers Thusness to be absolutely transcendental, T'ai-hsu regards it as both transcendent and immanent. He thinks that Ou-yang only knows Thusness as Void but does not know Thusness as Non-Void.[77]

Finally, instead of attacking the T'ien-t'ai and Hua-yen Schools as enemies of Wei-shih, as does Ou-yang, T'ai-hsu looks upon them as different roads to the same destination,[78] although he still feels that philosophically speaking, Wei-shih is superior.[79]

T'ai-hsu calls his theory new because, he says, it is eluci-

[73] T'ai-hsu, *Fa-hsiang wei-shih hsueh*, pp. 820–21.
[74] *Ibid.*, pp. 509, 621.
[75] Ta-yuan, "Comments on A *Decisive Analysis of Idealism*" (in Chinese), *Hai-ch'ao yin*, IV, No. 5 (November, 1924), 11.
[76] Ta-yuan, "Warnings on Criticisms of the *Awakening*" (in Chinese), *Hai-ch'ao yin*, IV, No. 7 (July, 1924), 13–14.
[77] T'ai-hsu, *Fa-hsiang wei-shih hsueh*, p. 465.
[78] *Ibid.*, p. 821. [79] *Ibid.*, p. 53.

dated with modern ideas,[80] makes use of modern science,[81] and agrees with Einstein's Theory of Relativity.[82] It is new also because while orthodox Idealism is close to Western Subjective Idealism, his system combines both Subjective Idealism and Objective Idealism.[83] Actually, his understanding of Western philosophy is extremely superficial, and he has not offered a new theory of ideation. What he has done is to harmonize the philosophy of Wei-shih, Hua-yen, and T'ien-t'ai,[84] combining their essential features and removing their contradictions. In fact, it was synthesis that motivated him. In his Wuchang Buddhist Institute, lectures were given on practically all Buddhist schools.[85] He himself promoted all sects, although he bore the label of Wei-shih.[86] He says that synthesis has distinguished the development of thought in Chinese history. He attempted to carry it a step further.

Unfortunately, he has not gone far enough. T'ai-hsu still clings to the philosophy of one system, though much enlarged and reformed. Ta-yuan claims that his master's Dharma-Character Idealism is a grand harmonizing of not only several Buddhist schools of thought but of Chinese classics and Western philosophy as well.[87] But this harmony is to be established within the Wei-shih School. In spite of all efforts at synthesis, he is not free from philosophical denominationalism. This is the reason why Hu Shih condemns T'ai-hsu's activities as a "stubborn effort to outlive historical usefulness." [88] In fairness to T'ai-hsu, however, we must say that although he did not go far enough, he did go a step

[80] *Ibid.*, p. 55. [81] *Ibid.*, p. 56. [82] *Ibid.*, p. 491.
[83] *Ibid.*, pp. ii, iv. [84] *Ibid.*, pp. 619–22.
[85] Ta-yuan, "The Changing Phenomenon of Buddhist Developments in China in the Last Fifteen Years" (in Chinese), *Hai-ch'ao yin*, XVI, No. 1 (January, 1935), 50. [86] Fa-fang, *op. cit.*, p. 6.
[87] T'ai-hsu, *Fa-hsiang wei-shih hsueh*, p. vii.
[88] Haydon, *op. cit.*, p. 248.

in the right direction and thus enhanced the Chinese spirit of synthesis.

HSIUNG SHIH-LI'S NEW IDEALISM

We now come to the third wave of modern Buddhist thought, Professor Hsiung Shih-li's "new wei-shih philosophy." Hsiung enjoys a large following among young Chinese philosophers, so that his movement constitutes a school of thought and has broad significance for China.

His philosophy is a part of Buddhist thought only in a negative sense, for it turns from Buddhism. Hsiung maintains that he is not a Buddhist but a Neo-Confucianist, and that he criticizes Buddhism rather than defending it. We have already seen how he revived and tried to reconstruct the Neo-Confucian Lu-Wang School.[89] We shall now see what he has done to the Buddhist Idealistic philosophy.

As a young man, Hsiung studied the *Ch'eng wei-shih lun* with Ou-yang.[90] He was also a student of Yang Shao-yu, executive of the Institute of Inner Learning. But he soon became dissatisfied with Idealism.[91] As he tells the story, "There was a period when I was inclined to Indian Buddhist thought. . . . I studied the philosophy of Asanga and Vasubandhu with Master Ou-yang and was thoroughly converted. Later on, I gradually rejected the theories of various schools. Putting aside all systems, Confucian as well as Buddhist, and with singleness of purpose, I searched within myself. . . . After a long time, I suddenly awoke to the fact that what I found inwardly agrees entirely with *The Book of Changes*. Thereupon I destroyed the draft on Idealism which I had written on the basis of Asanga and Vasubandhu and

[89] See p. 31, n. 82.
[90] T'ai-hsu, "Brief Comments on New Idealism" (in Chinese), *Hai-ch'ao yin*, XIV, No. 1 (January, 1933) 95.
[91] Yu-sun, in *Wen-hua yü chiao-yü*, No. 85 (March 30, 1936), pp. 26–27.

decided to build a new Idealism of my own." [92] In this development, he was deeply moved by the Neo-Confucianist Wang Ch'uan-shan (1619–92).[93] In one of the earliest publications, *Chen-hsin shu* ("Confession"),[94] he says, "As I read Wang Ch'uan-shan, I suddenly understood that principles and facts come from one source and that the hidden and the manifest are one thing." [95] Further, he says, "Wang followed Chang Heng-ch'ü [1020–77] [96] . . . whose basic teaching is that in the unceasing Great Transformation and Universal Current, the transforming and the transformed are one piece." [97] In sincere tribute to Wang, he says, "Wang has already spoken what I have to say." [98] "Among Confucianists Wang alone saw the truth." [99]

From his own statements, it is clear that the evolution of his thought started with Buddhism but developed towards Confucianism. In this process, he has accomplished two very important things. He has synthesized the Buddhist Schools of Being and Non-Being and he has synthesized Confucianism and Buddhism, or, rather, Confucianized Buddhism.

The key to his synthesis lies in the Confucian phrase, "Unity of reality and function." As one writer puts it, "the Dharma-Character School separates the unchangeable (Thusness) and the changeable (the eight consciousnesses) as two, leading to the defective theory that reality and function are mutually exclusive. Hsiung doubted the theory,

[92] Hsiung Shih-li, *Hsin wei-shih lun* ("New Idealism"), pp. 81–82.
[93] Wang was a typical Neo-Confucianist in the sense that, like Chu Hsi and other Sung Neo-Confucianists, he regarded *Li* (Principle) and *ch'i* (Matter) as the elementary principles of existence. Unlike Chu Hsi, who gives priority to *Li*, Wang gives priority to *ch'i*, saying that "wherever there is *ch'i*, there is *Li*."
[94] 1918. This work is not included in the *Shih-li ts'ung-shu* ("Collection of Works by Hsuing").
[95] Hsiung, *Hsin wei-shih lun*, p. 5. [96] See p. 37, n. 113.
[97] *Chen-hsin shu*, p. 31; *Shih-li yü-yao* ("Important Sayings by Hsiung Shih-li"), p. 30.
[98] *Hsin wei-shih lun*, p. 62. [99] *Shih-li yü-yao*, p. 67.

thought quietly for ten years, and finally realized that function and reality, the Current and the "master," phenomenon and noumenon, the changeable and the unchangeable, the movable and the unmoved, are all identical." [100]

Following the Buddhist pattern, Hsiung divides knowledge into two levels and calls them "Knowledge of Nature," and "Knowledge of Reason." [101] The former is the product of the Original Mind. It is "Reality intuiting itself," whether as the Cosmic Mind in the universe or the self in the individual. Although it is related to sense experience, it is not conditioned or bound by it. Through it all truth is discoverable. The latter, on the contrary, is a discriminating process, originating from the Knowledge of Nature but conditioned and "misled" by sense experience. "In other words," he says, "mental functions make use of the activities of Knowledge of Nature as their own activities, blindly cling to matter, and erroneously see an external world." [102] From this our "mind of habits" [103] is formed, which includes our total daily experience. It is habitual because it always has an irresistible tendency to externalize and through discrimination and analysis gives rise to the objective world of multiplicity. Because of this habit, there is always the tendency to be separated from the true Self, which has no externality.[104]

So far, Hsiung follows closely orthodox Buddhist Idealism in explaining the origination of the external world. Likewise, he follows it in refuting the idea of an independent external world. Proponents of an independent external world have based their conclusions on two theories, actualism and atomism.[105] Enlarging the arguments of orthodox Buddhist Idealism, Hsiung holds that to consider that a thing, whether a small object or the entire universe, can be independent of the

[100] Yu-sun, in *Wen-hua yü chiao-yü*, No. 85 (March 30, 1936), p. 25.
[101] *Hsing-chih, li-chih.*
[102] *Hsin wei-shih lun*, pp. 2–3.
[103] *Hsi-hsin.*
[104] *Hsin wei-shih lun*, pp. 3, 26.
[105] *Ibid.*, p. 9.

mind is nothing but a result of habit. As Buddhists have maintained throughout history, a thing has no self-nature but is merely an aggregate formed in the mind. For example, a vase has no independent reality apart from consciousness. There is no vase aside from sense consciousness and aside from the form and character organized by the mind consciousness.[106] Actualism is therefore indefensible. As to atomism, Hsiung dismisses it with the traditional standard argument that if atoms are measurable, they are no longer the smallest units, which is what atoms mean, but if they are not measurable, they cannot exist as objects.[107] Furthermore, how atoms can adhere to one another in order to become a thing, and how small units, atoms, can ever change to become large units such as a vase or the universe, has never been satisfactorily explained.[108]

In so far as the defense of Idealism goes, then, Hsiung is a typical Buddhist. But from here on, he diverges from Buddhist Idealism and travels in a different direction. While he maintains that an object-domain cannot exist independently from the mind, he does not deny its reality. He "revises" the theory of K'uei-chi that only the mind is real and that the object-domain externalized by the mind is Void.[109] "In truth," he declares, "the mind and the object-domain are really a complete unity. They possess an internal contradiction and a tendency to develop along two opposite directions." [110] As explained before,[111] the object-domain, or matter, tends by its nature to externalize and assume form, but the mind is free and, wanting to retain its pure self-nature, refuses to be externalized. This is the internal contradiction. This tension does not result in static equilibrium but in development, because the mind is the "master," is stronger, and has the upward tendency to realize itself as mind.

[106] *Ibid.*, pp. 9–14.
[107] *Ibid.*, p. 15.
[108] *Ibid.*, pp. 16–20.
[109] *Ibid.*, p. 8.
[110] *Ibid.*, p. 20.
[111] See above, pp. 36–37.

Although matter projected by the mind cannot be independent, it is not illusory, as Buddhist Idealists have always claimed. This radical difference between them and Hsiung is due to their difference in understanding causation. In orthodox Idealism, everything is produced by "seeds." These seeds are (1) real in themselves, or else they would not be able to produce consciousness, (2) different from consciousness, for cause and effect are by definition not identical, (3) equipped with the energy to produce, (4) numerous, since their products are numerous, and (5) different and independent from one another since each ideation is private and independent.[112]

To Hsiung this traditional theory of seeds, upheld by both Ou-yang and T'ai-hsu, is utterly unsatisfactory. He cannot allow cause and effect to be separated. Furthermore, traditional Idealism does not explain *how* the energy in seeds can produce. Here he presents his "new" explanation: "Although the emergence of consciousness or ideation depends on many causes, it must possess in itself some inherent, living, sufficient, and active energy. Our hypothesis is that this voluntary energy is the cause of ideation." [113] Each ideation is new, and each is an expression of new energy. The energy acts by itself, and although ideation works through nerves and sense organs, it is not their product, because it directs them rather than being directed by them. Also, although ideation arises at the stimulation of an object-domain, it is not just its reflection, because ideation transforms the object-domain. All this is due to energy, which works like electricity, coming as new wave after wave, without end.[114]

This energy is the expression of Knowledge of Nature. It is real in itself. But when expressed through nerves and sense organs, it is utilized by them as their own, and when mani-

[112] *Hsin wei-shih lun*, pp. 27–28. [113] *Ibid.*, p. 28.
[114] *Ibid.*, p. 29.

fested this way, it gives rise to the Knowledge of Reason; it makes distinctions and presents an external world.[115] Thus energy has two states, the state of being itself as reality, and the state of being expressed as function. Basically, function and reality are not two but one.

This position is radically different from that of the Buddhist Schools of Being, of which the Wei-shih School is one. According to the Wei-shih doctrine, consciousness apprehends all dharmas, transforms them, and manifests them as dharma-characters. These dharma-characters are real and hence are designated as Being. But in order to explain consciousness and dharmas, the Wei-shih School postulates "seeds" as their causes. That is to say, phenomenon is the result of the germination of seeds, and all seeds are contained in the *alaya*-consciousness. To Hsiung this is pluralism, diametrically opposed to his ideal of unity. In his way of thinking, multiplicity is not objectively real. It is merely the *function* of Reality, which in functioning manifests itself in all distinctions and varieties. The philosophy of Being, according to Hsiung, completely fails to understand that reality consists in function and that function is in essence the same as reality.[116] "Although they describe Thusness as the reality of all dharmas, they do not equate Thusness with seeds, nor do they regard seeds as manifestations of Thusness. This being the case, Thusness and seeds are two entirely unrelated things. Why then talk about Thusness? Furthermore, although they offer seeds as the causes of mind and matter, the producing cause and the produced result are also divided into two separate realms, one hidden and the other manifested. . . . To us, however, what is reality lies in function itself." [117] For these reasons, Hsiung rejects the Buddhist theory of Being.

As to the Buddhist Schools of Non-Being, Hsiung feels

[115] *Ibid.*, p. 29. [116] *Ibid.*, pp. 45–56. [117] *Ibid.*, p. 47.

that they are correct in denying the reality of phenomenon, but they consider the world of dharmas as illusory and fail to see that they are functions of Reality. "Both the Schools of Being and Schools of Non-Being do not allow the idea that Thusness manifests itself as the universe of multiplicity." This is their undoing.[118]

The main difference between Hsiung and the Schools of Being lies in their different concepts of energy. First of all, in the Wei-shih system, energy is latent behind phenomenon as its cause, and at the same time there is Thusness which is the noumenon. Thus there are two separate Realities. In Hsiung's New Idealism, there is only one Reality, for energy is Thusness itself.[119] Secondly, the Schools of Being bifurcates Nature into two parallel realms, whereas in the New Idealism these two realms are respectively reality and function, and they are at bottom the same.[120] Thirdly, energy in traditional Wei-shih is plural, whereas in Hsiung's system it is a complete totality.[121] Within this unity, however, there is the internal contradiction of Contraction and Expansion. Contraction tends to organize, concentrate, and assume concrete and material form, while Expansion tends to retain its self-nature of being free. The result is opposition and change and development. Energy being one, each Contraction or Expansion involves all others, just as every wave involves all waves and the entire ocean.[122] Finally, the Schools of Being attribute seeds to "perfuming." Thus seeds are not self-sufficient but require external influence. How this "perfuming" is possible has never been fully explained. In the New Idealism, however, energy, by its very nature, is self-sufficient and requires no external agency.[123]

It is clear that in his New Idealism, Hsiung has remedied many defects of orthodox Idealism. In the process, he inevi-

[118] Hsiung, *op. cit.*, p. 131. [119] *Ibid.*, p. 158. [120] *Ibid.*, p. 159.
[121] *Ibid.*, p. 160. [122] *Ibid.*, pp. 160–63. [123] *Ibid.*, pp. 165–66.

tably commits certain errors of his own. Without going into a detailed criticism of his system, we may point out that since Hsiung equates mind and matter with Expansion and Contraction as two phases of one Reality, he should not have designated his system as New Idealism.[124] Although he reminds us that he uses the term *wei* not in the sense of *only* but in the sense of *especially*, why cling to old terminology? It should also be mentioned that the idea of Reality being both ocean and waves is by no means foreign to Buddhism. As one critic of Hsiung points out, "the identification of function and reality has been a standard formula in the T'ien-t'ai and Hua-yen Schools. The very metaphor of ocean and waves comes from them." [125] Furthermore, to say that the mind that constructs the external world consists of habitual tendencies is to suggest that it works mechanically, and to say that the mind can be a habit and unable to control its tendency does not agree with Hsiung's fundamental idea that the mind is free.[126] That the mind can be free in one respect and bound by habits in another needs clarification. In spite of his repeated emphasis that reality and function are one, fundamentally he considers the manifested world as unreal.[127] This very fact makes him a Buddhist. Although he refuses to admit it, he is close to the intuitive school of Ch'an.[128] As a matter of fact, he himself says that he agrees with the Buddhist Schools of Non-Being when he says that Contraction and Expansion, as well as production and annihilation, have no self-nature but are merely manifestations

[124] T'ai-hsu, "Brief Comments on New Idealism," *Hai-ch'ao yin,* XIV, No. 1 (January, 1933), 97.

[125] Yin-shun, *P'ing Hsiung Shih-li ti Hsin wei-shih lun* ("Criticisms of Hsiung Shih-li's *New Idealism*"), pp. 16–17.

[126] Jan-hsi, "Comments on Hsiung's *New Idealism*" (in Chinese), *Hai-ch'ao yin,* XIV, No. 2 (February, 1933), 102–22.

[127] Chou Ku-ch'eng, *Chung-kuo shih-hsueh chih chin-hua* ("The Development of Chinese Historiography"), pp. 30–41.

[128] Yin-shun, *op. cit.*, pp. 16, 45.

of Constant Transformation.[129] He concedes that he may be called a Neo-Buddhist.[130] Because of his Buddhist heritage, he attaches no importance to objective investigation and experiment and relies exclusively on *t'i-jen* or intuitively witnessing Reality.[131]

Regardless of these defects, Hsiung has made two important contributions to modern Chinese thought. The first is that he has synthesized the Buddhist Schools of Being and Non-Being. In this, he accentuates the tendency of synthesis already prominent in Buddhism through the T'ien-t'ai and Hua-yen Schools to T'ai-hsu. Because of this synthesis, T'ai-hsu calls Hsiung's New Idealism a new Hua-yen School.[132] Others think that in Hsiung there is an attempt to synthesize not only the Buddhist Schools of Wei-shih, Ch'an, T'ien-t'ai, and Hua-yen, but also Confucianism, Taoism, Sankhya doctrines, and the modern theory of evolution.[133] In any case, Hsiung represents the strongest force in the already strong current of synthesis in Chinese thought.

The other contribution Hsiung has made is his Confucianization of Buddhism. In synthesizing Buddhism and Confucianism,[134] he continues the tradition of many Buddhists and Confucianists who saw complete harmony of the two systems, notably Wang Yang-ming, Wang Ch'uan-shan, and the three Pure Land Masters of the seventeenth century (L'ien-ch'ih, Han-shan, and Ou-i). But Hsiung goes further and converts Buddhist philosophy to Confucian ends. Buddhist theories of causation and ideation are designed to remove suffering and to transcend transformations, whereas Hsiung makes use of Buddhist theories to glorify the "great

[129] *Hsin wei-shih lun*, pp. 91, 101.
[130] *Ibid.*, p. 128.
[131] Jan-hsi, in *Hai-ch'ao yin*, XIV, No. 2 (February, 1933), 121.
[132] T'ai-hsu, in *ibid.*, XIV, No. 1 (January, 1933), 526.
[133] Yin-shun, *op. cit.*, pp. 16, 45; Chou T'ung-tan, "*New Idealism*" (in Chinese), *Quarterly Bulletin of Chinese Bibliography*, V, No. 4 (December, 1944), 60–67.
[134] *Hsin wei-shin lun*, pp. 111, 127.

virtue" of "production and reproduction," as all Confucianists have done before him.[135] In short, his theories are Buddhistic, but his objective is Confucian.

In turning Buddhist doctrines to Confucian ends, Hsiung certainly represents a new tendency in contemporary Chinese thought. No one can tell how this tendency will develop, nor predict how Ou-yang's orthodox Idealism and T'ai-hsu's Dharma-Character Idealism will fare in the future. But their activities surely indicate that Buddhist thought is still vital and even goes forth in new directions.

[135] Yin-shun, *op. cit.*, pp. 3–10; *Shih-li yü-yao,* I, 1A.

IV

The Religion of the Masses

Chinese religion has been largely a religion of the masses. They have borne the torch of religious development, and they have been its strength and support. First of all, Chinese religion has not been the creation of a few individuals but a gradual evolution out of the spiritual life of a great number of simple folk. None of the three traditional systems of Confucianism, Buddhism, and Taoism was founded in China by a savior. Recent research has definitely established that Buddhism does not owe its beginning in Chinese history to an imperial mission which returned from India most probably in A.D. 67.[1] Professor T'ang Yung-t'ung has conclusively proven that the

[1] Henri Maspero, "Le Songe et l'ambassade de l'empereur Ming," *Bulletin de l'École française d'Extrême-Orient,* X (1910), 95–130; T'ang Yung-t'ung, *Han Wei Liang-Chin Nan-Pei-ch'ao Fo-chiao shih* ("History of Chinese Buddhism from the Third to the Sixth Century"), pp. 22, 47–53. See also L. Carrington Goodrich, A *Short History of the Chinese People,* p. 61.

story of two Indian priests arriving in China with the mission is entirely unfounded.[2] Long before Emperor Ming had a dream of the golden image of the West, which caused him to send the mission, Buddhism had been a fairly popular practice in China,[3] existing in the forms of sacrificial rites, magic, charms, and alchemy, and most likely highly mixed with the folk religion promoted by a large group of priest-magicians called *fang-shih.*[4] According to T'ang,

> In Emperor Ming's decree [A.D. 65], references are made of the "temple of benevolence" [of the Buddha] and "vows with the deities." It can be shown from this that Buddhism was at that time merely a form of temple worship. King Ying of the state of Ch'u cultivated the *fang-shih* and produced many diagrams of omen. This being the case, the temple worship of Buddhism was only one form of magical formulae and crafts. For the Chinese at that time did not have very deep understanding of Buddhism and confused it with the doctrines of Taoist practices and the belief in spirits and immortals. Its fundamental tenet was the instructability of the soul, and its religious observances were modeled after temple worship. Buddhists and the *fang-shih* thus spoke the same language. Even toward the end of the Han period, An Shih-kao (c. A.D. 150), who translated the greatest number of Buddhist scriptures and was regarded as great master of the age, was recorded in the *Kao-seng chuan* ("Biographies of Eminent Monks") as thoroughly expert in astrology, geomancy, medical formulae, magic, and interpretation of sounds of birds and animals, and was very early renowned for his extraordinary ability. . . . From various evidences, we cannot help concluding that the spread of the influence of early Buddhism was due to its being a form of craft of worship suitable to the popular taste of the time.[5]

As to Taoism and Confucianism, not much need be said. We know that the so-called founding of the Taoist religion

[2] T'ang, *op. cit.*, pp. 16–30.
[3] *Ibid.*, pp. 49, 53.
[4] *Ibid.*, p. 53.
[5] *Ibid.*, p. 54.

in A.D. 143 by Chang Ling was but the culmination of an age-old movement promoted by the *fang-shih* among the masses several hundred years before the Christian era. We have already seen that the religious institution continuing under the name of Confucianism was not inaugurated by Confucius but an old heritage revived and transformed by the sage.

Not only were these three systems not founded by a few leaders, but there have been comparatively few religious leaders in Chinese history. Not a single member throughout Confucianism's long history of twenty-five hundred years may be labeled a religious leader. There were great priests in both Buddhism and Taoism, to be sure, but most of them existed before the twelfth century, and since that time there have been fewer and fewer prominent religionists. In recent Chinese history one cannot find a Ramakrishna or even a Kagawa. Today, aside from a few outstanding Buddhist abbots, one cannot think of a prominent religious teacher, preacher, theologian, or prophet, whether Confucian, Taoist, Islamic, or Christian. When Ch'en Tu-hsiu said that China is not a land of great religious leaders, he was stating a concrete historical fact.[6] It is amazing how few religious leaders China has produced, especially compared to the great number of eminent philosophers, poets, painters, statesmen, and so forth. If the life of Chinese religion had depended on a few leaders, it would have died out long ago. But Chinese religion has lived and continues to live, because it has been carried on by the masses.

Chinese religion has been largely a movement of the masses also in the sense that it has had little imperial or aristocratic patronage. This is not to deny that support has been given by emperors. For example, in A.D. 666, Emperor Kao Tsung of T'ang honored Lao Tzu as *T'ai-shang Hsuan-*

[6] *La Jeunesse*, II, No. 2 (October, 1916), 4.

yuan Huang-ti, the Most High Emperor of Mystic Origin, ranking above Confucius and Buddha. He also required princes and dukes and inferior nobles to study the *Tao-te ching* and ordered that temples be erected throughout the empire. But such sponsorship was sporadic. Compared with the case of Japan, where Buddhism owes its very inception and most of its sustenance for more than ten centuries to aristocrats, Chinese Buddhism can honestly claim to be a common man's religion. The same is true of Taoism, Islam, and Christianity.

Because Chinese religion has been comparatively free from governmental patronage, it has also been fairly free from governmental control. This is not to say that Chinese religion has been free from governmental regulation. However, although the government regulated the order of service in the sacrifice to Heaven and Earth and Confucius and the emperor personally officiated in the sacrifice, and although the different dynasties promoted various deities in rank and title, these activities were mostly ceremonial and had no influence on the practical religious life of the people. Indeed, they were scarcely known to the people at large. It is true that many times in Chinese history, the government prohibited witchcraft and divination, forbade people from becoming monks and nuns, and destroyed excessive temples. But most of these measures took place only in one period, from A.D. 400 to 960. Generally speaking, throughout Chinese history, the government did not pass judgment on religious beliefs, interfere with religious practices, or determine religious creeds. Of the three main features of the ancient cult, which has erroneously been called Confucianism in the West, and which Hu Shih once proposed to call the Sinitic religion,[7] only one had anything to do with the government, namely, the sacrifice to Heaven. The other two

[7] Sophia H. Chen Zen, *Symposium on Chinese Culture,* p. 33.

features, the honoring of ancestors and the worship of spirits, have been entirely affairs of the masses.

By the masses is meant the common, simple folk of China, who constitute some 85 percent of the population, and by religion is meant the three traditional systems of Confucianism, Buddhism, and Taoism. These systems have been called the "three religions" of China. To a limited extent, the use of the phrase "three religions" is justifiable. But the term is misleading in several ways. First of all, it suggests that the three systems are all religions and perhaps religions only. To the Chinese, the word *chiao* connotes three separate ideas: education, culture, and religion. When the word is used for Taoism or Buddhism, it may be any of the three, but when it is used for Confucianism, it means culture and moral education and almost never has the sense of religion. When a person is labeled a Confucianist, it means that he is a follower of Confucian doctrines, which include religion as an element, but not a follower of an organized, institutional religion.

The term "three religions" is misleading, in the second place, because it implies that Confucianism, Buddhism and Taoism are organized and institutionalized churches. This is true of both Buddhism and Taoism, which have a rigid hierarchy of priests and a strict system of ordination and transmission. But it is not true of Confucianism. Even within Buddhism and Taoism, such formalism affects the clergy only and has no relationship to the masses.

Again, the term "three religions" is misleading because it leads to the belief that the three systems are separate and parallel and that a Chinese is exclusively either a Confucianist, a Buddhist, or a Taoist. To be sure, there are six hundred thousand-odd Buddhist monks and nuns who have renounced their homes and society, shave their heads, wear robes that open to the left (instead of to the customary right) as a sign of deserting the world, adhere to vegetarianism, and lead a life of celibacy. These people are pure Buddhists in the sense that they follow the Buddhist religion and none other, although they do not hesitate to perform before non-Buddhist deities. There are also between three and four million Buddhist lay devotees, or "disciples at home," who put on the Buddhist garment and adopt vegetarianism on occasion but who worship non-Buddhist deities and ancestors as well. In addition, there are Taoist priests and "vegetarian women," far fewer in number than Buddhist priests and nuns. These Taoists may or may not forsake their homes, are vegetarians occasionally or all the time, and curl their hair. They are Taoists exclusively. There are also millions of Moslems, about three and a half million Roman Catholics, and close to six hundred thousand Protestants (or double that number if one includes the virtual Christians who have not been baptized)—all of whom follow only one religion. But the majority of China's millions, including the several thousand Jews who have forgotten their original cult, follow a religion which combines and overshadows Buddhism, Taoism, and the ancient cult. They do not follow three separate, parallel, and conflicting religions at the same time, but a syncretic religion embracing the ancient cult as its basis and Buddhist and Taoist elements as secondary features. Even when they visit a strictly Buddhist or Taoist temple, they do so not as Buddhists or Taoists but as followers of the religion of the masses.

TWO LEVELS OF RELIGION

I have always urged that instead of dividing the religious life of the Chinese people into three compartments called Confucianism, Buddhism, and Taoism, it is far more accurate to divide it into two levels, the level of the masses and the level of the enlightened. Professor Hocking has divided the Oriental religious personnel into four groups: the priests and monks, the lay mystics, the scholars, and the people.[8] In China the second group hardly exists. The other three may be separated into the two levels of the masses and the enlightened. By the masses is meant the 85 percent of the Chinese people who are devout but ignorant. By the enlightened is meant the intelligentsia and the illiterate farmers, fishermen, and similar humble folks who may use a smaller vocabulary but often express greater wisdom.

The masses worship thousands of idols and natural objects of ancient, Buddhist, Taoist, and other origins, making special offering to whatever deity is believed to have the power to influence their lives at the time. The enlightened, on the other hand, honor only Heaven, ancestors, and sometimes also Confucius, Buddha, Lao Tzu, and a few great historical beings, but not other spirits. The ignorant believe in the thirty-three Buddhist heavens, eighty-one Taoist heavens, and eighteen Buddhist hells. (Incidentally, the ratio of Buddhist heavens and hells shows the almost instinctive optimism of the Chinese, who believe the chances of going to Heaven to be twice as good as those of going to Hell.) As is well known, belief in Heaven and Hell was unknown in Chinese history until Buddhism introduced it into China. The enlightened Chinese flatly reject such belief. The masses believe in astrology, almanacs, dream interpretation, geomancy, witchcraft, phrenology, palmistry, the recalling of the soul, fortune-telling in all forms, charms, magic, and all varieties of superstitions. The enlightened are seldom contaminated by these diseases. The masses visit temples and shrines of all descriptions. The enlightened avoid these places, except the Temple of Heaven, ancestral halls, the Confucian temple, and occasionally the temples of great historical personages. The ignorant regard religious cere-

[8] William Ernest Hocking, *Living Religions and a World Faith*, pp. 84–93.

monies as magic; the enlightened regard them merely as pure form. The ignorant are fatalistic, believing that spirits have direct control over their fortunes and misfortunes; the enlightened are not believers in fate in this sense. To them, fate is that with which Heaven has endowed their nature. Their duty is to "establish" fate or destiny by fully realizing their nature as endowed or decreed by Heaven. The ignorant people go to deities primarily to seek blessings, particularly those of children, wealth, and long life. The enlightened people worship not to seek favors, but to pay respect. They have only thanks to give, no advantage to seek. They merely honor Heaven, ancestors, and teachers. The masses follow the beliefs and practices of the three systems and join various religious societies, with Taoism as the center. Hodous is correct in saying that "folk religion is behind and within the three religions." [9] I may add that it cuts across, includes, and extends beyond the three religions, with the Taoist element dominating. The enlightened, on the other hand, follow the three systems primarily as philosophies, with Confucianism as the center.

Perhaps the two levels can best be distinguished by the words *pai* and *chi*. The masses *pai*, that is, worship in the formal, orthodox, strictly religious sense, but the enlightened *chi*, that is, sacrifice or make offerings. Legge has pointed out that these offerings are oblations, not sacrifice in the ordinary Western sense of the term. The idea of propitiation or expiation is never present. The sacrifices "are the tribute of duty and gratitude, accompanied with petition and thanksgiving. They do not express a sense of guilt, but the feeling of dependence." [10]

Reserving the religion of the enlightened for a later chapter, let us look more closely at the religion of the masses and

[9] *China*, ed. by MacNair, p. 231.
[10] James Legge, *The Religions of China*, p. 53. See also W. E. Soothill, *The Three Religions of China*, p. 136.

see particularly what trends are evident in the last half century. When one comes to study the religion of the masses, one is appalled at the neglect by Chinese writers of this subject. The modern Chinese mind is strongly distinguished by its mass-consciousness. Modern Chinese poets, dramatists, artists, and educators all have devoted much of their attention to the people. Folk songs, folk designs, and folk stories have been collected and glorified, and surveys and studies have been made on the land holdings and on the diet, marriage, and other customs of the people. But religion has been singularly ignored. Not a single book on Chinese folk religion has been published in the last five decades. There have been books on Buddhism, of course, but they deal chiefly with Buddhist doctrines. The few books on Taoism and Islam have been devoted to history, literature, and basic teachings and offer little on actual present conditions. Religion does not even appear in statistical surveys. In the annual *Statistical Abstracts of the Republic of China,* statistics on religion are not included. In the 1935 issue of 1,247 pages, there are sections on population, sanitation, social pathology, and fishery, but none on religion.[11] The 1950 *China Handbook* contains chapters on Roman Catholicism and Protestantism but none on the traditional religions. For information about the religion of the Chinese masses, we still have to rely on Maspero, Soothill, Hodous, Doré, Day, Shryock, and Latourette.[12] These writers have dealt with the more obvious aspects. More recent writers, notably Yang, Noss, Wei, and Reichelt have reviewed the religion of the masses from a broader perspective and have studied its deeper significance.

[11] Nanking, 1935.

[12] Henri Maspero, "The Mythology of Modern China," in J. Hackin *et al., Asiatic Mythology,* pp. 252–384; Soothill, *op. cit.;* Clarence Burton Day, *Chinese Peasant Cults;* John K. Shryock, *The Temples of Anking and Their Cults;* Lewis Hodous, *Folkways in China;* Kenneth Scott Latourette, *The Chinese, Their History and Culture;* Henri Doré, *Researches into Chinese Superstitions.*

But they have hardly gone into the conditions of Chinese religions in the twentieth century. Nor have Ring, Everett, and Cranston.[13] Braden, Haydon, Pratt, Clennell, Hodous, and Hughes have pointed out certain recent tendencies, but the story is only half told and too briefly told,[14] and certain important developments have been overlooked.

As we turn to these developments, the first thing that strikes us is the general decline of the folk religion. Thousands of images have been smashed. Priests, monks, and nuns have been driven out of temples. Temples have been used for nonreligious or even anti-religious purposes or have been confiscated or destroyed. The City God, the guardian of city life, has vanished from many cities, and no new city has a place for him. The God of Grain, the chief deity of a local community, no longer reigns majestically. Instead, his arena is used in secular or unholy ways. Few new villages honor him with an altar. The use of charms and the practice of alchemy are being discontinued, and *feng-shui*, or geomancy, is fast becoming a thing of the past. The building of a new temple, familiar news in the old days, is now almost unheard of. Masses for the dead are becoming a rarity. Grown-up Chinese still have a vivid memory of seeing witches in their childhood days, but modern young Chinese would have to make an unusual effort to see one. According to one survey, of 175 temples, 58 percent were being used for purposes other than those for which they were erected.[15] No new immortal

[13] Y. C. Yang, *China's Religious Heritage;* John B. Noss, *Man's Religions;* Francis C. M. Wei, *The Spirit of Chinese Culture;* George C. Ring,, *Religions of the Far East;* John R. Everett, *Religion in Human Experience;* Ruth Cranston, *World Faith;* Reichelt, *Religion in Chinese Garment.*

[14] Charles Samuel Braden, *Modern Tendencies in World Religions;* A. Eustace Haydon, *Modern Trends in World-Religions;* James Bissett Pratt, *The Pilgrimage of Buddhism;* E. R. and K. Hughes, *Religion in China;* W. J. Clennell, *The Historical Development of Religions in China;* Lewis Hodous, "Confucianism," and "Taoism," in *The Great Religions of the Modern World*, ed. by Jurji, pp. 1–23, 24–43, respectively.

[15] Braden, *op. cit.*, p. 113.

has arisen to join the long and imposing list. And no new god has been added to the overcrowded pantheon. The last deification of a human being took place decades or perhaps centuries ago. As Hughes has pointed out, "no new gods have appeared in the last fifty years." [16] The latest deification, that of a simple fisher girl to be the Holy Mother on High, took place in the Ming Dynasty (1368–1644), although the Ch'ien-lung Emperor (1736–95) is worshiped in some places.

THE DECLINE OF TAOISM

This decline is true of folk religion in general, but it is especially true of Taoism. Since Taoism underlies the religion of the masses, its decline is tantamount to the collapse of the people's religion as a whole. It is generally considered that Taoism as a religion is already defunct. This is not to say that there are no more temples, shrines, idols, or priests, for although their number is rapidly decreasing, there are still too many for comfort. But the real spirit of the religion is dead, and its vitality is fast disappearing. There is nothing in it to promise, let alone insure, its survival. In an article on religious tendencies in China written as early as 1927, Bishop Tsu chose to omit discussion of Taoism entirely.[17] In the People's Consultative Conference in 1949, 7 out of 585 delegates meeting to set up the new government represented Protestantism, Buddhism, and Islam. Taoism was publicly and officially ignored; its existence was no longer recognized.

There is no doubt that Taoism is approaching extinction. There are at least five reasons for its disintegration. First of all, it has lost the essence of religion. The goal of Taoism was the realization of the Three Original Principles, that is, Es-

[16] Hughes, *op. cit.*, p. 139.

[17] Y. Y. Tsu, "New Tendencies in Chinese Religions" (in Chinese), *Wen She* ("The Literary Society Magazine"), II, No. 7 (May, 1927), 37–52.

sence, Vital Force, and Spirit, a goal that was crystallized through a series of philosophical developments. In the third century A.D. Wei Po-yang, in his *Ts'an-t'ung-ch'i* ("The Three Ways Unified and Harmonized"), unified and harmonized Taoist philosophy, the doctrines of priest-magicians, the philosophy of *The Book of Changes,* and the Yin Yang philosophy, with the ultimate aim of prolonging life through the practice of alchemy, whereby the *yin,* or passive cosmic force, and *yang,* or active cosmic force, could be harmonized and the vital energy (*ch'i*) of the universe concentrated in the individual's body. In the fourth century, Ko Hung (Pao-p'u Tzu) elaborated the techniques of alchemy and incorporated Confucian ethics into Taoist philosophy, all directed to the realization of the Three Original Principles. But this goal was forgotten soon after the thirteenth century. Today none of the Taoist classics are studied. Neither Wei's *Ts'an-t'ung-ch'i* nor Ko's *Pao-p'u Tzu* [18] has any meaning for present-day Taoists. Few Taoists are aware of the three basic scriptures based on Wei's work; namely, the *Lung-hu ching* ("Dragon and Tiger Scripture"), the *Huang-t'ing ching* ("Yellow, or Internal, and Realm, or External, Scripture"), and the *Yin-fu ching* ("Secret Accord Scripture"). The chief concern of Taoist priests has been with the search for earthly blessings and the perpetuation of superstitions.

Another reason for the rapid decline of Taoism may be found in the deterioration of its schools. The rise of schools in Taoism was a sure indication of its strength, vigor, and firmness of purpose. According to tradition, two schools emerged in the twelfth century, the Southern and the North-

[18] For English translations, see: Tenney L. Davis and Ch'en Kuo-fu, trans., "The Inner Chapters of Pao-p'u-tzu," *Proceedings of the American Academy of Arts and Sciences,* LXXIV (1941), 297–325; Eugene Feifel, trans., "*Pao-p'u-tzu,*" *Monumenta Serica,* No. 6 (1941), pp. 113–211, No. 9 (1944), pp. 1–33; No. 11 (1946), pp. 1–32.

ern, paralleling the Southern and Northern Schools of Ch'an in Buddhism. The Southern School is believed to have been founded by Wang Che of the Chin period (1115–1234). It aimed to cultivate man's nature, or the true self, through the arts of diet, medicine, and internal alchemy. Like the Southern School of Ch'an, it was a "self-power" school. The Northern School was founded by Liu Hai-ch'an in the Liao period (907–1125), aiming at the cultivation and prolongation of life, and the control and development of one's vital power, through the external means of charms, incantation, and similar crafts. As such, it was an "other-power" school, as in Buddhism. We have no clear record of these two schools, for what material we have is contradictory. According to another account, the Southern School was not concerned with the cultivation of man's nature, while the Northern School was concerned with both man's nature and life.[19]

Recent research, however, has definitely established that three Taoist schools arose in the twelfth century, all because the Chinese refused to submit to the invaders from the North who had forced the Chinese to move the capital of the Sung Dynasty to the South. As Ch'en Yuan says, "After the capital was moved southward, the founders of the three sects refused, as a matter of principle, to serve the Chin invaders. They gathered their followers and trained the people. They would eat only what they themselves produced. . . . They centered their doctrines around liberality and meekness."[20]

According to Professor Ch'en, the three sects were called the Ch'üan-chen (Complete Purity), Ta-tao (The Great Way), and T'ai-i (Great Unity) Sects. The Complete Purity Sect originally aimed at maintaining and preserving

[19] Liu Hsien-t'ing, *Kuang-yang tsa-chi* ("Notes"), *chüan* 3.

[20] Ch'en Yuan, *Nan-Sung ch'u Ho-pei hsin Tao-chiao k'ao* ("New Taoist Societies in the Northern Provinces at the Beginning of the Southern Sung Dynasty"), p. 3.

life at a time of chaos. The followers were escapists and hermits. Later on, the original character was lost and the sect became one of charms, omens, crafts, and alchemy. In the Yuan period (1206–1368), Wang Ch'ung-yang revived the sect and adopted as its goal the understanding of the mind and the realization of human nature. It advocated the elimination of desires and the suppression of emotions. The followers were taught to endure humiliation and "swallow bitterness." They were to conquer themselves and to benefit others. The Great Way Sect was begun by a Taoist priest, Liu Te-jen of the Chin period (1115–1234). It was distinguished by its practice of asceticism. The Great Unity Sect was founded by another Taoist priest, Hsiao Pao-chen, between 1138 and 1140, to promote the practice of charms and magic in an attempt to realize the Great Unit (Tao) and the Three Origins of existence (Heaven, Earth, and Man).[21]

The thing to note about these new schools in the twelfth century is that they came into existence for two very important purposes; namely, to boycott the invaders and to cultivate a special way of life. How they fared in the following centuries is still a matter for research. At any rate, two schools have continued to this day. In the South, there is the Cheng-i Sect, or the True Unity Sect, prevalent south of the Yangtze. It is traced to Chang Ling, the so-called founder of the Taoist religion, but it may have been founded by Liu Hai-ch'an of the tenth century. According to *The History of Yuan*, the True Unity Sect was the old school existing in Sung times, whereas the three schools that appeared in the twelfth century were new schools. If this is so, the present Southern School may be the survival of the older school or schools. It emphasizes man's nature, that is, man's spirit or true self, and relies on charms and magic formulae to preserve man's original nature. It depends on "self-power" and

[21] *Ibid.*, pp. 20–84.

is idealistic and informal. Its followers are all "family priests" or Taoists who remain at home with their families, and may either wear the Taoist robe all the time or only occasionally. They fast on occasions, recite Taoist scriptures, perform ceremonies, train pupils, and transmit the Taoist doctrines to them. They are vegetarians only on certain days. The head of the school is the "T'ien-shih," the Heavenly Teacher, who bears the presumptuous title invented for himself by the founder of the Taoist religion, officially accepted by the emperor in A.D. 1276, legally abolished in 1368, but popularly continued to this day, and who used to reside in the Dragon and Tiger Mountain in Central China, where a large domain was granted in 1015.

In the North there is the Ch'üan-chen Sect, or the Complete Purity Sect, which traces its inception to Lü Tung-pin (Shun-yang) of the T'ang Dynasty and which is also called the Shun-yang School. It also claims to have been founded by Wang Che in the tenth century. Actually, it was founded by Ch'iu Ch'ang-ch'un, who in 1220 was invited by the emperor to reside with eight disciples in the White Cloud Temple in Peking.[22] Although the school has followers in the South, it prevails chiefly in North China, with the White Cloud Temple as its center. Its original teaching was to be in harmony with Nature by being calm, tranquil, simple, and at peace with oneself. In order to achieve these states, one was urged to practice asceticism and to endure humiliation. Early followers were hard workers, performed their own labor, produced their own food, and were entirely self-reliant. The main objective was to control one's mind and to restore one's originally pure nature. This, of course, had to be preceded by a clear understanding of human nature and the hu-

[22] Lo-sang-p'eng-ts'o, "History of the Transmissions of the White Cloud Temple in Peking" (in Chinese), *Cheng-feng* ("Right Wind"), III, No. 1 (August 16, 1936), 71–73.

man mind.[23] In contrast to the Southern School, which emphasizes one's nature, this school emphasizes man's life, that is, man's vital energy (*ch'i*), and depends on medicine and diet to prolong life. As such, it is of the "other-power" sect of Taoism. It is materialistic and formal. Its followers are all regular Taoist priests, who renounce their homes, adopt vegetarianism, and live in monasteries. Like the family priests, they fast on certain occasions, recite the scriptures, train disciples, and officiate in ceremonies. But unlike the family priests, they wear the Taoist robe at all times, practice vegetarianism regularly, and do not marry. They do not drink wine.

Both schools have fallen into disorganization. For decades, the sixty-third direct lineal descendant of Chang Ling, the present "Heavenly Teacher," has had neither contact with nor influence over Taoist priests except through very weak links. The ordination of priests has been largely a local affair. The leader should not be called "Pope." The title "Heavenly Teacher" correctly implies that he is custodian of a body of knowledge but that he is neither an arbiter of morals nor a responsible spiritual leader. None of the successive line of "Heavenly Teachers" has attempted to set up a hierarchy or an extensive organization. The present Teacher conducted a school in the Dragon and Tiger Mountain to teach secrets and the Taoist Classics. Like his predecessors, he has no marked doctrinal peculiarities and adheres to no ascetic practice. In recent years he has been indulging in opium and in other earthly pleasures rather than attending to spiritual matters. To the ignorant masses, his chief divine duty has been to select dates as an astrologist, and, according to popular belief, to "command the wind and produce rain." When the Communists occupied the Dragon and Tiger

[23] Ch'en Chiao-yu, *Ch'ang-ch'un Tao-chiao yuan-liu* ("History of the Ch'ang-ch'un Sect of Taoism").

Mountain in 1927, his huge land holdings were confiscated and distributed among peasants, and he was driven out. Evidently he returned there after the Communists left in 1934. There was a rumor that he had become a beggar. But when I inquired about him in 1949, no Taoist priest could give me any information. The latest news is that, a refugee from the Communists for the second time, he went to Macao and decided that it was time for him to buy some books to read. The Taoist priests' indifference to him is very revealing. It shows how little control the "Heavenly Teacher" has had on other Taoists, and it also shows how little they care for him.

The Northern School has shown more vitality, comparatively speaking. The White Cloud Temple has been well kept, and some sort of ecclasiastical order has been maintained. But there is no longer any evidence of the original teachings. Corruption and even murder have given the place a bad reputation. With Communist control of Peking since 1949, the chance for the center to survive has practically been eliminated.

Besides these two centers—the Dragon and Tiger Mountain and the White Cloud Temple—there are local Taoist societies, but they are not correlated, and they were established primarily for the purpose of protecting temple property for the support of priests who have come to be generally regarded as social parasites. How weak Taoism has become can be seen from the fact that whereas both Buddhism and Islam have organized national associations, no such thing has been accomplished in Taoism.

Another reason for the rapid decline of Taoism is its lack of leadership. There is no Taoist priest remotely approaching the calibre of T'ai-hsu. Nor is there any Taoist lay leader worthy of the name. Indeed, leadership, whether clerical or lay, has been absent from Taoism for a thousand years.

During the last millennium, there has been no outstanding Taoist priest, philosopher, or teacher.

Still another reason for the rapid Taoist decline is its lack of a modern program. While both Buddhism and Islam, following the example of Christianity, attempted some sort of social program in educational, medical, and philanthropic service, Taoism remained inactive. Since the publication of 287 titles (114 of which are not included in the Taoist Tripitaka) in the *Tao-tsang chi-yao* ("Important Works of the Taoist Tripitaka") in 246 stitched volumes in 1906, there has not been any significant Taoist publication. The only new enterprise it undertook was the promotion of herb medicine, with which it has long been identified. Of all possible social services, it chose a chauvinistic cause. There was no attempt to promote evangelism or education.

The chief reason for the Taoist collapse is, of course, its total devotion to the search for earthly blessings—wealth, health, longevity, happiness, children.[24] With the advancement of science and education in China, the Chinese masses learn that fulfillment of human desires does not come from chasing away evil spirits and praying to benevolent deities. Modern medical science is fast replacing the God of Medicine, and rural school children go to the temple of Wen-ch'ang, God of Literature, not to pray but to play.

For various reasons, then, the Taoist cult is rapidly deteriorating. When the process is complete, will there be anything left of it? There is no doubt that it will remain a pure philosophy, as it has always been to the educated Chinese. As education reaches the masses, this will become part of their philosophical heritage. The philosophy opposes Nature to man and has therefore been throughout Chinese history a counterpart to humanistic Confucianism. It glorifies Tao

[24] Day, *op. cit.*, pp. 11–14, gives lists of values sought in Chinese religions drawn by various writers.

as the Way, or Nature, Reality, cosmic order, from which ensue emptiness, tranquillity, and enlightenment, "long life and lasting vision," as taught by Lao Tzu (sixth century B.C.?),[25] and in which all things and opinions are equalized and "spontaneous and unceasing transformation of things" go on forever, as was taught by Chuang Tzu (fourth century B.C.).[26] It teaches the doctrine of *wu-wei,* that is, following Nature, non-artificiality, inaction, or passivity, meaning that artificiality must not replace spontaneity and that the state of Nature must not be disturbed by human activities, superficial morality, or pseudo-wisdom. Even in a dynamic, restless period like ours, this philosophy will not be discarded but may be needed all the more.

For the same reason, Taoism will certainly continue to be a Chinese way of life for the educated and the uneducated alike. As Professor Dubs says, "religious Taoism has been dying for centuries, and modern science is speeding up the process. Philosophical Taoism, however, with its exaltation of mysticism, naturalism and simplicity, securing solace in misfortune by cultivating inward calm, laissez faire, skepticism of doctrinaire programs, and optimism, cultivating bodily as well as spiritual health, is likely to remain an important part of China's heritage." [27]

Similarly, Taoism will persist as a guiding principle of Chinese art, as its doctrines of spontaneity, simplicity, and *ch'i* (rhythmic vitality or vitalizing spirit) have been the great source of power in the movements of the brush stroke and of inspiration in the poetic conception of expression.

[25] For translations of the *Tao-te ching,* see *The Way and Its Power,* trans. by Arthur Waley; "The Book of Tao," trans. by Lin Yutang, in his *The Wisdom of Laotse,* pp. 41–325, and also in his *The Wisdom of China and India,* pp. 583–624.

[26] For translations of *Chuang Tzu,* see Chuang Tzu, *Chuang Tzu,* trans. by Fung Yu-lan, Chaps. 1–7; *Chuang Tzu: Mystic, Moralist, and Social Reformer,* trans. by Herbert A. Giles.

[27] *China,* ed. by MacNair, p. 289.

In festivals, too, Taoism will maintain the powerful influence on the Chinese people that it has always had. Here some religious tradition will go on. The romantic, carefree, and gay carnival spirit of its Immortals will continue to soften Chinese life and to give it charm and color. This does not mean the survival of the superstitious belief in immortals as spiritual beings who inhabit the Realm of Great Purity and wander freely in this world in various forms to promote good and remove evil. The most popular set of Taoist immortals, the Eight Immortals, representing all kinds of people—old, young, male, female, civil, military, rich, poor, afflicted, cultured—became chiefly important for their artistic significance perhaps as early as the twelfth century.[28] By the fourteenth century, their connection with both art and religion was overshadowed by the utilitarian, for from that time they were usually associated in art and the drama with birthday felicitations. But it does mean that the gay, spontaneous, romantic spirit as expressed in the Immortals and in symbols, ceremonies, and folklore will always be felt in Chinese festivals. Through popular occasions, Taoism will live on. Even the Communists, though not the kind of people especially keen about promoting tenderness and gaiety in life, have perpetuated the Spring Holidays during the old New Year, which has always been the high point of festivity and religious observance.

Finally, and most intriguing of all, perhaps some Taoist deities will not be forgotten but will be remembered, and, indeed, adored, as Kuan-yin has been. Instead of remaining the object of offers of food and incense in exchange for children and well-being, Kuan-yin,[29] the Great Mercy and Great Compassion Goddess of Mercy who "sees the cry of suffer-

[28] For a brief discussion of the Eight Immortals, see my article, "Hsien," in *An Encyclopedia of Religion*, ed. by Ferm, p. 151.
[29] See above, p. 88.

ing," has become a most popular figure in Chinese folklore and art. In stories, in art objects, and on the stage, Kuan-yin has been an inexhaustible fountain of inspiration and comfort in the moral and spiritual life of the Chinese people. Who can tell for sure that in the course of time other Taoist figures, too, will not become the force that Kuan-yin is? Is there not a possibility that Taoism as a religion will cease to be a set of superstitions and will become a source of spiritual motherhood, as in effect Kuan-yin has been to the millions of Chinese? If the West has felt the need of the Virgin Mary, will the Chinese not need her counterpart?

THE DEVELOPMENT OF TRADITIONAL RELIGIOUS SOCIETIES

From the foregoing, we can say that the soul of Taoism will enjoy immortality but that its body is dying. As an organism, it has been metamorphosing into religious societies. This process has been going on for several centuries, and there have been many such societies. We shall only mention three, the Tsai-li Society, the White Lotus Society, and the Ways of Following the One.

The Tsai-li (Principle Abiding) Society is also called Li Chiao and Li Men, both names meaning the Religion of Principle. It was founded during the transition between the Ming and Ch'ing Dynasties by Yang Ts'un-jen, a native of Shantung. Yang was a Taoist with a high civil service degree. The society was expanded by a second "founder," Yin Yen-sheng, Yang's pupil, who began to preach the doctrine in Tientsin. The sect participated in the White Lotus uprising in 1813–14, and in consequence its members were persecuted and its public halls closed. In 1883, it was again outlawed and persecuted.[30]

[30] Wang Chih-hsin, *Chung-kuo tsung-chiao ssu-hsiang shih ta-kang* ("An Outline History of Chinese Religious Thought"), p. 218; Wang Chao-hsiang, "The Religion in Chinese Secret Societies" (in Chinese), *Wen She*, II, No. 3 (January, 1927), 50–51.

According to its basic document, the *Tsai-li tsung-lun* ("General Statement on the Tsai-li Sect"), "We are the Principle Abiding Sect because we follow the Principle of the sages and transmit the doctrine of Heaven and Earth. . . . Hence we abide by *Li* [Reason, Principle]." Its ethical principles may be summed up in sixteen Chinese characters, meaning "Spiritual awakening," "Escape suffering," "Obtain happiness," "Discipline the body and the mind," "Rectify the heart and cultivate the person," and "Return to the root." [31] Consequently, the sect is distinguished by abstinence from smoking, snuffing, and drinking. It admonishes its members to be diligent and thrifty, and many poor and lazy people have become hard-working and well-to-do under its influence. For this reason it has a strong appeal to rural folk.[32]

Religiously, the sect follows both Buddhism and Taoism. In its public halls, the central position of the altar is occupied by Kuan-yin. There are also altars for the Buddhist bodhisattva Maitreya and the temple guardian Wei-t'o, as well as for the two founders of the sect. Observances including worship, chanting, fasting, and the like, are no different from the general practice of the masses. Close secrecy surrounds its initiation, vows, sign communications among members, and so forth.

The sect is now prevalent mostly in North and West China and along the Yellow River in the provinces of Hopei, Shantung, and Honan, with public halls all over these areas, especially in large cities like Peking and Tientsin. Members are mostly from the artisan and laboring classes, followed by farmers and merchants, with a small number of intellectuals. It is so similar to the White Lotus Society in its main features that it is often considered a branch of it.

[31] *Ibid.*, p. 50.

[32] Chan Chan-hsi, "Facts about Religious Societies" (in Chinese), *K'ung-chiao Hui tsa-chih* ("Confucian Society Magazine"), I, No. 1 (1912), 13–16.

Much has been said of the White Lotus, and much confusion has enveloped the subject. According to one story, it was founded in 1133 by Mao Tzu-yuan of Soochow as a Buddhist sect emphasizing repentance, suppression of desires, vegetarianism, abstinence from drinking, and refraining from taking life.[33] According to another version, the society was established in the last years of the Sung Dynasty (960–1279) by Tuan Yung, who organized it as a Buddhist sect. It attracted many people, especially peasants, and soon spread from Shansi and Shensi to Honan, Hopei, and Shantung. In addition to prayers, offering incense, the use of charms, and incantation, members also practiced boxing and fighting with spears, for the avowed purpose of resisting the invading Chin. They served Sung loyally. During the reign of Wu Tsung (1308–1311) of Yuan, Han Shan-t'ung rose in Wanchow in Hopei and proclaimed himself the leader. His son organized more peasants and rose against the Mongols, adopting a red scarf as their identification. In 1356, he actually proclaimed himself an emperor, and maintained his throne for thirteen years. During the Manchu Dynasty (1644–1912), members of the White Lotus rebelled several times, notably in 1794, 1801, and 1813. The society now spreads over the Yellow River region, especially Honan, Shantung, and Hopei.

The sect has branched out into many secret societies. In the North, its branches include such groups as the Way of Pervading Unity, the Big Sword Society, the Small Sword Society, the Heavenly Gate Society, the Non-Ultimate Society, the Eight Trigram Society, the Yellow Sect, the Fans Society, the Society of Filial Sons, and the Society of White Robes. Some of these are predominantly political, others

[33] Shigematsu Shunsho, "The Early Period of the White Lotus Sect" (originally in Japanese), in Komai Kazuchika, *Chung-kuo li-tai she-hui yen-chiu* ("A Study of Societies in Chinese History"), trans. by Yang Lien, pp. 144–46.

predominantly religious. Of the more political groups the most important one is the Big Sword Society. It was formed in Shantung by Chang T'u-fu during the reign of the Kuang-hsu Emperor (1875–1908) to resist the exploitation of government officials. Eventually it destroyed Christian churches. In its religious practice, it worships Heaven and Earth, the sun, the moon, and stars, the Black Tiger as the protector of the human body, and the tortoise and snake as the dual guards of human life. Members carry charms and recite incantations to ward off evil. It is especially strong in the southern part of Shantung. It is said that there are at least a million members there.[34]

Another branch in the North, the Eight Trigram Society, became the notorious Boxers and, still later, the Society of Red Spears. It covers Shansi, Shantung, Hopei, Honan, and Anhui. In 1916, members actively resisted both bandits and government troops. In 1924–25, they disarmed a whole division belonging to the warlord Wu Pei-fu and defeated two regiments belonging to another warlord, Chang Tso-lin.[35] Repeatedly attacked by government troops, the society has shifted its centers of activities to Szechuan, Hupei, Hunan, and Kiangsu.[36] In religion, the society worships the Jade Emperor, Kuan-yin, Kuan Ti, and many stars. Historically it evolved out of the alchemy school of Taoism rather than the Yellow Emperor–Lao Tzu School. It believes in the identity of man and gods and is entirely utilitarian in its superstitions.[37]

In South China, the main branches of the White Lotus are the Triad Society and the Elders Society. The Triad So-

[34] *Shina himitsu kessha no shinjosei* ("New Tendencies in Chinese Secret Organizations"), p. 10.

[35] Kao-miao, "The Red Spears Society and Peasants" (in Chinese), *I-shih pao* ("Welfare Daily"), Tientsin, June 13, 1936.

[36] Wang Chiao-wo, "The Religious Concepts of the Red Spears Society and Their Patterns of Belief" (in Chinese), *Wen She*, III, No. 8 (January, 1928), 56–60.

[37] *Ibid.*, pp. 58–59.

ciety is variously called San-tien (Three Dots), San-ho (Triple Harmony), Heaven and Earth Society, and T'ien-li Society ("Heavenly Law"). It was founded in 1647 in the Shao-lin Monastery in Fukien, for political purposes. From there it spread to Kwangtung and Kwangsi. Gradually it extended to Formosa and the South Seas. Its history is traced to the Early Five Founding Fathers and the Later Five Founding Fathers.[38] It follows a number of Buddhist and Taoist practices and worships Emperor T'ai Tsung (627–49) as an indication of patriotism. It participated in the revolt of 1774 and also in the T'ai-p'ing Rebellion.[39] In recent years it took an active part in the revolution of Sun Yat-sen.[40] It is still strong in South China and is especially strong among overseas Chinese. In the United States, the society is known as Chih Kung Tong.[41]

According to other sources, the society is a branch of Hung Men.[42] Whether one is the branch of the other, or whether the names are interchangeable, is a moot point.[43]

The Elders Society, or Ko-lao Hui,[44] variously called in different parts of China,[45] originated also in Fukien, somewhat later than the Triad Society. One theory is that in 1853, the Triad Society was resisting the Manchus in South China

[38] Lo Yuan-kun, *Chung-kuo chin pai-nien shih* ("Chinese History in the Last Century"), I, 341.
[39] J. S. M. Ward and W. G. Sterling, *The Hung Society, or the Society of Heaven and Earth*, I, p. 7.
[40] Lo Erh-kang, *T'ien-ti Hui wen-hsien lu* ("Documents of the Heaven and Earth Society"), p. 2.
[41] Carl Glick and Hong Sheng-hwa, *Swords of Silence; Chinese Secret Societies Past and Present*, pp. 44–53.
[42] Liu Lien-k'o, *Pang-hui san-pai-nien ko-ming shih* ("A History of the Revolutionary Activities of the Secret Societies in the Last Three Hundred Years"), pp. 71–72.
[43] Lo Erh-kang, *op. cit.*, p. 2. See also Gustave Schlegel, *Thien Ti Hwai, the Hung League; or Heaven and Earth League, a Secret Society with the Chinese in China and India*, trans. into Chinese under the title *T'ien-ti Hui yen-chiu*.
[44] Liao Tai-ch'u, "The Ko Lao Hui in Szechuan," *Pacific Affairs*, XX, No. 2 (June, 1947), 161–73.
[45] Lo Yuan-kun, *op. cit.*, p. 342.

and the Elders Society arose in Central and North China in sympathetic response.[46] In any case, it spread over almost all China but is now particularly strong in Central, North, and West China. It has been strongly anti-Manchu. It was so powerful in the nineteenth century that even leading government generals like Tseng Kuo-fan (1811–1872) and Tso Tsung-t'ang (1812–1885) had to join it.[47] Today it is the most extensive, well organized, and influential of China's secret societies.

All these four branches of the White Lotus—the Big Sword Society, the Red Spears Society, the Triad Society, and the Elders Society—represent the radical tendency of secret societies and are more political than religious in nature. The Way of Following the One (Kuei-i Tao), however, is strictly religious. It is prevalent in Shantung, Hopei, and Honan. Until 1948 there was no information about it in any written work.

Followers of the sect claim that it is an offshoot of the Way of Former Heaven (Hsien-t'ien Tao) founded by Li T'ing'yü (fl. 1640–60). Its history is vague. At any rate, from 1887 to this day it has been a persistent religious movement.

Members of the sect emphasize devotion, as expressed in such practices as bowing four thousand times every day with the head touching the ground, reciting verses, and fingering rosaries. They prefer a life of independence, diligence, and thrift. They avoid wealth and glory and dedicate themselves to a life of hard work, vegetarianism, self-cultivation, saving others, and setting living beings free. They believe in the merciful salvation by the Mother of No-birth, who is the Source, Creator, and Preserver of all living beings. She is the One, worshiped in Confucianism, Taoism, and Buddhism

[46] Liu Lien-k'o, *op. cit.*, pp. 71–72.

[47] Chih-yü, "On the Organization and History of Chinese Secret Societies" (in Chinese), *Hua-ch'iao jih-pao* (*China Daily News*), New York, February 23, 1943.

under different names, and she is the one vehicle of salvation in this troubled sea of suffering. From Taoism the sect has borrowed the use of charms, the belief in divination, and alchemy of various kinds; from Buddhism the doctrines of suffering and salvation; and from Confucianism the basic ethical teachings, especially that of the original goodness of human nature. It advocates the avoidance of "six harms," namely, fame, sex, wealth, indulgence in food, falsehood, and jealousy, and promotes the practice of "eight virtues," that is, sincerity of the will, rectification of the heart, carefulness in speech, seriousness in handling affairs, respect for the old, affectionate love for the young, integrity for the self, and urging others to do good. This religious life is centered in the home rather than in temples. No one knows how many followers there are, but its persistence testifies to the tenacity of old religious societies.[48]

THE RISE OF NEW RELIGIOUS SOCIETIES

Not only have old societies thrived. New societies have grown up in the last few decades. The twentieth century has been for China a period of intellectual doubt, spiritual upheaval, and economic and political chaos. New societies have arisen partly for escape and partly for spiritual uplift. Since most of these societies were short-lived and kept no records, and since scholars and historians have avoided them as insignificant, little information about them is available. Among them, brief mention may be made of the Society of World Religions,[49] organized in Szechuan by T'ang Huan-chang in

[48] Li Shih-yü, *Hsien-tsai Hua-pei pi-mi tsung-chiao* (*Religions secrètes contemporaines dans le nord de la Chine*), 131–37, 149–58. This is the only written information about this sect. Three other contemporary secret religious societies hitherto not described are related here at length, namely, (1) the Yellow Heaven Sect or Huang-t'ien Chiao (pp. 10–31), (2) the Way of Pervading Unity (pp. 131–65), (3) the Heavenly Way of One Mind or I'hsin T'ien-tao (pp. 166–75). The second will be described below. Of the other two each is confined to one small area.

[49] *Shih-chieh Tsung-chiao Ta-t'ung Hui.*

1915; the International Society of Holy Religions,[50] founded by Wang Chia-shu in Peking;[51] the Hsi-hsin She (Society for the Purification of the Heart), established in 1917 (1920?) in Taiyuan by one of General Yen Hsi-shan's staff, which aimed at "preserving the heart, cultivating one's nature, manifesting virtue, and loving people," and has kept the Confucian temple in good condition, established schools and libraries, conducted lectures and publications, devoted Sunday as the day for cleansing one's heart, and designated a special hall for introspection;[52] the Universal Ethical Society,[53] established in Tsinan in 1921, which spread over the country after having received impetus from "genius" Chiang Hsi-chang, distributed Confucian and Taoist literature, recognized the good in all great teachers, opposed war in the First World War, and offered lectures by K'ang Yu-wei;[54] the Ethical Study Society,[55] founded in 1924 (?) with headquarters in Peking and a few branches in the provinces, which emphasized sound morals, study, quiet sitting, and the cultivation of self nature.[56] None of these was very influential, and it is doubtful that any trace of them is left.

Four new societies, however, deserve close attention because of their vast influence; namely, the Tao Yuan, the T'ung-shan Society, the Wu-shan Society, and the Way of Pervading Unity (I-kuan Tao). The Tao Yuan (Society of the Way), also known as Tao-te She or the Society of the

[50] *Ch'üan-ch'iu Sheng-chiao Ta-t'ung Hui.*

[51] *China Mission Year Book,* 1924, p. 65.

[52] Huang Yen, ed., *K'ung-chiao shih-nien ta-shih* ("Important Events in Confucianism in the Last Ten Years"), VII, 60.

[53] *Wan-kuo Tao-te Hui.*

[54] *China Mission Year Book,* 1924, p. 61; *China Christian Year Book,* 1926, p. 79.

[55] *Tao-te Hsueh-she.*

[56] *China Mission Year Book,* 1924, p. 61. For a list and short descriptions of twenty-odd societies, old and new, large and small, see Karl Ludvig Reichelt, *Religion in Chinese Garment,* pp. 165–73. The account gives a confused picture of the relationship among the societies themselves and their relationship to Chinese religions.

Way and Its Virtue, originated in Tsinan in 1921 (1919?),[57] having arisen from a revelation in a planchette appearing to its founder a year before. Within two years, it spread over North China and the Yangtze area, especially in Peking and Shantung, with one branch in Japan. In 1921, there were thirteen branches with two thousand members. By 1927, there were thirty-eight branches in Shantung alone, and eighteen in each of Kiangsu and Hopei, so that there must have been over a hundred in the country. It claimed thirty thousand members.[58] Its building consists of five *yuans* or halls, one each for worship, scripture reading, meditation, preaching, and charity. It worships the Ultimate Sage and Primeval Old Ancestor as the Great Unity below whose altar are the names of Confucius, Lao Tzu, and the Buddha and the symbols representing Christianity and Islam. Its doctrines emphasize the community of Heaven and man in matters of the spirit, and the spirit of world brotherhood.[59] For its members, it urges meditation, cultivation of the inner life, the belief in planchettes, and the use of spirit photography. For others, the society practices charities and other forms of social service, operates hospitals, and establishes banks with small deposits for poor people. The emphasis on charity led it to assume later the name of Universal Red Swastika Society, and it carried on extensive Red Cross work.[60]

The T'ung-shan She or Fellowship of Goodness (Society for Common Good) was started around 1918 (1911? 1913?) [61] in Peking by Wang Ch'ao-tsung and others. In

[57] Wang Chao-hsiang, in *Wen She*, II, No. 3 (January, 1927), 48.
[58] *Ibid.*, p. 49. [59] *Ibid.*
[60] Braden, *op. cit.*, pp. 130–31; *China Mission Year Book*, 1924, pp. 62–63; *China Christian Year Book*, 1926, p. 77–78.
[61] Wang Chih-hsin, *op. cit.*, p. 219, says the society was founded in 1921. According to Wang Chao-hsiang, in *Wen She*, II, No. 3 (January, 1927), the year was 1922 or 1923. John C. De Korne, who has written the most

1923 the Society claimed more than a thousand branches in all parts of China proper and Manchuria. It advocates the "inner work" of worship, meditation, and vegetarianism and the "outer work" of charity and maintaining schools. In spite of its Buddhist background, it strongly opposes monasticism and the renunciation of the family.[62] Like the Tao-yuan, it follows all three religions, and attracts mostly the educated. The arrangement of its halls resembles closely that of the Tao Yuan, but it worships the three images of Confucius, Lao Tsu, and the Buddha.[63] It stresses evangelism through the methods of personal visits, regular meetings, and literature.[64] It believes that illness can be cured by quiet sitting. Like other religious societies, it keeps close secrecy and is primarily utilitarian in purpose.[65]

The Wu-shan She or Society for the Intuition of the Good (Association for Awakening Righteousness), also called the Society of the Six Holy Religions,[66] was founded in Szechuan about 1915 by T'ang Huan-chang. He traced the society to an early period and called himself the seventh "founder."[67] From Szechuan it extended to Peking, Nanking, Shantung, and Shanghai. Like the Fellowship of Goodness, it practices meditation, charity, spiritual cultivation, spirit photography, and use of the planchette to receive messages from divinities, but it keeps more secrecy. It teaches fasting and meditation to prolong life. Most of its followers are uneducated people.

---

detailed account of the society, *The Fellowship of Goodness,* says the society was first officially registered with the government in 1917 but earlier existence can be traced to 1914 (*op. cit.*, p. 15).

[62] De Korne *op. cit.*, pp. 47, 59.

[63] *China Mission Year Book,* 1924, pp. 60–61.

[64] Wang Chao-hsiang, in *Wen She,* II, No. 3 (January, 1927), 43–44.

[65] *Ibid.*, also Wang Chih-hsin, *op. cit.*, pp. 219–20.

[66] *Liu-sheng Tsung-chiao Ta-t'ung Hui.* See Wang Chih-hsin, *op. cit.*, p. 219.

[67] *Ibid.*, p. 219; Wang Chao-hsiang, in *Wen She,* II, No. 3 (January, 1927), 45–46.

Later it took the name of New Religion for World Salvation.[68] As a religion, it follows Confucianism, Taoism, Buddhism, Islam, Christianity, and Judaism. In organization, it closely resembles Roman Catholicism. It is headed by a bishop who is elected through revelation. In belief, the society traces everything to the First Cause, or Primeval Ancestor. He is the True Lord of Christianity and Islam. Impelling messages from the spirit world are his mandates. Associated with him is Lü Tsu, one of the eight Taoist Immortals.[69]

The three societies just described have been on the decline in the last decade or so. The Way of Pervading Unity (I-kuan Tao), however, gained strength and extended its activities during the Second World War. As in the case of the Way of Following the One, there was no literature about it until 1948, and to this day even its name is unknown to most scholars. Its origin is obscure. Its members claim great antiquity, but the best guess is that some elements of the Boxers started secret activities soon after the Revolution of 1911 and the movement rapidly grew after 1928 when Chang T'ien-jan (d. 1947) propagated his teachings.

The sect believes that the One is the root of all things and as a principle penetrates through and pervades in all existence. The universe evolves from the realm of *Li* (Principle or Law), which is infinite and a priori, to the realm of *ch'i* (material force) through its active and passive principles (*yin yang*), and then to the phenomenal world. We are now in the midst of the third catastrophe in the history of human existence, and it is through the mercy of the Mother of No-birth, the Creator of all, and our own moral and spiritual efforts that the world will be saved. All systems—Confucianism, Taoism, Buddhism, Christianity, and

[68] *Hsin Chiu-shih Chiao.*

[69] *China Christian Year Book,* 1926, pp. 78–79; *China Mission Year Book,* 1924, p. 60.

Islam—with all their sages, gods, and Buddhas, are vehicles for this salvation. In the end all people will be saved.

Followers of the sect emphasize "internal" and "external" efforts equally. The former includes self-cultivation, purification of the heart, reduction of desires, and control of the mind. The latter includes the use of charms and planchette, the practice of the "three secrets" of finger signs and magic phrases, abstinence from meat and tobacco and alcohol, incantation, worshiping images of all religions, offering and sacrificing, study and recitation of Buddhist and Taoist canons, preaching, and charity. Like most secret religious societies, it attracts chiefly the ignorant and illiterate. There is no way to reckon the number of its followers or its temples. During the Second World War it was very active in almost the entire territory occupied by Japan, especially in North China. Since the war, however, it has been suppressed and its activities have quieted down. How it will fare under the Communist regime only time will tell.[70]

It will be noticed that most of these societies grew up in Shantung shortly before or after the First World War. There is no doubt that general chaos in this period generated disillusionment. The Intellectual Renaissance of 1917 had in the first decade created more doubt than certainty. Besides, because of its strategic position at the mouth of the Yellow River with very fertile soil, Shantung has always been a center of contest in wars, whether civil or international. These wars, the suffering they produced, and the social and economic difficulties due to overpopulation encouraged people to seek help in these societies. But they are all negative in outlook, utilitarian in purpose, and superstitious in belief. Consequently they have been condemned by Chinese intellectuals. Liang Ch'i-ch'ao, for example, declared that they were "poison to the people," and Wu Chih-hui said that their

[70] Li Shih-yü, *op. cit.*, pp. 32–37, 45–75.

net result was to "pour poor men's rice into the pockets of witches." [71]

SIGNIFICANT TRENDS

The ignorance and superstition surrounding these societies, old and new, are distressing. They deserve the attack of intellectuals and are already being suppressed by the new government in China.[72] This is not the first time they have been banished, but each time they have survived under cover only to emerge stronger later on. As economic and political forces, they are not to be lightly dismissed. From the religious point of view, they seem to represent escapism, reaction, the backwash of gradual but sure recession. No one can deny these elements. But over and above them, they demonstrate certain tendencies in China's religious life that are exceedingly meaningful to us. These tendencies are not only evident in the religious societies but also in Taoism itself, in Islam, in Buddhism—in short, in the religion of the masses in general. In fact, they are equally evident in the religious attitude of the intellegentsia. If we believe that the future grows out of the past, it is not too much to say that these tendencies give us a preview of what the future of Chinese religion is likely to be.

Two interesting observations on religious trends in China should be noted. One, the most recent, is by Earl H. Cressy, veteran missionary in China. He found (1) a feeling for the need of religion; (2) a search for a spiritual foundation of the international order; (3) an increase in the prestige of Christianity; (4) Fellowship among Religious Believers; and (5) research on religions in China.[73] The other, more

[71] Liang Ch'i-ch'ao, "Criticism of the Anti-Religious Alliance" (in Chinese), *Che-hsueh* ("Philosophy"), No. 6 (June, 1922), p. 5; *Wu Chih-hui hsueh-shu lun-chu* ("Academic Writings of Wu Chih-hui"), p. 89.

[72] New York *Times*, August 19, 1950.

[73] Earl H. Cressy, "Recent Developments in the Religions of China," *The Journal of Bible and Religion,* XV, No. 1 (April, 1947), 79.

comprehensive observation is found in Braden's *Modern Tendencies in World Religions.* He enumerates six trends: (1) anti-Christianity, (2) anti-religionism, (3) nationalism, (4) liberalism but not anti-religionism, (5) reform and revival of old religions, and (6) syncretism.[74] A note of clarification should be added to the effect that nationalism refers to the Chinese Nationalist government's decision to regulate the Christian church and Christian schools in China in the 1930s. There is no doubt that China, with its new national consciousness, was extremely nationalistic in the 1920s and 1930s. All universities, including Christian institutions, were required to register with the Nationalist government. In this, the government was absolutely right. But for a time, many Christians were barred from government positions because of their faith, and in this the government was absolutely wrong. But there was no nationalism in religion itself. As we have noted previously, Buddhism has never tried to identify itself with national life. The Taoist religion was not even aware of the national consciousness. Religion was not a war issue. In fact, Chinese religion itself has been subjected to the virtues and vices of Chinese nationalism just as other institutions have been. It has not been an instrument of the government. Instead, it has often found itself in opposition to it. This leads to the first tendency we are to discuss; namely, the tendency from patriotism to revolt. Following this, we shall discuss other tendencies—this-worldliness, ethical emphasis, laymen's movements, and syncretism.

From Patriotism to Revolt. Students of the history of Chinese religions are struck by the fact that the Taoist schools and traditional religious societies all started as patriotic movements against invaders. This dominant note expressed itself repeatedly in the resistance against the Chin, the Mongols, and the Manchus, and it was struck strongly

[74] Braden, *op. cit.*, pp. 94–96.

in the infamous Boxer uprising of 1900 against Westerners. This note of patriotism still rings, but over and above it there is an increasingly strong note of revolt against internal oppression. In recent centuries, the uprisings against the Manchus were chiefly in the nature of revolution against an oppressive government, whether foreign or native. This note is especially powerful in the secret religious societies, as we have seen.

Of course, the religious societies are not the only groups bent on self-defense against tyranny. Among the nonreligious societies, the Green and Red Brotherhoods are the most vigorous.[75] These Brotherhoods have often been confused with various branches of the White Lotus Society.[76] Actually, although they have elements in common with it, they are distinct entities and are different in character from that society.

The Green Brotherhood was organized in 1806 in Shantung by Ch'en Yuan, who secretly organized boatmen, longshoremen, and transportation workers to disrupt the transportation system of the Manchu government. It is so named because it originated in East China, for green is the traditional color of the east. Its Robin Hood character may be traced to the *hsia-shih*, or knight-errants, of the fourth century B.C. The tradition of wandering knights who fight to right wrongs has always been strong in Chinese history, and Chinese chronicles are full of accounts of such movements which have been dramatized in novels and on the stage. The Brotherhood enhanced this tradition in their fight against the Manchus. Ch'en's first uprising took place in Hunan with four thousand men and was quickly defeated. But within ten years of the founding of the Brotherhood, it had six hundred thousand members in North and East China. The defeat of the T'aip'ing rebellion, in which they partici-

[75] Ch'ing Pang, Hung Pang.

[76] Wang Chih-hsin, *op. cit.*, p. 217.

pated, caused them to disperse. For a time the Brotherhood disintegrated. One of its leaders, Lin Chün, who forgot for a time the anti-Manchu purpose of the society, attacked the T'aip'ing rebels and served under Tseng Kuo-fan. When Tseng disbanded his forces, Lin went to the Twin Dragons Mountain in Central China and organized the Red Brotherhood, the Hung Pang. The word *hung* ("red") was chosen because it was the traditional color for the South, and because it sounds the same as the Hung Society, which was also fighting the Manchus. When Tseng finally invaded the Twin Dragons Mountain, Lin's followers scattered over Shantung and Hopei. There they met members of the Elders Society and became their sworn brothers because of their common purpose in fighting the Manchus.

Undoubtedly, many people belong to the Red or the Green Brotherhood as well as to the White Lotus Society, and many are not aware of their difference. One difference is that while revolution is the main objective of the Brotherhoods and religion only secondary, for the White Lotus Society, religion is primary and revolution secondary. Another difference is that while the Brotherhoods emphasize chivalry, it is not particularly stressed in the White Lotus.[77] What makes them look similar is their common spirit of revolt.

It should be said that this spirit of revolt is basically in the interest of self-defense. It is political in the sense of rebellion against an intolerable government but not in the sense of identifying the church with the state. Neither Buddhism nor Taoism has been interested in politics as such. The historic Buddhist declaration, "We monks will not salute kings," speaks not only for Buddhism but for Taoism also. The so-called worship of the emperor in the Temple of Long Life before 1912 carried with it no idea of the divinity of the emperor, as in Japan, but was merely an expression of hope

[77] Chih-yü, in *Hua-ch'iao jih-pao*, New York, February 23, 1943.

for the sovereign's longevity. The bowing before Sun Yat-sen's portrait, the reading of his will, and the three-minute silence in the weekly memorial periods under the Nationalist government are not considered by the Chinese as constituting a new cult. Granting the religious nature of such customs, still they do not make Chinese religion political or nationalistic. We have seen that there has been a movement to make Buddhism international. In Chinese Islam, too, many efforts have been made recently to cultivate friendly relations with other Islamic countries. Both before and during the war, because many soldiers and generals were Moslems, patriotism ran high. But most Chinese Moslems still adhere to their traditional vow to "fight for our religion but not for our country." This bold and bitter manifesto underlies the note of revolt against oppression, for Chinese Moslems, being mostly poor people, have been for centuries victims of aggression by the government and the gentry, and they have fought not for religious freedom, which they have always enjoyed, but for social and economic justice.

This-Worldliness. The social and economic interest of Chinese religions has always been profound, because the religion of the masses is distinctly this-worldly. In the discussion of modern Buddhism, we have already pointed out that in outlook, Buddhism has moved from other-worldliness to this-worldliness. This tendency is true of Chinese religion in general. Only in Buddhism have Heaven and Hell been taken seriously. But even there, salvation is to be achieved "where you are" and "in this very body," and "Every color and every fragrance are no different from the Middle Way." In other religions, Heaven and Hell are either absent or pushed to the background. In none of the modern or traditional religious societies do they occupy a central position. In most of the societies they are not even mentioned. To be sure, many societies have indulged in the superstitious practice of praying to spirits in Heaven, but it is significant that members of these societies seldom hope to become immortals and ascend to Heaven. On the contrary, they ask spirits to descend from Heaven to the world. When Hodous said that Chinese religious thought runs from man to God, rather than from God to man as in the West, he was stating a solid fact.[78] As one Chinese writer points out,

> The religious motive of the Chinese people is saturated with the spirit of the present world. . . . This is why the God of Wealth and Kuan-yin are popular objects of worship. The Chinese people, aside from worshiping Heaven, especially worship Earth. They worship Yen Wang more than the Jade Emperor, because the relationship between Heaven and our practical life is not as direct as between it and Earth. Heaven has to depend on earth to produce and sustain man. For this reason, from ancient times to the present day, the Gods of Grain and Ground have been universally worshiped, and the local God of Soil has a shrine in every village. The reason that each county has a City God is because the deity governs the soil of the area and has an intimate relation to the life of the people. And the reason that the Jade Emperor is worshiped less than Yen Wang is because while the Jade Emperor only rules in Heaven, Yen Wang rules man as well as Hades.[79]

It is hardly necessary to remind us that the extreme superstitions, the many variations of alchemy, and the large horde of spirits in Taoism are all calculated to prolong life on earth. In all its various forms, the religion of the masses aims at earthly blessings. We may dismiss all this as primitive. However, we cannot be blind to the glaring fact that the Chinese masses keep their eyes on the ground so far as religion is concerned.

[78] Haydon, *op. cit.*, p. 169.
[79] T'ang Chün-i, *Chung-hsi che-hsueh ssu-hsiang chih pi-chiao yen-chiu chi* ("Essays on the Comparative Studies of Chinese and Western Philosophical Thought"), p. 222.

Ethical Emphasis. Because of their preoccupation with this world, the religious societies, old and new, have given very little study to spiritual beings. Their primary interest has been man and his good life on earth. The highest deities and the founders of the great religions are revered not as mysterious sources of magic power, but as models and an aid for a good life. To this end, meditation, incantation, and even the planchette are used as means, but not renunciation of the family, extreme asceticism, or self-immolation. The chief emphasis in the practices of the cults have been on charity for others and cultivation of the inner life for the self. Such are the central emphases of the Fellowship of Goodness and the Wu-shan society, whose practical ethics have been strongly influenced by the Five Precepts and Ten Virtues of Taoism: not to kill, drink alcohol, lie, steal, or commit adultery; and (1) filial piety, (2) loyalty, (3) love, (4) patience, (5) remonstration of evil deeds, (6) self-sacrifice to help the poor, (7) setting living beings free and planting trees, (8) building roads and digging wells, (9) teaching the unenlightened and promoting welfare, and (10) reading scriptures and worshiping deities.

The Ten Ideals of the Fellowship of Goodness are: straight heart, a high type of service, unrestricted virtue, clear instruction, law observance, diligence in moral culture, desire for progress, harmony, maintenance of high ideals, and the unification of the soul.[80]

The Decalogue of the Tao Yuan consists of these: (1) Do not dishonor parents; (2) Do not lack virtue; (3) Do not lack goodness; (4) Do not lack righteousness; (5) Do not lack mercy; (6) Do not conceal goodness of others; (7) Do not be cruel; (8) Do not have secrets; (9) Do not have envy or spite; (10) Do not blaspheme.[81] Members of the Red Spears Society vow not to drink or gamble but to be filially

[80] De Korne, *op. cit.*, p. 57.

[81] Braden, *op. cit.*, pp. 130–31.

pious toward parents, respectful towards elders, harmonious with neighbors, and righteous with regard to money.[82] The Tsai-li Sect preaches such positive virtues as filial piety, respect, neighborliness, patience and tolerance, "rectification of the heart and cultivation of the person," and "self-discipline and the restoration of social order." [83] The "eight virtues" of the Way of Following the One have already been mentioned. Most of the societies have names indicating their central emphasis on moral culture.

Because of this elementary concern with morality, there is no place in these cults for myths, miracles, or mysticism. Fanatic mass conversion and revivalism are unheard of. The religious approach is largely individual, and this individual approach has given the followers a strong sense of individual moral responsibility. Each must work out his own salvation. For this reason, there does not exist in these cults an elaborate machinery for evangelism, conversion, or missionary work.

Individualism and self-salvation is possible because there is in all men the Buddha-nature, the Taoist pure nature, or the Confucian *Li* (Reason, Principle). In direct contrast to Christianity, these societies, like the three traditional systems, accept no idea of original sin. Instead, they hold that human nature is originally good. This absence of the concept of original sin has disturbed many a Christian missionary, who simply cannot understand how religion is possible without a dogma so basic in his own. His natural conclusion is that the Chinese people have not advanced to that stage. Even so fair-minded and learned a person as Soothill thought that the Chinese notions of sin were "crude." [84] He hopefully forecast that the Chinese were "prepared" for the conversion to the doctrine of original sin, without realizing that

[82] Kao-miao, in *I-shih pao*, Tientsin, July 13, 1936.
[83] *Tsai-li tsung-lun.*
[84] Soothill, *op. cit.*, pp. 208–26.

unless the Chinese throw overboard their entire philosophical, religious, and ethical heritage solidly based on the belief in the universal goodness of human nature, his chances are very small.

From the unmistakable ethical emphasis in present-day Chinese religion, it is safe to predict that the future development of religion in China will be deeply this-worldly and ethical. It is significant to note that the greatest measure of success of Christianity in China has been along these lines, whereas its theology and doctrines of immortality have largely fallen on deaf ears. To grow on Chinese soil, Christianity must be long on the humanistic and short on the theological side. One is justified in saying that Chinese development of Christianity has already followed the ethical tendency. As Latourette rightly observes, "the Chinese heritage is largely one of personal and social ethics. From the standpoint of China's most influential philosophy, Confucianism, a religion is to be judged by its power to produce worthy character and a just social order. Presumably, it is this note which Chinese Christians will stress in their contribution to the Christianity of the twentieth century." [85]

The Layman's Movement. Since the focal point of Chinese religion is ethical, and since everyone, because of his innate good nature, can save himself, it follows that religiously speaking, each is as important as the other. Consequently, in most ancient and modern cults there is no clergy. In the traditional systems, whatever clergy there has been, has been relatively unimportant. There is no clergy in Confucianism. In Taoism, the priests do hardly more than perform ceremonies. Their role is passive. They are ordered by the people rather than leading them. In Buddhism, while the clergy has tight control over temples, they have very little control over the religious life of the people. As we have

[85] *China*, ed. by MacNair, p. 311.

seen,[86] in the last several decades, even the ecclesiastical leadership was being gradually taken over by Buddhist laymen. The relative strength of the layman and the relative weakness of the clergy have been a blessing for Buddhism. In India, early Buddhism was confined to the monastery and therefore lacked the support of the masses. As a result, Indian Buddhism was too weak to withstand the onslaught of Islam and was practically wiped off the Indian scene. In China, on the contrary, it has become rooted in the masses rather than the clergy, and it has lived through fortunes and misfortunes alike. In short, it is the layman who has given Chinese religion its vitality, strength, and leadership. Under such circumstances, Christianity can hardly escape the same influence. Since the National Christian Council of China was established in 1922, the center of Christianity in China has gradually shifted from the clergy to the layman.[87]

The best evidence of the layman's movement in Chinese Christianity is the Jesus Family. Founded by Ching Tienying in Machuang in Taian, Shantung Province, in 1921, the Jesus Family consists of a number of small families who live, work, share property, and worship together as a large family. In January, 1950, there were 179 such large families, involving about ten thousand people. Every one of these members has the responsibility of economic production and preaching the gospel. Theirs may be the Chinese Christian's challenge to Communism.

The importance of the layman in Chinese Christianity is fully realized by Francis Wei in his proposal for a "four-center church" for China. He would have, first of all, a number of "church cells" consisting of thirty to fifty families. Then there would be social service centers comparable to

[86] See above, p. 86.

[87] Wu Yao-tsung (John Wu), "Christian Thought in the Last Thirty Years" (in Chinese), *Lun-t'an* ("Herald"), Nos. 6–7 (July, 1948), p. 8.

civic centers. There are already the Christian colleges. All the three centers are to be interdenominational and supported and managed by laymen. Only in the fourth, the center of "Christian pilgrimages" situated in beautiful spots up in the mountains for religious recreation and retreat, would there be a minister.[88] Without going into a detailed discussion of Wei's interesting proposal, we must say that his reliance on the layman for the development of Christianity in China shows his clear understanding of the religious genius of his people.

Syncretism. Parallel with the ascendance of the layman has been the growth of syncretism. There has been in the entire religious movement not a single attempt to replace all religions with one. On the contrary, the general direction in the last fifty years, as in the last fifteen hundred years, has been toward the harmony and synthesis of all religions. We have already mentioned that the Way of Following the One and the Fellowship of Goodness follow the three traditional systems. We may now add that the latter derives its practice of meditation from Buddhism, rules of longevity from Taoism, and ethical standards from Confucianism.[89] To these three systems, the Tao Yuan and the Way of Pervading Unity add Islam and Christianity, and the Society for the Intuition of the Good includes Judaism also. The fundamental document of the Tsai-li Sect says, "Buddhism teaches the preservation of life and the attainment of longevity. Taoism teaches the cultivation of life and the achievement of enlightenment. And Confucianism teaches the establishment of life and the realization of one's destiny. They are three religions but their principle (*li*) is one." [90] The number of inter-religious conferences which have been

[88] Francis C. M. Wei, *The Spirit of Chinese Culture*, pp. 160–69.
[89] C. Yates McDaniel, "Buddhism Makes Its Place in the New Era," *Asia*, XXXV, No. 8 (August, 1935), 540.
[90] *Tsai-li tsung-lun*.

held and relief projects which have been carried out in recent years are examples of the trend toward harmony.[91]

This syncretic spirit has long been prominent in Chinese religious life. Many years ago, Edkins observed that "China is the only instance of a country where three powerful religions have existed together for ages without one of them being successful in destroying the other two." [92] The reasons for this amazing phenomenon, according to him, were: (1) that the Chinese "are superstitious but wanting in conscientiousness"; (2) that it was a matter of circumstances, the three systems being supplementary to each other; (3) that the three systems are all supported by the weight of authority.[93] He also said that the syncretic spirit is a result of politeness. The first explanation is absurd, the third historically inaccurate, and the second inadequate though correct. However, he was sound when he observed that Taoism, Confucianism, and Buddhism all teach the doctrine of the original goodness of man and that the path of reformation and perfection lies in following out our nature, and that this common teaching has combined them together.[94] It is amazing that Reichelt, who understood Chinese Buddhism well, completely failed to apprehend the syncretism in Chinese religion. He thought it was a result of a "loosely articulated system" of thought and that the Chinese followed several religions at the same time because they felt a sense of "special obligation" to various deities.[95]

To understand the real meaning of syncretism in Chinese religion, one must go back to the period when the conflict of religions was solved. Ever since the Taoist priest Wang Fu of the Western Chin Dynasty (265–317) fabricated the story that Gotama was the reincarnation of Lao Tzu, there

[91] *China Christian Year Book,* 1926, p. 76.
[92] Joseph Edkins, *Religion in China,* p. 57.
[93] *Ibid.,* pp. 59–65; 74. [94] *Ibid.,* pp. 73–74.
[95] Reichelt, *Religion in Chinese Garment,* pp. 173–74.

was a heated controversy between the Buddhists and the Taoists, a quarrel lasting off and on for some three hundred years. In the North, the struggle was mostly for power and often resulted in actual hostility. In the South, the dispute chiefly centered around doctrines. The Taoists, who were joined by some Confucianists, denounced Buddhism on three grounds: that it was unsuitable to Chinese conditions and life, that Taoism was more basic whereas Buddhism was secondary, and that the destructibility of spirit disproved transmigration, the very foundation of the Buddhist faith. The Buddhists countered with the assertions that Lao Tzu was a disciple of the Buddha and that Buddhism was more fundamental than Taoism and Confucianism because, while these religions offered a good way of life, Buddhism alone penetrated to the nature of existence. To prove their claim, both Taoists and Buddhists forged holy canons and did other things fully as absurd as what is being done by some religious protagonists in the world today. The controversy between Taoists and Buddhists became so intolerable that in 574 Emperor Wu ordered more than twenty thousand Buddhist monks and Taoist priests back to lay life.

Fortunately for China, long before this "catastrophe," Buddhists, Taoists, and Confucianists began to resolve their tension. It is significant that even at the height of their agitation, they did not condemn other religions as untrue or as the work of the Devil. They conceded a degree of truth in other religions and could not help admitting that other religions also offered a good way of life. Once the contestants started along this direction, they inevitably arrived at a point where all religions met and became identified as one. The upshot in Chinese history is the well-known "harmony of three religions" or the "unity of three religions." For the last fifteen hundred years, the three systems have been mutually penetrated, interrelated, and partially identified. They have become "three roads to the same destination," as the Chinese people are fond of saying. Or, as the famous Chinese proverbs have it, "The three religions are one family"; "Like flowers, leaves, and seeds, they all come from the same root"; "Taoist alchemy, Buddhist relics, and Confucian ethics are identical." [96]

The harmony of the three religions is understood in three senses. First of all, it is understood in the sense of equality, that is to say, that all religions are equal. As Ku Huan (390–483), the Taoist, put it, "Taoist and Buddhist scriptures match and complement each other," and, "Taoism and Buddhism are equal in illuminating and in transforming people." [97] Many Chinese scholars noted the fact that different religions developed under different conditions and met different needs, but they are all "convenient means" to the same end. "Confucius sought order and peace in society," remarked Sun Ch'o (320–77) of Chin Dynasty, "and the Buddha sought enlightenment in the fundamental nature of existence, but their goals are the same." [98] Hence the general conviction that while Confucianism is worldly and Buddhism other-worldly, they lead to the same results. By the same token, it is often maintained that "Confucianism and Taoism are equal."

Religious harmony is also understood in the sense of mutual identification. "The enlightenment that transforms a person into a Buddha," said Sun Ch'o, "is none other than the awakening which Mencius said the sage achieves for himself and helps others to achieve." [99] It was repeatedly pointed out that the three sages, Confucius, Lao Tzu, and Gotama, taught the full realization of man's true nature.

[96] For similar proverbs, see Clifford H. Plopper, *Chinese Religion Seen through the Proverb*, p. 72.
[97] Ku Huan, *I-hsia lun* ("Essay on Foreign and Chinese Religions"). See Seng-yu, ed., *Hung-ming chi* ("Essays Lucidating the Doctrine"), Chap. 6.
[98] *Yü-tao p'ien* ("Explaining Truth"), in Seng-yu, ed., *Hung-ming chi*, Chap. 3.
[99] *Ibid.*

The Taoist attainment of immortality is equivalent to the Buddhist attainment of Nirvana. The Taoist desire for no death, to most Chinese, is in effect the same as the Buddhist search for freedom from birth. Philosophically, the Taoist doctrine of Non-Being can be identified with the Buddhist doctrine of the Void.

Finally, religious harmony is understood in the sense of One Source. Many writers, such as Emperor Wu of Liang, insisted that "In origin all sages are one" and that "The source of truth is one."[100] To K'an Tse (fl. 241), "All three religions have their source in Heaven which they obey."[101] As Chang Jung (444–97) said, "Both Taoism and Buddhism, in their tranquil origin, are one. Only when they responded to external conditions have they become different."[102] "In their transcendental nature," said Chou Yü (d. 485), "they are no different. Differences appear only in the empirical sphere."[103] The consensus of opinion, from the fourth to the eighth century, was that both Tao and Dharma are derived from *Li* or Law, and Law is One. Also, this Law is intelligible because there is a Universal Mind, and the Universal Mind is One.[104] The result of these discussions has been the age-long harmony of the three systems.

It is against this intellectual and historical background that the Chinese people have built many "temples of three sages," and that the average Chinese wears a Confucian crown, so to speak, a Taoist robe, and Buddhist sandals.

[100] T'ang Yung-t'ung, p. 467. [101] Wang Chih-hsin, *op. cit.*, p. 109.
[102] *Men lun* ("On Religions"), in Seng-yu, ed., *Hung-ming chi*, Chap. 6.
[103] Chou yü, *Sun-tsung lun* ("Three Sects"); see Seng-yu, *loc. cit.*
[104] The material on the harmony of religions is drawn from a paper, "The Harmony of Religions," which I presented at the Mid-Century Institute in Boston University in March, 1950, and which has been published in *The Bostonian*, April, 1950, pp. 19, 43–44; *World Outlook*, June, 1950, pp. 10–12; *The Christian Leader*, CXXXII (July, 1950), 230–32; *Chinese Press* (San Francisco), July 28 and August 4, 1950. For a bibliography on the controversy and truce among Chinese religions, see Lien-sheng Yang, *Topics in Chinese History* (Cambridge, Harvard University Press, 1950), p. 53.

When Chang Jung died, he held in his left hand a copy of the Confucian *Classic of Filial Piety* and the *Tao-te ching,* and in his right hand the Buddhist *Lotus Sutra.* He died a typical Chinese.

This harmony is indeed an extraordinary accomplishment. What is more extraordinary, however, is that when the world is full of religious tensions and when China herself is beset with conflicts between the old and new, and between the foreign and the indigenous, religious tension is conspicuously absent. The fact that practically all continuing religious cults have perpetuated the tradition of religious synthesis clearly indicates that syncretism is a mandate of the Chinese people. They have always looked upon religious particularization with suspicion and regard people who follow only one religion as odd.

Against this strong tendency, Christianity drives ahead. Referring to the Conference of All Religions in 1926, the *China Christian Year Book* admits that "probably only a minority of the Christian missionaries look with favor on this liberal movement." [105] Chinese Christians and foreign missionaries have held three attitudes toward Chinese religions. The first is that Christianity should and will replace them. As Y. C. Yang says, Chinese religions are "broken lights" that have "had their day." [106] The second attitude is that at their best, Chinese religions are a preparation for Christianity. To James Legge, Christ alone gave moral precepts which Confucius and Lao Tzu combined to give.[107] Soothill thought that Confucius was a preparation for Christianity.[108] Plopper expresses a similar sentiment in saying that Chinese religions are a "splendid preparation . . . for the coming of the real Saviour." [109] The third attitude is represented by Francis Wei, who thinks that "special strength

[105] *China Christian Year Book,* 1926, p. 76.
[106] Y. C. Yang, *op. cit.,* p. 195.
[107] Legge, *op. cit.,* p. 263.
[108] Soothill, *op. cit.,* p. 203.
[109] Plopper, *op. cit.,* p. 368.

and virtues of all the religious traditions may be brought into the Christian Church." [110] N. Z. Zia, a prominent Christian writer, says that for a religion to grow on strange soil, it must get acclimated and absorb its most nutritious elements. There are three things in Confucianism which Christianity would do well to adopt, according to him. The first is the idea of mutuality, which in its original meaning of *jen* means that unless men live in society harmoniously, they cannot fully develop their nature. This concept is sufficient as an ideal because it is self-evident and can be an excellent supplement to the Christian idea of God, which is a postulate and not self-evident. The second is the Confucian idea of Central Harmony or Golden Mean, which will soften the many extremes in Christianity. And the third is the spirit of tolerance, which will provide a workable formula in inter-human relations on the basis of Confucian ethical pluralism.[111]

All three attitudes bar religious synthesis, although Zia's position comes very close to it. But there is another attitude, as held by the former chancellor of Yenching University, Wu Lei-ch'uan. He said that the Confucian virtues of Wisdom, Love, and Courage are equivalent to the Christian Faith, Hope, and Love; that the Confucian concept of *ch'eng* (sincerity, truth) is the same as the Christian concept of God; that the Confucian doctrines of *chung shu*, that is, being true to one's good nature and following the same principle in the relations with others, are the same as the Christian Golden Rule.[112] In saying this, Wu reflects the traditional sentiment about the harmony of all religions. Wu's attitude is by no means the general attitude among Chinese Christians, but it can safely be said that it is a growing one.

[110] Wei, *The Spirit of Chinese Culture*, p. 204.
[111] N. Z. Zia, "Contributions of Confucianism to Christianity" (in Chinese), *Chen-li yü sheng-ming* ("Truth and Life"), XIV, No. 2 (June, 1948), 80–88.
[112] Neander C. S. Chang, *Kuo-nei chin shih-nien lai chih tsung-chiao ssu-ch'ao* ("Religious Thought in China in the Last Ten Years"), pp. 416–22.

To be sure, synthesis must be made on the highest level, not on the level of superstition or utilitarianism. When the best in every religion is assimilated, all religions will gain.

There is a popular story among the Chinese called "the three laughing gentlemen," from which we may draw a moral. One day, a Confucianist, a Taoist, and a Buddhist gathered in the morning. The Buddhist hermit, who had vowed never to walk beyond a certain bridge, saw his two friends off in the afternoon. Unconsciously he crossed the bridge. Just at that moment, a tiger roared, and the three gentlemen instantly burst into laughter. It took imminent danger to wake the three scholars up to the fact that they were one and behaved in the same way. Do we need another war to realize that different religions can and must be harmonized as one?

V

The New Awakening of Islam

In spite of its thirteen centuries in China, Islam has remained a foreign religion on Chinese soil. Cut off from the world Islamic community at large and isolated from Chinese culture and life, it thrives by itself. Since its introduction into China [1] it has had almost no contact with the outside Islamic world until our own time. In consequence, none of the intellectual movements of world Islam substantially affected the Chinese Moslems. Neither of the two greatest Islamic theologians, Ashari (873–935) and Ghazzali (1058–1111), both of whom radically transformed Islamic thought, had much influence

[1] According to Ch'en Yuan, the most authoritative historian of Chinese religions, the first official diplomatic relations between China and the Arabic world were established in A.D. 651. Following Professor Ch'en, Chinese scholars generally regard this date as the beginning of Islam in China. See Ch'en's "A Brief History of the Introduction of Islam into China" (in Chinese), *Tung-fang* (*Eastern Miscellany*), XXVI, No. 1 (January, 1928), 116–17.

on China. While Sufi mysticism is strong in the Northwest,[2] its influence in other parts of China has been mild. And China has not produced a single Sufi mystical poet! Modern Islamic reforms in Arabia, Egypt, and India in the nineteenth century had no counterpart in China.

Likewise, Islam within China has been intellectually isolated. While Buddhism, Taoism, and Confucianism have cross-fertilized one another, Islam has stayed outside these intellectual streams. This isolation makes Chinese Moslems the largest separate religious community in Chinese history. No one knows how many Moslems there are in China. Conjectures have ranged all the way from three to fifty million.[3] Marshall Broomhall estimated in 1910 that the number was from 4,727,000 to 9,821,000, and he tended to support the higher figure.[4] Japanese surveys in the early 1920s gave the figures of 9,207,000 and 10,262,000.[5] Chinese government statistics of 1924 put the number at between fifteen and twenty million.[6] A Moslem writer quotes the figure of 48,104,240.[7] Chinese Moslems have generally accepted the round number of fifty million. Challenging this high estimate, the *China Handbook*, 1937–43, a government publication, has this to say: "Followers of Mohammedanism, Islam, in China claim to number 48,000,000 with 30,000,000 in the Northwest. The number is greatly exaggerated considering the fact that the entire Northwest—Sinkiang, Kansu, Chinghai, Ninghsia, Suiyuan, and Shensi—has only a total population of 22,000,000. A more reasonable esti-

[2] F. H. Rhodes, "A Survey of Islam in China," *Moslem World*, XI, No. 1 (January, 1921), 56.
[3] Kenneth Scott Latourette, *The Chinese, Their History and Culture*, p. 654.
[4] *Islam in China*, p. 216.
[5] By the Intelligence Department of the Japanese War Ministry in 1921 and by the Research Department of the Southern Manchurian Railroad Administration in 1925, respectively. See *Friends of Moslems*, XVII, No. 1 (January, 1943), 4.
[6] *Chung-kuo nien-chien* ("China Year Book"), 1924, p. 1917.
[7] *China Year Book*, 1936–37, p. 1501.

mate is from 10 to 15 million persons with 5,000,000 in the Northwest." [8] The 1937–45 issue of the *Handbook* repeats the same figures.[9] But the 1950 issue jumps to the highest figure, fifty million.[10] The tendency, however, is towards a much lower estimate. One author, writing in a scholarly magazine, puts it at "below thirty million." [11] An outstanding Moslem scholar says that Chinese Moslems number between thirty and forty million.[12] In a letter to the present writer, Canon Claude Pickens, Jr., who knows Chinese Islam intimately, considered from fifteen to twenty million a fair estimate and called attention to the fact that there are more Moslems in China than either Egypt, Turkey, or Iran.

Regardless of the exact number of its members, the Islamic minority is a huge one. Once its isolation is broken, radical transformations are bound to follow. At present no spectacular change is taking place. There is neither revival as in Buddhism, institutional decline and philosophical reconstruction as in Confucianism, or total degeneration as in Taoism. Nevertheless, certain trends and developments are observable. These may be described as: (1) a tendency towards liberalism, (2) new attitudes towards the Qur'an, (3) intellectual awakening, (4) closer identification with national life, and (5) a new "Law-seeking" movement. These represent a small but significant beginning, and we shall now turn our attention to them.

[8] (New York, Macmillan, 1943), p. 29.
[9] (New York, Macmillan, 1947), p. 27.
[10] *China Handbook*, 1950 (New York, Rockport Press, 1950), pp. 26–27. This figure is accepted by Ali Ahmed (*Muslim China*, p. 39).
[11] Wang Wen-hsuan, "On Reading Ku Chieh-kang's Essay on Chinese Islamic Culture" (in Chinese), *Yü-kung* (hereafter cited as *Chinese Historical Geography Magazine*), VII, No. 4 (April, 1937), 189–90.
[12] Pai Shou-i, *Chung-kuo I-ssu-lan shih kang-yao* ("Essentials of the History of Chinese Islam"), p. 66.

TENDENCY TOWARDS LIBERALISM

The liberal tendency in present-day Chinese Islam is mild but none the less definite. Such a tendency is not surprising since it agrees with the spirit in which Islam was founded and also with the typical Chinese religious temperament. It may be detected in Chinese Islamic organization, in the development of Islamic sects, and in Chinese Moslems' attitude towards the Qur'an.

National Organization. Traditionally, Chinese mosques, like mosques in other Islamic lands, are independent. There are no higher or lower mosques. Nor are there central and branch mosques. Each mosque is governed by recognized community leaders or District Elders who elect their own *imam,* who is chosen by the community for one or several years for his good character, scholarship, and mature age, and who is charged with general supervision of the mosque and leadership in prayer. The *imam* and the Elders invite an *ahung* (*ahong*), whose duty it is to preach the doctrine, explain the laws, officiate in name-giving, circumcision, weddings, and funerals, and settle disputes. He is not a priest in the strict sense of the word but a teacher and adviser. His authority is not derived from any divine or ecclesiastical source but from the common consent of the community. In a few cases, women have become *ahungs.*[13]

The offices of the *imam* and the *ahung* have been, as a rule, appointive, but in some cases they have been hereditary.[14] However, Islamic organization is essentially democratic, for each mosque is independent and the *ahung* exercises no final authority in doctrinal interpretation or moral

[13] Elizabeth Z. Pickens, "Moslems in China," *Moslem World,* XXXIV, No. 4 (October, 1944), 255.
[14] Lo Chen-p'eng, "Islam in Kaifeng" (in Chinese), *Chinese Historical Geography Magazine,* VII, No. 4 (April, 1937), 159.

judgment. The absence of a central authority among Chinese Moslems in general and for each mosque in particular is an amazing phenomenon. Islam is held together not by any organizational authority but by community feeling. Many of them merchants and caravan workers, Chinese Moslems travel extensively. On their journeys they are given shelter in mosque compounds or in Moslem homes, often with financial aid to return home when such aid is needed.

There is no tendency to alter this fundamentally democratic system. On the other hand, hereditary positions are decreasing in number. As we shall see, the position of the *ahung,* already weak traditionally, is becoming even weaker now. And, as in the cases of Buddhism and Christianity, the center of the religion is moving outside the mosque. At least so far as secular activities are concerned, the center of Chinese Islam is now in a lay organization, the Chinese Islamic Association.

The first national organization among Chinese Moslems, the Chinese Mohammedan Mutual Progress Association,[15] was founded in Peking in 1912 by Wang Hao-jan (1848–1918), who had returned in 1908 from extensive study in Islamic countries. The association established some primary schools, published a semimonthly periodical, and undertook a Chinese translation of the Qur'an. It expanded rapidly and by 1923 claimed to have three thousand branches throughout China. When the war came in 1937, patriotic Moslems in Changchow organized the Chinese Islamic National Salvation Federation [16] to counteract the Japanese-sponsored All-China Moslem League. This federation united all existing Moslem organizations into a national so-

[15] Chung-kuo Hui-chiao Chü-chin Hui.
[16] Chung-kuo Hui-min Chiu-kuo Hsieh-hui, later changed to Chung-kuo Hui-chiao Chiu-kuo Hsieh-hui.

ciety and was formally established in Hankow in 1938. Five years later it became the Chinese Islamic Association.[17] It has undertaken many activities, such as the establishment of schools, sending students abroad for advanced study, inviting foreign Islamic scholars to teach and lecture, importing Qur'anic and other Islamic literature from India, Egypt, Arabia, and Turkey, conducting lectures and discussions on Islam for both Moslems and non-Moslems, publication, establishment of young men's associations, other youth groups, and women's organizations, medical service, relief, and patriotic activities.

It will be seen that the movement for a national association has been exclusively for mutual aid, social reform, and national salvation. As such, it enhances the community feeling of Chinese Moslems and strengthens the bond between them and their non-Moslem neighbors. It has nothing to do with Islamic doctrine or church authority. Like the Buddhist national association, it suggests no intention of building up a national church or creating an Islamic pope. If anything, it forms a new center outside the mosque for Islamic activities. It must be added, however, that the mosque is by no means becoming less useful. On the contrary, aside from its traditional religious functions, it has undertaken many new activities. In Nanking, for example, there are within the mosques "knowing Allah" associations, Moslem fellowship associations, young Moslems' associations, and the like.[18] But the main point to note is that in not increasing the authority of the mosque or the *ahung*,

[17] Chung-kuo Hui-chiao Hsieh-hui. In 1929 prominent Moslems in Shanghai founded the Chinese Moslem General Association (Chung-kuo Hui-chiao Kung-hui), which soon disappeared because of lack of support. Four years later the Chinese Moslem National Association (Chung-hua Hui-chiao Tsung-hui) came into existence in Nanking, with branches in the provinces.

[18] Shih Chueh-min, "Moslem Life in Nanking" (in Chinese), *T'ien-shan,* ("Sinkiang Mountain") I, No. 3 (December 15, 1934), 94.

Chinese Islam continues the traditional liberalism of the religion.

Development of New Sects. The liberal tendency is better seen in the development of the Modern Sect, or the "New New Sect," which is a reaction against the conservatism of the New Sect in the last several centuries. Chinese Islam belongs to the liberal tradition of the Sunnite or Orthodox Schools of Law, the Hanifite, which insists that the Qur'an is to be applied differently according to different situations. Partly because of this fact and partly because Chinese Islam has been isolated from the Islamic world, Islamic customs in China have deviated from the prescriptions in the Qur'an. When the Chinese imperial ban on traveling abroad was lifted in the seventeenth century, some Chinese Moslems made the pilgrimage to Mecca and discovered that Chinese customs were not in accord with those followed in Arabia. They returned to start the movement to go back to the literal observance of the Qur'an. The result has been the split of Chinese Islam into two sects, Old and New. In 1781 Ma Ming-hsin of Kansu preached a new doctrine, emphasizing, first, that the Qur'an should be recited aloud, and, secondly, that there should be a central authority for the mosque.[19] When the inevitable conflict with conservative Moslems ensued, Ma's followers killed over a hundred of them. The Manchu government, which did not look with any enthusiasm upon the prospect of Moslems being organized under a central authority, promptly suppressed the Moslem civil war. The affair cost four or five thousand lives.

Although since this bloody incident, controversy between the two sects has remained nonviolent, in recent decades it has been at times quite heated, especially in Peking and

[19] Pai Shou-i, *Chung-kuo I-ssu-lan shih kang-yao*, p. 51.

Tientsin.[20] The New Sect [21] insists that a certain chapter of the Qur'an should be recited once only instead of three times as held by the Old Sect,[22] that at prayer clasped hands should be raised once instead of twice, that after a meal there is no need to raise clasped hands in greeting, and that in singing the praise of Allah the voice should be low instead of high. With reference to religious service, the New Sect does not allow any substitute for an *ahung* in preaching, whereas the Old Sect permits such arrangement. The two sects also disagree on the basis for calculating the period of fasting, with the New Sect adhering strictly to the Arabic method and the Old Sect following the Chinese lunar calendar. The New Sect believes that at funerals mourners should take off their shoes and stand on a mat while praying for the dead, whereas the Old Sect holds fast to the tradition of standing on the ground with shoes on.[23] The New Sect also directs that the corpse be laid on the ground, whereas the Old Sect insists on its being on a platform. There is also disagreement as to whether there should be honoraria for preachers. In short, the New Sect insists on returning to Islamic traditions, but the Old Sect prefers to keep the customs that have developed in China through the centuries.

So far as the observance of religious rites is concerned, then, the New Sect manifests a spirit of conservatism. But the conservatism stops there. The controversy between the two sects has nothing to do with ethical or theological matters. In general, the Old Sect is more lax in dietary and moral habits, but the New Sect represents no tendency to-

[20] Wang Shao-min, "Miscellaneous Reports on Moslems" (in Chinese), *Chinese Historical Geography Magazine*, VII, No. 4 (April, 1937), 167.

[21] Hsin Chiao. [22] Chiu Chiao.

[23] Yang Te-yuan, "Controversy between Old and New Islamic Sects" (in Chinese), *Ch'en-hsi* ("Morning Light"), II, No. 10 (November 15, 1936), pp. 5–10.

wards puritanism or asceticism. Some of its members even burn incense.[24] As we have observed, the controversy between the sects has quieted down in recent years.

In the meantime, the "New New Sect," or Modern Sect, arose.[25] It was founded by Ma Fu-ch'u (1794–1874) of Yunnan some eighty years ago and is now prevalent along the coast. It is the most liberal of all sects. In education it emphasizes religious ethics rather than the traditional course of "knowing Allah." Its interpretation of the Qur'an maintains that the spirit rather than the letter of the holy scripture should be followed. In personal habits it advocates "modernism," such as wearing European styles of clothing. In organization it attaches less importance to the *ahung*. Thus this sect travels even further than the Old Sect, which had already carried the liberalism of the liberal Sunnites to a higher degree. As a new force counteracting the conservatism of the New Sect, the Modern Sect has tremendous possibilities for the simple reason that it is growing in modern cultural centers of China. Besides these main sects, there are in the Northwest many small ones, such as the Brand New Sect [26] and several Sufi orders such as the Che-ho-yeh (Jahriyah).[27] The latter has an abbot like the Buddhist lama. It is heavily superstitious, and is generally despised by other schools.[28]

[24] Broomhall, *op. cit.*, p. 253. [25] Hsin Hsin Chiao.
[26] Tsan-hsin Chiao. [27] From the Arabic, meaning to pray aloud.
[28] Moslems in certain parts of China, Kwangsi, for example, are not divided into sects. For discussions of certain minor Chinese Islamic sects, see M. Hartmann, "Muhammadenism (in China)," in *Encyclopedia of Religion and Ethics*, ed. by Hastings, VIII, 894. For a bibliography on Chinese Islamic sects, see Claude L. Pickens, *Annotated Bibliography of Literature on Islam in China*, pp. 36–37. Seven minor factions in Northwest China are briefly described in a short article in the *Ta Kung Pao*, Tientsin, May 8, 1934, which has been translated in *Friends of Moslems*, VIII, 4 (October, 1934), 46–48.

NEW ATTITUDES TOWARDS THE QUR'AN

From the foregoing it is unmistakable that the conservative attitude of the New Sect towards the Qur'an is more than offset by the Old and Modern Sects. This liberal attitude towards the Islamic Bible can also be seen from another angle. Traditionally, the Qur'an was to be recited only, and recited in Arabic. The new tendency, with practically no opposition at all, is to read and study it outside of religious services and to do so in the Chinese language. Hence the persistent effort to translate the Qur'an.

Curiously enough, the first comprehensive attempts to translate the Qur'an into Chinese were made by non-Moslems. It is true that the earliest translation was by a Moslem, Ma Fu-ch'u, but he left only five unpublished chapters.[29] In 1927 Li T'ieh-cheng, a non-Moslem of Peking, published the first complete Chinese translation.[30] It is based on the Japanese version by Sakamoto Kenichi and Rodwell's English version.[31] A year later S. A. Hardoon, a wealthy British Jew in Shanghai, sponsored a translation under the editorship of Chi Chueh-mi, a Buddhist scholar, who was assisted by an *ahung* and some specialists on Chinese language and literature. It was carefully checked with the English version of Muhammad Ali (1917). This is the first Chinese translation from the Arabic and was published

[29] According to his biography, he finished twenty chapters but did not publish them. Fifteen of these were destroyed by fire. The other five eventually came into the possession of Chao Chen-hou, who brought them to Shanghai on his way to Mecca and handed them over to the Mohammedan Educational Association of that city. The association published them in 1927 under the title *Han-i pao-ming chen-ching* ("Chinese Translation of the Divinely Decreed True Scripture"). Since the translation is not entirely correct, it is suggested that it may have been the work of Ma's pupils. See Fu T'ung-hsien, *Chung-kuo Hui-chiao shih* ("History of Chinese Islam"), p. 222.

[30] *K'o-lan ching* ("Qur'an").

[31] *The Koran*, trans. from the Arabic by J. M. Rodwell; *Koran Kyo*, trans. by Sakamoto Kenichi, 2 vols. (1929–30).

in 1931.[32] Both Li's and Chi's versions are unsatisfactory to the Moslems because of many errors, especially in the version by Li, who did not know Arabic.

The first complete translation by a Moslem was the one by the Sino-Arabic scholar Wang Ching-chai (Wen-ch'ing). He first made a complete translation from the Arabic into colloquial Chinese, but he put this aside and published only a selection from it. In 1926 he started another translation in classical Chinese based on the Constantinople edition of A.D. 1608. It took seventeen years of careful scholarship in both Arabic and Chinese, with frequent consultation of the English version of Muhammad Ali. It was published in Peking in 1932 by the Chinese Mohammedan Mutual Progress Association, under the title *Ku-lan ching i-chieh*, and holds much favor with Chinese Moslems. In 1945 Wang made another translation in colloquial Chinese, which was published under the same title. No doubt the most scholarly translation is by Ma Kin (Chien), foremost Islamic scholar and first professor of Islamic culture in a Chinese university, who made a translation from Arabic into colloquial Chinese. It was scheduled for publication in 1949.[33]

The persistent efforts to translate the Qur'an, a project long overdue, are commendable, especially in view of the fact that practically all of them were individual and sponta-

[32] *Han-i Ku-lan ching* ("Chinese Translation of the Qur'an").
[33] Other translations are: (1) By Yin Shu-jen, who, under the auspices of a Ceylonese Moslem in Hong Kong, undertook in 1926 to translate Muhammad Ali's English version into Chinese. It was not yet finished in 1940. (2) By T'ien Chen of the Mohammedan Educational Association of Shanghai, who in 1928 attempted a translation from Arabic with the assistance of Ma Te-ch'eng, an Arabic scholar. Some chapters have been published in a magazine. (3) By Yang Tzu-hou, who in 1934 compiled the Qur'an through a verbal translation by Ma Mou-shun. Some chapters have been published in the *Ch'en-hsi* magazine. (4) By Yang Chung-ming of Tientsin. He began a translation in 1936, but none of it has been published. (5) By Liu Ping-ju and Hwa Ju-chou of Yangchow. Only the first part was published.

neous. There are several explanations for the long delay. One theory is that since Islamic customs were not in accord with Chinese practices, there was the fear of grave consequences if the Qur'an was translated.[34] This theory is correct so far as the Ch'ing Dynasty (1644–1912) is concerned, for as we shall see, the Manchu rulers were hostile towards Islam. When Liu Chih (Chieh-lien) and Ma Fu-ch'u translated Islamic works into Chinese, they chose works which were agreeable to Confucianism and avoided those incompatible with Chinese culture or offensive to the Manchu rulers. But the theory does not explain why no effort was made in the previous nine centuries.

Another possible explanation is that the Qur'an, like a work of poetry, is untranslatable.[35] But great Buddhist works of similar nature and style have been translated into Chinese with great success. The real explanation is Islamic isolation. Since there was little contact between Chinese Moslems and the outside world, there was no exchange of Chinese and outside Islamic scholars as there was between Chinese and Indian Buddhist scholars. Consequently, Chinese Islam did not have the good fortune that Buddhism had in such early and famous translators as Kumarajiva and Hsuan-tsang. And since Chinese Islam was also isolated from Chinese intellectuals, it remained outside the intellectual atmosphere of China. The strong and increasing interest in textual studies among Chinese intellectuals, Confucian, Taoist, and Buddhist alike, did not attract the Moslems.

One thing is sure, however. The failure to translate was not due to any opposition to translation as such. Nor was there any belief that the authority to interpret the Qur'an

[34] Yang Te-yuan, "The Evolution of Chinese Islamic Culture" (in Chinese), *Ch'en-hsi*, III, No. 4 (April 15, 1937), 8.
[35] H. A. R. Gibb, *Modern Trends in Islam*, p. 4.

rested solely with the *ahung*. The new movement to translate and study, therefore, represents no revolt against any religious authority or monopoly.[36] It is primarily a result of the general intellectual awaking in Chinese Islam.

The long-range effect of the translation and consequently of the more direct and more extensive study of the Qur'an cannot be foretold. We can be sure, however, that the results will be important, considering the fact that the split into the Old and New Sects was due to a desire to interpret the scripture literally. The present tendency seems to be along liberal lines. There is also the general desire to emphasize the compatibility between the Qur'an and modern science. Such a tendency is found in all Islamic lands, and China is no exception.[37] As in other Islamic countries, too, Chinese followers cling to the doctrine that the Qur'an is the inspired word of Allah and is eternal, and that Muhammad is the ultimate sage. But unlike the Modernists in many Islamic countries, Chinese Moslems exhibit no tendency to concentrate on and glorify Muhammad as a mystical personality and an emotional companion.[38]

INTELLECTUAL AWAKENING

For the present the immediate effect of the new attitudes toward the Qur'an is intellectual rather than emotional or religious, that is, they are expressions of a new intellectual awakening. This is expressed in two directions, education and publication. Their stories may be briefly told.

Education. In connection with Moslem education Wang Hao-jan's name, already mentioned, stands out conspicuously. The era of modern education for Chinese Moslems

[36] One Chinese writer says that the translation ended the monopoly of the Qur'an. This is not justified. See Y. Y. Tsu, "New Tendencies in Chinese Religions" (in Chinese), *Wen She* ("The Literary Society Magazine"), II, No. 7 (May, 1927), 4.

[37] See A. Eustace Haydon, ed., *Modern Trends in World-Religions*, p. 13; Gibb, *op. cit.*, p. 72.

[38] Gibb, *op. cit.*, p. 74.

began with him. In his pilgrimage to Mecca he was appalled at the comparative educational backwardness of his fellow Moslems. When he returned in 1908, he brought two Turkish scholars with him. Immediately he established a normal school in Peking in which various subjects besides Islamic doctrines and literature were taught and for which Chinese as well as Arabic was used. In the following year he established a primary school for Moslem children. Thus in one stroke he inaugurated three epoch-making movements—the use of Chinese in teaching, general education, and universal education.

These movements are revolutionary because hitherto Islamic education was confined to the mosque, restricted to religious subjects, and aimed almost exclusively at training religious leaders. The earliest known movement for Islamic education was started by Hu Teng-chou (1522–97) of Shensi. After a trip to Mecca, he felt the desperate need for education for Chinese Moslems. He established a school in his mosque, invited students to attend with free board, and taught them himself. The movement was carried on and extended by his pupils. In time it spread. By the end of the nineteenth century, the curriculum in Moslem schools had become fairly standardized, comprising fourteen subjects—eight taught in Arabic (five on the Arabic language and literature, two on the Qur'an, and one on theology) and six conducted in Persian (two on religious doctrines, one on rites, one on ethics, one on scriptural commentaries, and one on philosophy).[39]

The schools then divided into two opposing groups. The Shensi group used Arabic exclusively, emphasized intensive study, often specialized on one subject, such as "knowing Allah." The Shantung group, on the other hand, used Persian as well as Arabic and emphasized extensive

[39] Pai Shou-i, *Chung-kuo I-ssu-lan shih kang-yao*, p. 45.

study.[40] There was no difference in religious beliefs between the two factions, but in regard to education the Shantung group was definitely the more liberal.

It was against this background that Wang, a member of the Shantung group, launched the radical changes. It is to the credit of Chinese Moslems that there was no opposition to his innovations. Instead, Wang obtained enthusiastic support. In addition to Wang's effort, other Moslem groups were also promoting education. Under the leadership of Tung Tsung, Moslems in Chinkiang, Kiangsu province, organized the East Asia Moslem Educational Association in 1908, and the thirty-six Chinese Moslem students in Japan formed the Chinese Moslem Students Educational Association in Tokyo in the following year.[41] But the harvest that is being reaped comes from the seed sowed by Wang.

In terms of quantity, the harvest is not gratifying. In 1936 the total number of Moslem high schools in all of China was only eleven, three for religious education and eight for general education.[42] In 1948, there were only 570 Moslem students in college.[43] In 1949, in an outstanding Islamic cultural center in China, Shatien in Yunnan, which has sent more students for further study abroad than any other Islamic community and which produced the renowned Moslem scholar Ma Kin, of the population of five thousand there were only two college graduates and some thirty high-school graduates. There was only one grade school, with 360 pupils, but no high school.[44] In all, according to 1950 fig-

[40] P'ang Shih-ch'ien, "Church Education in Chinese Islam" (in Chinese), *Chinese Historical Geography Magazine*, VII, No. 4 (April 16, 1937), 101.

[41] Pai Shou-i, *Chung-kuo I-ssu-lan shih kang-yao*, p. 63.

[42] Chao Chen-wu, "Chinese Islamic Culture in the Last Thirty Years" (in Chinese), *Chinese Historical Geography Magazine*, V, No. 11 (August 1, 1936), 15–17.

[43] *I-chen* ("Future of Islam"), No. 22 (Aug. 29, 1948).

[44] Chiang Ying-liang, "A Survey of a Moslem Agricultural Community: Shatien, Yunnan" (in Chinese), *She-hui ching-chi yen-chiu* ("Social Economic Studies"), No. 1 (January, 1951), pp. 195–98.

ures, the Chinese Islamic Association set up or coordinated some twenty high schools and more than two hundred primary schools.[45] There is only one Islamic college, the Islamic Theological College, which was opened in the Chungking mosque in 1945. Education for women has hardly begun, and only one of the high schools is for girls, although the number of girls in lower schools is increasing.

The general educational situation, then, is disheartening. This unfortunate situation is partly due to the extreme poverty of Chinese Moslems. It is partly due to their own resistance to education. Some of them still believe that to study Chinese books is to betray their religion.[46] In the Northwest, Moslems used to employ substitutes to attend school in place of their children. Others asked such questions as, "My older son is already in the army. Why should you take my younger son to school?" [47]

However, although statistically the general picture is dark, there are bright spots in it. For one thing, the high schools are spread out all over China—in Peiping, Shanghai, Tsinan, Wanhsien, Hangchow, Kunming, Chinghai, Lanchow, Kweilin, Sian, and Ninghsia. For another, half of these are normal schools, testifying to the determination to train more teachers for more extensive education.[48]

Equally encouraging is the determination to seek further study abroad. Ma Ming-hsin studied abroad and returned in 1777. Some eighty years ago, Ma Fu-ch'u went to study in Arabia. After that Hai Wei-liang went to India and Wang Tseng-shan went to Turkey. In 1921 the movement gained momentum when Wang Ching-chai went to study in Egypt

[45] *China Handbook,* 1950, p. 27.
[46] Pai Ch'ung-hsi, "Chinese Islam and World Islam" (in Chinese), *Hui-chiao wen-hua* ("Islamic Culture"), I, Nos. 3 and 4 (July, 1943), p. 3.
[47] Yang Te-yuan, "Educational Problems of Chinese Moslems" (in Chinese), *Ch'en-hsi,* II, No. 12 (December 15, 1936), 4
[48] Pai Shou-i, *Chung-kuo Hui-chiao hsiao-shih* ("Short History of Chinese Islam"), p. 44.

and his pupil Ma Hung-tao went to study in Turkey.[49] All of these were private enterprises, privately financed, but in the 1930s organizational support was given to such projects. In 1931 the Islam Normal School in Shanghai sent Ma Kin to Egypt. Three others went with him. Six students followed in the next year, three in 1934, and five in 1935. In 1936 the Ch'eng-ta Normal School of Peiping sent five students to Azhar University, and in the same year Na Chung became the first Chinese student to obtain a degree in that institution.[50] In 1937 Yunnan province sent three students to Azhar, and Shanghai sent five. There were in that year eighteen Chinese students in Egypt, half of them from Yunnan.[51]

One more trend in Moslem education should be noted; namely, military education. In the last two decades, several thousand Moslem students have been trained in military academies.[52] This is due generally to the traditional military occupation of Chinese Moslems but more particularly to the ascendency of many Moslems to political and military power.

Publication. As in education, slow but sure progress has been made in Moslem publication. Chinese Moslems did not write on their religion in Chinese until Wang Tai-yu (d. 1644?) wrote several works in that language and Ma Wen-ping (Chung-hsiu, Chu, b. 1640) wrote the well-known *Ch'ing-chen chih-nan* ("Introduction to Islam") in ten *chüans* (parts) in 1646.[53] The custom of writing in Chi-

[49] Chao Chen-wu, in *Chinese Historical Geography Magazine,* V, No. 11 (August 1, 1936), 18.

[50] Fu T'ung-hsien, *op. cit.,* p. 219.

[51] *China Year Book,* 1936–37, p. 1505.

[52] *Yueh-hua* ("Lunar Corona"), No. 35 (May 27, 1948).

[53] Many Chinese Moslems, of course, wrote in Chinese before these writers. Pickens (*op. cit.,* p. 20) mentions Ma Huan of the fifteenth century. Even before him, many wrote in Chinese, such as Mi Fei (1051–1107). But they wrote on nonreligious subjects.

nese on religious subjects was begun by these men.[54] Since them, the most famous and most authoritative Moslem writer was Liu Chih (fl. 1720) whose works are classics,[55] and the most productive was Ma Fu-ch'u, who left no fewer than thirty-three works,[56] some in Arabic, some in Chinese, and some in both.[57] During the 267 years of the Ch'ing Dynasty, some two hundred works in Chinese were produced.[58] Compared to the scholarly output in Buddhism or Taoism in the same period, this is no small amount. But as has been observed, half of these are non-scholarly and unreliable,[59] such as *A Record of the Coming of Islam*[60] and *The Origin of Chinese Islam*,[61] both of which were used by Broomhall.[62]

Since the establishment of the Republic in 1912, there has been comparative freedom of publication. As a result, about ten important works on Islam have been translated from foreign languages, including *Haqigat ad-Diyana al Islamiyya* by Hussain al-Jisr, and *Outline of Islamic Monotheism*, by Muhammad Abduh, both translated by Ma Kin.

Among original works, five are on the introduction to and history of Chinese Islam, one on Arabic grammar, one

[54] Yang Te-yuan, "The Evolution of Chinese Islamic Culture" (in Chinese), *Ch'en-hsi*, III, No. 4 (April 15, 1937), 7.

[55] *T'ien-fang hsing-li* ("Islamic Philosophy"), 1704, five *chüans* (parts); *T'ien-fang tien-li tse-yao chieh* ("Essentials of Islamic Rites Explained"), 1706, twenty *chüans; T'ien-fang Chih-sheng shih-lu* ("Life of Muhammad"), 1721, ten *chüans.*

[56] Twenty-two on religious doctrines, three on astronomy and geography, three on Arabic language and literature, and five representing systematization of works by former writers.

[57] Pai Shou-i, *Chung-kuo I-ssu-lan shih kang-yao*, p. 61.

[58] On Chinese traditional Islamic literature, see: Claude L. Pickens, *op. cit.*, pp. 38–48; A. Vissière, "Etudes sino-mahométanes," *Revue du monde musulum*, tome treizième (1911), pp. 30–63.

[59] Yang Te-yuan, in *Ch'en-hsi*, III, No. 4 (April 15, 1937), 8.

[60] *Hsi-lai tsung-p'u*, by Ma Ch'i-jung, 1882.

[61] *Hui-hui lai-yuan*, by Lin San-chieh, new ed., 1904.

[62] *Op. cit.*, pp. 62, 68.

on Islamic rites, one on Arabic astronomy, and several others on miscellaneous subjects.[63] One authority on Islam estimates that translations and original works in the last thirty years total some thirty or forty titles.[64] As early as 1923, one Moslem publisher in Peking had seventy-six titles, Chinese and bilingual. Another had a stock of Persian and Arabic works numbering 128.[65]

In the field of periodicals, the first Chinese Moslem periodical appeared in Tokyo in 1906 and was published by the Chinese Moslem Student Educational Association. Only one number was issued.[66] The first published in China was the *Ch'ing-chen yueh-pao* ("Islamic Monthly"), which appeared in Yunnan in 1915. In the next three decades there were about seventy periodicals. These may be classified under four headings, some dealing chiefly with Islamic doctrine, some with Islamic culture, some with problems of Moslems in the Northwest and border regions, and others published as institutional and school bulletins.[67] Only nine have been able to appear regularly. In 1937 there were twenty-eight, including eleven published in Peiping.[68] Those with the longest history are the *Yueh-hua* ("Lunar Corona"), which first appeared in 1928, and the *I-kuang* ("Light of Islam"), which was first published in 1930. Centers of publication are Peiping, Shanghai, Kunming, Nanking, Canton, Changteh, Sian, and Tientsin, Peiping being the greatest of all.[69] Most of the periodicals were interrupted by the war. In 1947 there were only nine.[70] In general, they

[63] Chao Chen-wu, in *Chinese Historical Geography Magazine*, V, No. 11 (August 1, 1936), 21.
[64] Pai Shou-i, *Chung-kuo I-ssu-lan shih kang-yao*, p. 68.
[65] Mark E. Botham, "Modern Movements among Chinese Mohammedans," *Moslem World*, XIII, No. 3 (July, 1923), 296.
[66] Pai Shou-i, *op. cit.*, p. 63. [67] Fu T'ung-hsien, *op. cit.*, pp. 227–28.
[68] *China Year Book*, 1936–37, p. 1504.
[69] Pai Shou-i, *Chung-kuo Hui-chiao hsiao-shih*, p. 44.
[70] *Friends of Moslems*, XXII, No. 2 (April, 1948), 26–27.

have a small circulation of several thousand copies each, and only a few are national in scope.

Aside from these books and periodicals there has been no large set of books. There is nothing to compare with the large sets of Buddhist dictionaries.

It is clear, then, that in both education and publication Moslem achievement has been small, especially in relation to the large number of Chinese Moslems. There are a few small libraries, but there are no libraries or research institutes comparable to those in Buddhism or Christianity. Nevertheless, from a long and deep slumber, the intellectual awakening in Chinese Islam is gaining new vitality. In one respect the awakening is especially significant. We have seen that the Chinese language is used in both education and publication. This fact is significant because the language binds the Moslems and other Chinese in a common society and hence contributes substantially to the breakdown of Islamic isolation. Had Arabic been insisted on as the holy language, then isolation from the Chinese community would have been reinforced. The use of English in Christian missionary schools in China, while beneficial in many ways, certainly has delayed Christianity's becoming a real part of China. Happily, Chinese Moslems have come to avoid this mistake. Because of this foresight and other factors, they are becoming more and more strongly identified with the Chinese national life.

CLOSER IDENTIFICATION WITH NATIONAL LIFE

We have repeatedly referred to Moslem isolation in China. It is now necessary to explain this peculiar phenomenon. Several factors account for the setting apart of Chinese Moslems from the rest of the Chinese. Historically, when the Arabs came to trade in China in the eighth and ninth centuries, mostly in Canton and Yangchow, they met among themselves for religious worship. They enjoyed religious freedom, but they confined religious observance to themselves. They made no effort to evangelize the Chinese people in Islam, chiefly because they considered their sojourn in China to be temporary. They did not build permanent religious edifices until the Sung Dynasty (960–1279).[71] Only then did they become permanent residents in China, marrying Chinese women, raising families, and transmitting their religious heritage from generation to generation. In other words, Islam became established in China not because of missionary zeal, as in the case of Christianity, nor because the Chinese sought its gospel, as in the case of Buddhism, but incidentally and unconsciously. During the next dynasty, the Yuan (1206–1368), a number of Moslems became high government officials and renowned scholars in Confucian philosophy, literature, art, and architecture. In the civil service examination of 1333 alone, ten Moslem scholars obtained the highest degree.[72] Moslem scholars introduced into China Arabic astronomy, medicine, Central Asiatic languages, music, dance, and the art of canon making.[73] Islam may now be considered not only to have taken root but also to have bloomed in China. But it has not formed an integral part of Chinese cultural life. The atmosphere of foreignness remained and has continued to this day.

The geographical factor also contributes to the compara-

[71] Chinese Moslems accept the generally held theory that the Huai-sheng Mosque in Canton was built in the seventh century. The earliest evidence of the history of the mosque, however, is a tablet dated 1274, when the building was repaired. See Cheng Shih-k'o, "Arab Activities in Canton in the Middle Ages" (in Chinese), *Huai-sheng* ("Thinking of Muhammad"), No. 4 (October 5, 1948); Pai Shou-i, *Chung-kuo I-ssu-lan shih kang-yao*, pp. 16–17; Wang Chih-hsin, *Chung-kuo tsung-chiao ssu-hsiang shih ta-kang* ("Outline of the History of Chinese Religious Thought"), p. 144. The Ch'ing-ching Mosque in Chuanchow was built between 1131 and 1162.

[72] Ch'en Yuan, *op. cit.*, p. 121.

[73] Chin Chi-t'ang, *Chung-kuo Hui-chiao shih yen-chiu* ("Studies in the History of Chinese Islam"), pp. 148–52; Pai Shou-i, *Chung-kuo Hui-chiao hsiao-shih*, pp. 19–29.

tive isolation of the Chinese Moslems. They are now mainly distributed in Yunnan, Shensi, Kansu, Hopei, Honan, Shantung, Szechuan, Sinkiang, and Anhwei, numerically in the order mentioned.[74] Those whose ancestors came to China by sea are now spread out in South China, with Canton as the center, and in East China, with Nanking as the center. Those whose ancestors came overland now thrive in the Northwest, whence they have spread also to Honan, Shantung, and Hopei in North China and further to the Northeast (Manchuria). The origin of those in Yunnan, Kweichow, and Szechuan is uncertain.[75] In Kansu the northern and western parts of the province are almost entirely Moslem, and in the capital city, Lanchow, the southern section is exclusively Moslem. The "Oxen Street" outside the city wall of Peiping is inhabited entirely by Moslems and is a community of more than a thousand families.[76] In Tsinan, Changchow, and Tientsin, the Moslems live in a section outside the city gate. In Tungchow they congregate in the southeastern corner of the city.[77] Such are the striking examples of Moslem concentration, which naturally sets them apart from the non-Moslem Chinese. These concentrations are mostly for convenience in worshiping and in adhering to the food laws. Thus they are either accidental or voluntary, and with some exceptions the question of segregation has not arisen.

In addition to the historical and geographical factors, there is also the occupational distinction. For some reason not easily explained, few Chinese Moslems have taken to farming or other productive occupations. Because of their

[74] For numerical distribution of Chinese Moslems and mosques, see *China Year Book*, 1936–37, p. 1501.
[75] Kao Lao, "Historical Distribution of Moslems in China" (in Chinese), *Eastern Miscellany*, XIV, No. 10 (October, 1917), 50–54.
[76] *Ibid.*, pp. 54–55.
[77] Chin Chi-t'ang, "The Moslem Race" (in Chinese), *Chinese Historical Geography Magazine*, V, No. 11 (August 1, 1936), 32.

peculiar dietary habits, they have generally avoided government service, in which refraining from eating pork would have been a formidable difficulty. It is undoubtedly because they have chosen freedom to follow their food laws that they have gone into restaurant, inn, and caravan businesses. They are also butchers, leather workers, and dealers in curios, jewelry, and metal work. In most parts of China these are almost distinctive Moslem occupations. In certain localities some occupations are exclusively Moslem, such as leatherwork in Ninghsia, bath houses in Changchow, and sedan transportation in Taishan.[78] In many cities Moslems have their own trade guilds.[79]

These factors are sufficient to make them different from their fellow Chinese. However, these may be considered accidental and external. There are certain things inherent in Islam that keep the Moslems alien; namely, their peculiar character and customs. They greet one another in Arabic and Persian. Many wear white headdresses resembling turbans. They seldom allow their women to ride on horseback. Generally speaking, they abstain from alcohol and from pork. In the Northwest they practice circumcision. They do not use coffins in burial. Their marriage and funeral rites are unique. In many places they call their villages *ying* (barracks) and *fang* (quarters), evidently from their military heritage. Their community feeling is exceptionally strong. They are well disciplined and have strong faith.[80] They are famous for their athletic interest and ability. They seldom become beggars. They shun usury, divination, geomancy, or

[78] Fu T'ung-hsien, *op. cit.*, p. 169; Yu Ho, "Moslems in Changchow" (in Chinese), *Ch'en-hsi*, I, Nos. 24–26 (October 15, 1935), 31–33; *China Mission Year Book*, 1924, p. 81; Lai Wen-ts'ai, "The Future of Chinese Moslems" (in Chinese), *Yueh-hua*, No. 42 (July 8, 1937).

[79] Shih Chueh-min, in *T'ien-shan*, I, No. 2 (November 15, 1934), 41; I, No. 3 (December 15, 1934), 94.

[80] Chang Yü-fei, "Religion in the New Northwest" (in Chinese), *Hsin hsi-pei* ("New Northwest"), I, No. 2 (March, 1939), 23–26.

acting on the stage.[81] In these and other ways they behave differently from the Chinese.

The most important factor responsible for Moslem isolation, however, is Manchu persecution. From the inception of Islam in China, there was no conflict until the Manchus conquered China. As has already been mentioned, there were Moslem scholars and high government officials during the different dynasties, especially in the Yuan, when there was imperial patronage and mosques were built by imperial order. Partly because Moslems participated in civil service examinations and partly because they never attacked Confucianism, they were never persecuted except by the Manchus. There was no anti-Islamic movement comparable to the anti-Buddhist movement by Han Yü (768–824) and the anti-Christian movement by Yang Kuang-hsien (1597–1669). When other foreign religions suffered in the persecution of 845, Islam was not affected. During the Ming Dynasty (1368–1644) prohibition of foreign dress, foreign language, and foreign names necessarily affected the Moslems, but they were not singled out for discrimination.

The Manchus, however, adopted a deliberate policy of setting the Moslems against the Chinese in order to divide and rule. During this long dynasty, although Moslems, like other Chinese, enjoyed the privilege of taking the civil service examinations and becoming government officials—and there were prominent ones—they were discriminated against in many ways by the Manchus. Punishments were heavier. In certain places Moslems and Chinese were segregated. Marriage between Chinese and Moslems was not allowed, and communication between them in general was made difficult.[82] The result was a series of rebellions, in Kansu in

[81] Chin Chi-t'ang, in *Chinese Historical Geography Magazine*, V, No. 11 (August 1, 1936), 32–33.
[82] Pai Shou-i, *Chung-kuo Hui-chiao hsiao-shih*, p. 34.

1648 and 1781, in Yunnan in 1820–28, 1830, 1846, and 1855–76, and in the Northwest in 1755, 1764, and 1862–76. Those of 1855–76 and 1862–76 cost millions of lives.[83]

These rebellions made the Chinese Moslems extremely group-conscious. They became exclusively loyal to their own kind. Besides, some of the rebellions were caused not by Manchu oppression but by Chinese and Moslem antagonism. Civil wars embittered both parties, and the cleavage between them became deeper and deeper.

As the twentieth century arrived, however, the situation changed for the better. Chinese and Moslem relations slowly improved and Moslem isolation began to break down. On the one hand, the Chinese and the Moslems united to overthrow the Manchu regime. With the establishment of the Republic, Sun Yat-sen's doctrine of "harmony and equality of the five races" put the Moslems on equal footing with the Chinese. On the other hand, Moslems themselves made definite efforts to shatter their isolation. Some of these efforts may now be reviewed.

First and foremost, an increasing number of Moslems no longer consider Chinese Moslems as a different race but are emphatic in declaring that they are Chinese. They resent being classified as a racial minority. Traditionally they have been called Hui people, a name of uncertain origin but probably derived from Uighur, through which place many ancestors of Chinese Moslems have come to China. Now they prefer to be called followers of the Hui religion. It is true that most Chinese Moslems have a larger build, longer face, deeper eyes, and heavier beard than other Chinese. It is also true that they have some thirty family names such as Na, Ha, Sa, and T'ieh, held by no other Chinese.[84] But Mos-

[83] Pai Shou-i, *op. cit.*, pp. 49–59; Ma I-yu, *Chung-kuo Hui-chiao shih-chien* ("History of Chinese Islam"), p. 99.

[84] Chin Chi-t'ang, in *Chinese Historical Geography Magazine*, V, No. 11 (August 1, 1936), 32–35. The name Ma, however, is not exclusively Moslem.

lems are quick to point out that they are descendants of a mixture of races, including the Chinese. Throughout history, many Chinese entered the religion through adoption, marriage, and accepting the faith of their Moslem military and government officials.[85] Certain groups of Moslems still speak a foreign language, notably those in "Oxen Street" in Peiping, who speak Arabic, and some groups in the Northwest, who speak Mongolian or Turkic. However, these constitute a very small number and are therefore quite exceptional. Racially, many Moslems insist that they are Chinese.

This feeling on the part of Moslems has brought them closer to the Chinese and has greatly improved mutual understanding. In the past Chinese ignorance of Islam has led to absurd statements such as that Moslems worshiped pig-headed idols and that they practiced polyandry. These insults provoked riots.[86] To create better understanding, Moslems are now making use of radio broadcasts, publications, and lectures, not for evangelical purposes but purely to promote more cordial relations with non-Moslem Chinese.

On the political front, Moslems are actively and successfully identifying themselves with national life. During the war they joined the People's Political Council and the State Council.[87] In 1948 there were eighteen members in the National Legislature.[88] In the army, Moslems have grown much in influence. They have a glorious military tradition behind them. In A.D. 757 four thousand Arab soldiers assisted in the suppression of An Lu-shan's rebellion. During the Yuan Dynasty many foreign Islamic soldiers and commanders were introduced by the Mongol rulers. Moslems

[85] Pai Shou-i, *Chung-kuo Hui-chiao hsiao-shih*, p. 30.
[86] Fu T'ung-hsien, *op. cit.*, pp. 187–94.
[87] Derk Bodde, "Chinese Muslim Minority," *Far Eastern Survey*, XV, No. 18 (September 11, 1946), 283. See also *Friends of Moslems*, XVII, No. 2 (April, 1943), 25.
[88] *Ta-lu pao* ("Highway Journal"), Nanking, August 10, 1948.

helped in founding the Ming Dynasty. The famous Cheng Ho, a eunuch, who led seven expeditions to the South Seas between 1405 and 1431, involving in the first expedition 27,870 men and sixty-three ships, was a Moslem from Yunnan. Moslems in China never used the sword to propagate their religion, but they built up an enviable military reputation. Under the Nationalist government many Moslems rose to national prominence; notably, Ma Hung-kwei, Ma Pu-fang, and Ma Hung-pin, for many years undisputed military governors of the Northwest, and Pai Ch'ung-hsi, brilliant "scholar-general" and for many years chief of staff. There were many others.[89]

Thus in the political sphere, especially as military officers, Chinese Moslems have participated intimately in national affairs. While there are still Moslems in the Northwest who swear to "fight for our religion but not for our country," Moslem patriotism is increasingly evident. They had an ample share in the revolution of 1916. In the war with Japan they gave an excellent account of themselves.[90]

Incidentally, Moslem ascendency in military influence has produced some changes in Moslem occupation and residence. A large number of Moslems left their traditional distinctive occupations to join the army and moved away from their ancestral homes.[91] These changes are as yet slight, but they help to weaken Moslem isolation.

In the long run, Moslems will not become really Chinese until they are baptized by China's intellectual culture, or, to put it differently, until they come into close contact with

[89] *China at War*, VII, No. 6 (December, 1941), 30–31.

[90] For Chinese Moslems under Japanese occupation, see Derk Bodde, "Japan and the Muslims of China," *Far Eastern Survey*, XV, No. 20 (October 9, 1946), 311–13; "Chinese Muslims in Occupied Areas," *ibid.*, XV, No. 21 (October 23, 1946), 330–33.

[91] In one locality of Kwangsi, for example, 20 percent of the Moslems earned their livelihood in the government and in the army, and practically all of them moved away. See Mu, "Survey of Moslems in Suchiao, Kwangsi" (in Chinese), *Ch'en-hsi*, I, Nos. 24–26 (October 15, 1935), 34.

Chinese intellectuals. As it will be pointed out in the chapter which follows, the Chinese literati have been the ones in Chinese history to direct the developments in education, government, religion, and art. Although a number of Moslem scholars were prominent in various periods, they did not form an integral part of Chinese intellectual life; at least they did not do so as Moslems. This is illustrated by the famous story about Mi Fei (1051–1107), the celebrated painter, whose habit of cleanliness amazed his Confucian and Buddhist friends but whose Islamic religion was unknown to them.[92]

Fortunately, the contact with Chinese intellectuals has now been made. In 1933, upon the petition of the Chinese Islamic National Salvation Federation, the government made the study of Islamic culture a regular feature in the curriculum of some government universities. Ma Kin and two other Moslem scholars were appointed professors in two national universities.[93] Non-Moslem magazines exhibited a new interest in Islam, and non-Moslem writers wrote on it. The *Chinese Historical Geography Magazine*, a non-Moslem scholarly periodical, devoted two special numbers to Islamic religion and culture.[94] These new developments, with the increase in the number of modern Islamic publications and schools, will open the way for crosscurrents between Islamic and Chinese thought.

Whether Islam will become more Chinese intellectually remains to be seen. In some respects Moslems remain stubborn. For example, they are adamant in refusing to intermarry with non-Moslems unless the other party accepts the Islamic faith.[95] As late as 1948 the Moslem general in the

[92] Yang Te-yuan, in *Ch'en-hsi*, III, No. 4 (April 15, 1937), 8.
[93] *China Handbook*, 1937–45, p. 27.
[94] *Chinese Historical Geography Magazine*, V, No. 11 (August 1, 1936), and VII, No. 4 (April 15, 1937).
[95] In Sinkiang, Moslems take Chinese, Mongolian, and Tibetan wives without requiring them to adopt Islam, but they seldom allow their daughters to marry non-Moslems.

Northwest military headquarters prohibited intermarriage between Moslems and others.[96] Moslems are not in a hurry to give up their peculiar customs and habits. In Chengtu, for example, they only celebrate Moslem festivals and ignore the Chinese New Year,[97] and in the Northwest they refuse to contribute to or participate in community theatricals because these involve non-Islamic religious practices.[98]

This is not to suggest, however, that Islam can remain completely aloof from Chinese transformation. In the past it has succumbed to Chinese influence. The dome, so often characteristic of the Islamic mosque, has been replaced in China by a four-sided roof. Except for the white headdress, the attire of Moslems is Chinese. Under Chinese influence, Moslems in China have never required their women to wear a veil and have never allowed first cousins to marry.[99] The marriage ideal is for a man to have two instead of four wives, although many do have more.[100] Circumcision is not practiced in most parts of China. Shops do business as usual on Friday. In many cases pork is eaten in company with non-Moslems. The Moslem attitude towards Muhammad as a sage is essentially the same as the Chinese attitude towards Confucius. Liu Chih wrote his famous books in Confucian terms and made a conscious attempt to present Islam in the light of Neo-Confucian philosophy. His *T'ien-fang hsing-li* ("Islamic Philosophy") followed the style of Neo-Confucianism of the Sung period. His *T'ien-fang tien-li* ("Islamic Rites") followed the five human relations of Confucian-

[96] *Ta-lu pao*, Sept. 16, 1948.

[97] Hu Shih-wen, "Moslems in Chengtu" (in Chinese), *Chinese Historical Geography Magazine*, VII, No. 4 (April 16, 1937), 45.

[98] Y. P. Mei, 'Stronghold of Muslim China," *Moslem World*, XXXI, No. 2 (April, 1941), 180.

[99] Women in certain Islamic groups in Sinkiang do wear veils. They are, however, rare exceptions.

[100] Chin Chi-t'ang, in *Chinese Historical Geography Magazine*, V, No. 11 (August 1, 1936), 32; Ch'en Yuan, *op. cit.*, p. 123.

ism.[101] And his *T'ien-fang Chih-seng shih-lu* ("Life of Muhammad") followed the pattern of Chinese histories. While Moslems do not worship idols or ancestors, they regard Heaven in Chinese religion as the same as Allah.[102] In some cases Moslems even promoted Confucianism. The first Confucian temples in Yunnan, for example, were built by a Moslem, Chan Ssu-ting (1211–79).[103] In short, Islam in the past has been influenced to some extent by Confucianism. The future development of Chinese Islam may not be Confucian, but if Chinese transformation of Buddhism can be taken as a precedent, it is almost sure to become Chinese. What has happened to Buddhism in Chinese history may well happen to Islam.

A NEW LAW-SEEKING MOVEMENT

One thing that made Buddhism strong and eventually transplanted it from India to China and made it Chinese was the fact that for several centuries hundreds of Chinese Buddhists braved almost insurmountable dangers to go to India to "seek the Law." They returned with Indian scholars, books, images, and new spiritual blood. Is there a similar movement in Chinese Islam today? There may not be a well-established movement, but a beginning is noticeable. We may take as indications pilgrimages to Mecca, students studying abroad, and good-will missions.

Before the 1930s very few Chinese Moslems made pilgrimages to Mecca. In the eleven years prior to 1934, however, no fewer than 834 Chinese Moslem pilgrims went to the holy city. By 1937 there were about 170 a year.[104] After the war there were about 200 a year. Much of this activity

[101] This is denied by Ma Lin-i. See his *I-ssu-lan chiao kai-lun* ("Introduction to Islam"), p. 29.
[102] Wang Chih-hsin, *op. cit.*, p. 144.
[103] Ch'en Yuan, *op. cit.*, p. 122.
[104] Derk Bodde, in *Far Eastern Survey*, XV, No. 18 (September 11, 1946), 283.

has been promoted by the Chinese Islamic Association.[105] They all went by sea. In 1947, forty Chinese Moslems attended the Hajj. Of the more than two thousand who applied for permission to make the pilgrimage to Mecca, half were from Sinkiang alone. In 1948, two hundred visited Mecca.

The numbers of those traveling abroad to study have already been discussed. As to good-will missions, in 1938 the Chinese Islamic Association dispatched a Chinese Moslems Goodwill Mission to the Near and Middle East. The group reached Mecca in time for the Hajj in February and met many fellow Moslems from other Islamic countries. They visited Egypt, Lebanon, Syria, Iraq, Iran, Turkey, and India. In December, 1939, another mission went to the South Seas and also visited Malaya, India, Arabia, and Iran. Two more missions went abroad in the next three years.

These activities will bring Chinese Moslems closer to their fellow religionists in the Islamic world. They will also help to bring China as a nation closer to Central and Near Eastern countries. Before 1942 China maintained diplomatic missions in Turkey and consulates in Egypt and Arabia. In 1943 the ministry in Turkey was raised to an embassy, and in 1944 the Chinese government exchanged ministers with Afghanistan and established a consulate in Iran. In all these diplomatic relations, young Chinese Moslems became the staffs, in some cases recommended by the Chinese Islamic Association. In this way they contribute to good international relations.

But Moslem interest in these outside contacts is not political. For example, Chinese Moslems have shown no interest in the Moslem League. The interest is primarily religious. Out of this interest may come a concerted movement that will help Islam to grow and bloom in China in the same way as Buddhism.

[105] *Ta-lu pao*, Aug. 10, 1948.

VI

The Religion of the Intellectual

The religion of the Chinese intellectual is of special importance in our understanding of religion in modern China. This is true for several reasons. First of all, throughout Chinese history it was the intellectuals who set the pattern and determined the directions in the development of education, government, art, and religion. They, rather than the military generals or the feudal lords, controlled the government. They were the educators. They, instead of the professional artists, were the guiding spirit in the movement of Chinese art. In religion, it was the intellectuals, not the ecclesiastical authorities, who formulated the basic concepts and fixed the course of its philosophical and historical evolution. As Hocking has observed, the scholar of China is "an important guide to the possibilities of growth." [1] If the masses are the body of Chi-

[1] William Ernest Hocking, *Living Religions and a World Faith,* p. 87.

nese religion, the intellectuals are the mind. This has been true throughout the ages. It is true today.

Secondly, what Chinese intellectuals have thought of religion in the last half century may well foreshadow religious developments in China for many decades to come. A number of these intellectuals whose opinions have seriously affected religion in the recent past are in the new regime and may influence the Chinese Communists with respect to their relation to religion.

In the third place, the religion of the Chinese intellectuals is most likely going to be the religion of the Chinese people as a whole. With the development of science and education in China, ignorance and superstitions in the religion of the masses are bound to be removed. As the masses cast aside these objectionable features, they will follow the enlightened beliefs and practices of the intelligentsia, for with education the masses will become enlightened themselves. It is a common phenomenon in Chinese society that as a man becomes educated either through schooling or through experience, he rejects the beliefs and practices of the ignorant masses and turns to those of the literati.

In recent decades Chinese intellectuals have shown an increasing interest in religion. One reason for this is that they have been the most energetic promoters of Western culture, and it was impossible for them to ignore religion, which forms an essential component of that culture. Secondly, the controversy over Confucianism as a state religion or as a religion as such stimulated debates on the subject. Thirdly, Chinese intellectuals, in their initial revolt and subsequent revaluation of traditional institutions, had to consider religion, which underlies many of those institutions. Fourthly, in their violent reaction against Western imperialism, they have looked upon Christianity as one of its instruments and have therefore devoted much attention to the Christian religion and through it to religion in general. In the fifth place, some well-known intellectuals and high government officials were converted to various religions, notably Liang Sou-ming and Tai Chi-t'ao to Buddhism, Chiang Kai-shek to Protestantism, former premier Lu Cheng-hsiang to Catholicism. Although these cases were few and neither attracted national attention nor left any noticeable effect on Chinese religious life, they nevertheless aroused a certain amount of interest among the Chinese intelligentsia. Lastly, the rapid rise and spread of dialectic materialism in the last thirty years could not help invoking serious thought about religion, which it vigorously attacks.

These interests have led to a series of movements which may conveniently be divided chronologically. The first period, from 1917 to 1927, may be called a period of debates on religion. The second period, from 1927 to 1947, may be called a period of affirmation. The third period, from 1947 on, may be called a period of uncertainty.[2]

THE PERIOD OF DEBATES

The decade of debates on religion may further be divided into five periods. We shall see that Chinese intellectuals went from (1) the advocation in 1917 of substituting aesthetic education for religion, to (2) a general discussion on religion in 1921, to (3) an anti-religious movement in 1922, to (4) an anti-Christian movement in 1922–27, and to (5) a controversy in 1923 over science and philosophy of life.

The Substitution of Aesthetic Education for Religion. The theory that aesthetic education surpasses the best of religions sounds naïve and shallow, but it left a deep impression on Chinese intellectuals, many of whom honestly

[2] Compare Charles Samuel Braden, *Modern Tendencies in World Religions*, pp. 97–112. The account leaves out the important turning point and the later period of religious affirmation.

believed that it could replace religion. It was proposed by one of the most mature intellectuals, Ts'ai Yuan-p'ei, then chancellor of the Peking National University, the center as well as the source of China's Intellectual Renaissance. In an article in *La Jeunesse* in 1917, Ts'ai, a Han-lin scholar or member of the old Imperial Academy, contends that aesthetic education has the good but not the bad aspects of religion and is therefore the best substitute for it. To him, "Religion has become a thing of the past in the West, for problems about its contents have been solved by scholars through scientific studies." [3] He maintains that religion arises because of men's spiritual activities—intellect, will, and emotion. Among primitive peoples, he says, religion fulfills the spiritual needs in all three spheres, but in modern times these three have gradually declared their independence from religion. For example, since the discovery of evolution, there is no longer any need for religion to explain the creation of the human species. This is proof, he argues, that the intellect has freed itself from religion.

Likewise, the will has been emancipated from religion. According to him, religionists have accepted moral precepts as the will of God, deductively apprehended and unchangeable, whereas modern scholars, applying the "general laws" of psychology and sociology to ethics, and using the inductive method of science, have found no absolute or eternal standards of ethics. "This is proof that the will has become independent of religion." [4]

The emotions are intimately related to religion, Ts'ai admits. They are strongly and beautifully expressed in religious architecture, murals, music, and famous mountain resorts. But even here the tendency to be independent of religion is evident, he contends. In the Southern and Northern Dynasties (A.D. 386–589), Buddhist paintings faithfully

[3] *La Jeunesse*, III, No. 6 (August, 1917), 1.

[4] *Ibid.*, p. 2.

portrayed heavens and hells. By the Sung Dynasty (960–1279), however, nature became the controlling theme in Chinese painting. Ts'ai thinks that the general direction in the development of art has been toward freedom from religious shackles. Thus freed, art is the purest and most beautiful form of emotional expression. As a handmaid to religion, art is contaminated by religious intolerance. Purged of religious evils, it can be the best means of education. It makes no distinction between oneself and others. It transcends the realm of opposition and discrimination. It rises above the utilitarian consideration of advantages and disadvantages. It is not infested with the selfish desire for personal fortune such as eternal life in Paradise. It cultivates one's noble nature. And it identifies us with the Greatest and the Strongest (Reality) as one.[5]

The theory, simple as it is, immediately became tremendously popular among Chinese intellectuals. The general feeling was that here was a definite solution to a difficult problem, and a constructive and attractive one at that. To a number of writers the defects of the theory are obvious. One writer, for example, points out that art expresses a scene, emotion, or a mood, whereas religion has the motive of betterment and salvation of the world.[6] Liang Sou-ming also reminds us that while art does have religious qualities, it is not religion, just as a conversation may be poetic but is not poetry. To him as a Buddhist, religion is transcendence over life and death, which is clearly beyond the province of art.[7] We may add that Ts'ai's own objective in aesthetic education, namely, the identification of the self with Reality, is a deeply religious one, so that his aesthetic education may enhance but does not replace the religious process. Never-

[5] *Ibid.*, pp. 3–5.
[6] *China Christian Year Book*, 1929, p. 137.
[7] *Min-Toh*, III, No. 2 (February, 1922), 7–8.

theless, in spite of its shortcomings, the proposal stirred discussion over a decade and fired the imagination of many a Chinese intellectual.

It is significant that Ts'ai did not merely reject religion but sought a substitute for it, thus tacitly recognizing that religion *had* fulfilled real spiritual needs. It is also significant that his substitute for religion should be a form of education. This is perfectly in line with the Chinese attitude towards religion, for, as we shall point out later, to the Chinese people in general and to the intellectuals in particular, religion is in essence a form of education. It is also in line with the typical Chinese philosophy of naturalism and humanism, for education through art presupposes nothing supernatural or superhuman. Lewis Hodous is quite correct in grouping Ts'ai's attempt with the humanistic and naturalistic movements started by others, including Hu Shih.[8] Hodous also compares Ts'ai's effort with the Confucian effort to harmonize the individual and society through the exercises of ceremonies and music. While the similarity is unmistakable, it must be added that Ts'ai was by no means engaged in promoting or defending Confucianism. He aimed at eliminating religion whether as a spiritual discipline or as a social institution. In this he did not succeed, but he did arouse a serious discussion on the nature and function of religion and thus ushered in the second phase of the Period of Debates; namely, that of general discussions on religion, in 1921.

General Discussions on Religion. These discussions were an important event, sponsored by an important organization at the height of the Intellectual Renaissance. The Young China Society, one of the main forces in the Renaissance, was founded in 1918 and included as members many men of profound influence on modern China; to wit: the famous writers, Wang Kuang-ch'i and Tsung Pai-hua; the dramatist

[8] A. Eustace Hayden, *The Modern Trends in World-Religions*, pp. 176–77.

T'ien Han; the librarian Yuan T'ung-li (T. L. Yuan); the political party leaders Ch'en Ch'i-t'ien, Tseng Ch'i (1891–1951), and Li Huang; and, charter members of the Communist Party, Li Ta-chao (1866–1927), Chou Fu-hai (1897–1946), and (mark the name) Mao Tse-tung.[9] Distinguished at the outset by its leftist tendencies, the society was thoroughly antagonistic towards religion. On August 28, 1920, the executive committee of the society in Peking unanimously approved the recommendations of its Paris branch that "no person with religious faith shall be admitted to membership and that members with religious faith shall voluntarily withdraw." [10] Among the members in Paris were Li Huang and Tseng Ch'i, who later became the twin leaders of the Young China Party which participated in the ill-fated coalition government of 1939–49.

It was to the credit of the society that protests immediately came from its own members, especially those who entertained no religious faith. The result was three series of public lectures on religion in Peking and in Nanking in 1921 delivered by such prominent thinkers as Bertrand Russell, who was lecturing in Chinese universities at the time, Liang Souming, Chou Tso-jen, brother of the famous Lu-hsun (Lusin) and a celebrated writer in his own right, and Lu Chih-wei (C. W. Luh), later chancellor of Yenching University. The lectures were printed in the journal of the society with extensive comments of approval and disapproval.

The lecturers were about evenly divided for and against religion. As a scientist, Wang Hsing-kung opposes science to religion, emphasizing the finality of analysis and experiment, and refuses to tolerate anything supernatural or mysterious. He argues that "if the universe is determinate, then religious

[9] *Shao-nien Chung-kuo* ("The Journal of the Young China Society"), II, No. 10 (April, 1921), 70–72.

[10] *Ibid.*, II, No. 4 (October, 1920), 87. See also Kiang Wen-han, *The Chinese Student Movement*, p. 54.

worship is futile because life and death, and fortune and misfortune, are all predetermined. To interpret determinism in the sense that greater human effort will bring greater results, he continues, is further to affirm the futility of worship. If the universe is nondeterminate, then life and death, and fortune and misfortune, are all a matter of chance and worship is useless."[11]

To this tune of scientific supremacy, Li Yü-ying (Shih-tseng), well-known anarchist and fellow revolutionist with Sun Yat-sen, adds the note of a naturalistic moralist. As a result of the advancement of knowledge, he declares, there is nothing mysterious or "sur-natural" any more. God is sur-natural, his existence cannot be proved, and therefore he cannot be accepted. Just as the development of science has reduced alchemy, divination, and witchcraft to absurdity, so it will reduce religion to superstition. As to morality, it is nothing other than "the nature of things to love life." As such it can replace religion as it can replace social conventions.[12]

Following the scientist and the anarchist, the sociologist Li Huang views belief in Paradise, hope for immortality, and the dependence on divine inspiration as obstacles to social progress. In his way of thinking, "The spirit of socialism is directed towards this world, whereas that of religion points to Paradise. Socialism is rational and not magical, scientific and not mystical."[13]

Not so theoretical but much more vehement and therefore more effective was the philosopher Bertrand Russell. He congratulated China for her great fortune of having none of the "poisonous" religions of Europe and none of the religious wars that spread blood throughout European history. He told his Chinese audience that European religions were per-

[11] *Shao-nien Chung-kuo*, II, No. 8 (February, 1921), 2–8.
[12] *Ibid.*, pp. 32–36. [13] *Ibid.*, p. 49.

secution, intolerance, and dogma. Institutional religion, he says, has "murdered people," suppressed invention and thought, and caused immeasurable sacrifice, including human sacrifice. As to individual religion, it restricts man's will, feelings, and conduct, and thereby the free development of the individual. Morality is not improved by religion, he maintains, for strong religious beliefs make one's behavior mechanical and one's attitude conservative.[14] Because he was a Westerner, because he was the greatest European thinker to have lectured in China, and because he had become an idol to Chinese intellectuals with whom he associated, he became some sort of a religion himself, exerting a profound influence on the modern Chinese mind and furnishing much vigor for the Chinese attack on religion. Commenting on these lectures, Li Huang concludes that in the future mankind will be free from religion. Specifically, he says, the China of tomorrow will need no religion because (1) China must be modern and the modern world renounces religion; (2) China needs a rational approach in her reconstruction and religion is opposed to rationality; (3) China needs truth, initiative, equality, and freedom, all of which are alien to religion; (4) China will have none of the intolerance of religion; (5) China will overcome whatever difficulties she may encounter in her regeneration not through religion but through moral cultivation and aesthetic training.[15] Looking back to history, Ts'ai Yuan-p'ei reminds the Chinese that China has never been intimately connected with religion, and, looking to the future, he assures them that there will be no religion but only philosophy.[16]

On the opposite side, there was an equal number of lecturers who defended religion. They did not justify religion on

[14] *Ibid.*, pp. 28–42. (For a fuller summary of this lecture, see Kiang, *op. cit.*, pp. 54–55.)
[15] *Ibid.*, III, No. 1 (August, 1921), 19, 35–36.
[16] *Ibid.*, pp. 75–76.

dogmatic or subjective grounds. On the contrary, their arguments were on a highly philosophical plane, revealing a high degree of intellectual objectivity and emotional calmness. This is all the more noteworthy because they were facing a hostile audience, the general tenor of whose thought was strongly anti-religious.

Of the three lecturers defending religion, Liang Sou-ming was a Buddhist layman, C. W. Luh was a Protestant, and T'u Hsiao-shih (1893–1932) was not a follower of any religion. Liang describes religion as "something transcending knowledge and aiming at emotional motivation and comfort to the end that the mind becomes at peace and one's destiny fulfilled." [17] It is religion, he says, that maintains life and prevents it from disintegration. All religions have two common elements; namely, the function of providing comfort for the soul, and anti-intellectualism. The latter is true because all religions are transcendental and mystical. Neo-Confucianism may be sufficient to provide satisfaction in life and human motivation, but only religion can transcend life as we find it.[18]

Here as elsewhere, Liang is persistent in stressing the Buddhist note of transcending the present world. Such emphasis on other-worldliness did not appeal to the realistic and pragmatic crusaders for the Renaissance. But his anti-intellectualism hit the opponents of religion on their strongest spot. They have predicated their reasoning on the ultimate position of science and reason. Both Luh and T'u attacked this as their chief target. The former points out that science can only discover cause on the basis of effect but cannot predict the result of any given cause. Besides, religion deals with life as a whole of which science is only a part. Luh defines religion as "emotional reaction" to the "highest value in life" and as definitely beyond the scope of science. He

[17] *Shao-nien Chung-kuo*, III, No. 1 (August, 1921), 10.
[18] *Ibid.*, pp. 11–22.

says that religion can affirm individual freedom, while science cannot.[19]

Along similar lines of thought, T'u equates religion with the effort to "emancipate man from all bondage of natural existence and to become one with transcendental Reality." In this process direct religious experience is its own final evidence. Such experience is emotional, not rational, and cannot be denied, regardless of its nature, since it is direct and real. Being a matter of direct experience, religion is not in conflict with science, aesthetic education, or morality, since each of these is only a particular kind of attitude towards life, whereas religious experience covers life as a whole. Being intuitive, concrete, and synthetic, religious experience does not necessarily conflict with science but can be harmonized with it. The same is true of history, since history cannot ignore absolute and eternal truth cherished in religion, although, as a record of the process of human developments, it deals only with relative truth.[20]

From the above, it is clear that the position of both opponents and proponents of religion is uncompromising. Only Chou Tso-jen, the celebrated writer, took the middle-of-the-road position. To him, both literature and religion identify us with the highest deity, unite society as one, and look to the future. Therefore, in spite of attacks by science, religion still retains a valuable position in literature. He rejects narrow, exclusive, or superstitious religion, but he is agreeable to a religion of a pantheistic or an ideological type.[21]

The amazing thing about Chou is that while as a leftist he

[19] *Ibid.*, II, No. 10 (May, 1921), 9–12.
[20] *Ibid.*, pp. 28–31. Kiang, based on secondary sources, presents T'u's view as contrasting religion with science. He quotes T'u as saying that "the religious view of the universe is teleological, whereas the scientific view of the universe is mechanical. This is the most important point at which the two are diametrically opposed to each other." The quotation is correct but is taken out of context.
[21] *Ibid.*, pp. 8–9.

was fully expected to denounce religion in total, he comes out with affirmation, half-hearted though it is. From this it is clear that the discussions on religion were emotionally calm and intellectually profound, in this respect far above the violent and irrational debates on state religion of about a decade earlier. There is nothing dogmatic, authoritarian, or anti-foreign in these discussions. They led to two results. One is that the Young China Society in June, 1921, rescinded its action against religious faith. The other is that they set Chinese intellectuals to review the true character of religion and raised Chinese thought about religion to a high intellectual level. They did not abate the anti-religious tide in China, for in the year following these lectures there was a movement against religion in general and against Christianity in particular. But they forced critics of religion to take it seriously and not to dismiss it as mere superstition. Debates on religion were now carried on with intellectual dignity. We must not overlook the strongly intellectual character of the anti-religious and anti-Christian movements. It would be a great mistake to look upon them as fanaticism or anti-foreignism.

The Anti-Religious Movement. The anti-religious movement may be traced to the early years of the Republic when, in the controversy over a state religion and over the question whether Confucianism was a religion, religion itself was opposed. The movement was intensified by the declaration by Ch'en Tu-hsiu in 1918, far-reaching in its influence, that "all religions are idols and rackets" that must be destroyed.[22] It reached a climax in 1922 in the activities of the Great Federation of Anti-Religionists.

The federation was formed early that year when it was announced that the World Christian Student Federation would meet in Tsinghua College in Peking, in April. Im-

[22] *La Jeunesse,* V, No. 2 (May, 1918), 89.

mediately following the announcement, students in Shanghai voiced their protest, which was strengthened by students and professors in Peking and other centers of the Renaissance. Telegrams were dispatched and manifestoes were issued. Starting as an attack on Christianity itself, it was broadened to an attack on religion in general. Ts'ai Yuan-p'ei, Li Yü-ying, and others were invited to lecture.[23] In its proclamations the Great Federation, in denouncing religion as poison, had the character of an emotional outburst against Christianity. But physical violence was entirely absent. The World Christian Student Federation conference was conducted smoothly and without disturbance. As a member of the conference, the present writer was hardly aware of the intellectual storm. Critical of religion as the movement was, it was not merely "youthful enthusiasm and mass emotion." [24] Critics reached their conclusions only after serious reflection. Although their arguments betrayed a lack of understanding of the true meaning of religion, their criticisms were not entirely unfounded. As summarized by a Christian writer who had analyzed some one hundred articles at the time, the main points were: that religion is the product of primitive peoples; that it is superstition and as such has been superseded by science and philosophy; that it is dogmatic, intolerant, and claims supremacy over other aspects of culture; that it is unfavorable to human progress; that it hinders individual development and social advancement; that it is hypocritical; that morality issues from human nature and needs no help from religion; and that mankind can better its lot by improving its environment, promoting the arts, and achieving real knowledge.[25] These arguments represent the general opinion of critics of religion.

[23] For details, see Kiang, *op. cit.*, pp. 61–64.
[24] *Ibid.*, p. 67.
[25] Neander C. S. Chang, *Kuo-nei chin shih-nien lai chih tsung-chiao ssu-ch'ao* ("Religious Thought in China in the Last Ten Years"), pp. 463–64.

It should be noted, however, that the attack on religion by intellectuals was not at all unanimous. Five distinguished intellectuals and leaders of the Renaissance, including Chou Tso-jen and Ch'ien Hsuan-t'ung (1887–1938), who were neither followers nor supporters of any religion, joined in issuing a warning to the Great Federation of Anti-Religionists that the fundamental point to stress was freedom of belief, which the members of the federation should be the first to respect.[26] Liang Ch'i-ch'ao in his "anti-anti-religious" declaration urged the federation not to overemphasize rationality in the discussion of religion, since religion is a matter of emotion, but to stress the constructive rather than the negative aspects of religion.[27] As the storm blew over, Chinese intellectuals settled down to a reconsideration of the true nature of religion. If the movement was socially disturbing, it was intellectually educative.

The Anti-Christian Movement. During the entire anti-religious movement, Christianity was the principal target. The anti-Christian movement was not limited to 1922–27, though those were its most active years.[28] Among the earliest diatribes against Christianity, the most ill-tempered was an article by Chu Chih-hsin (1885–1920), a hero in the political revolution, entitled "What is Jesus?". He describes Jesus as an illegitimate child, selfish, ruthless, revengeful, narrow-minded, hypocritical, "nothing but an idol with no importance in history." [29] The article led a long series of attacks on Christianity.

P. C. Hsu has classified critics of Christianity in three groups: the rationalists, the nationalists, and the Com-

[26] Neander C. S. Chang, *op. cit.*, p. 99.
[27] "Criticism of the Anti-Religionists" (in Chinese), *Che-hsueh* ("Philosophy"), No. 6 (June, 1922), pp. 2–3.
[28] For a good account of the anti-Christian movement, see Wu Yao-tsung (John Wu), "Christianity in the Last Thirty Years" (in Chinese), *Hsin t'an* ("New Altar"), Nos. 6–7 (July, 1948), pp. 6–9.
[29] *Min-kuo jih-pao* ("Republican Daily"), Canton, December 25, 1919.

munists.[30] Among the leaders of the rationalists are Hu Shih and Yü Chia-chü. Their arguments are based on two broad assumptions; that science is all-powerful, and that philosophy is superior to religion. Their arguments are also directed against belief in miracles, Creation, Heaven and Hell, and similar dogmas. Among the nationalists are Ch'en Ch'i-t'ien, Tseng Ch'i, and Li Huang. They emphasize Christian intolerance, Christian persecutions and wars, and imperialism. They view Christianity primarily as an instrument of Western exploitation. The Communists, headed by Ch'en Tu-hsiu, combined both lines of arguments. As summarized by Neander Chang, the attacks on the Christian religion are: (1) that it is unscientific, as testified by its legends, accounts of miracles, and revelations; (2) that it is illogical, for the idea of an omnipotent God is inconsistent with the actual, imperfect world; (3) that it is contrary to social ideals because it relies too much on superhuman power for social reformation and uses Heaven to allure people; and (4) that it is not suitable to China's needs which the Intellectual Renaissance alone will fulfill.[31]

It should be added that while the anti-Christian current was strong among most Chinese intellectuals, some of them did have a good word to say. Chiang Shao-yuan, a non-Christian authority on religion, speaking from the historical point of view, informs his readers that historically Christianity has progressed with time and has changed Western thought in the process.[32] Another writer, speaking from the objective point of view, carefully distinguishes the Christian religion and the Christian church. The latter, he observes, has committed many sins, but the former, centering around

[30] Hsu Pao-ch'ien, "The Anti-Christian Movement and Our Future Policies" (in Chinese), *Sheng-ming* ("Life"), VI, No. 5 (March, 1926), 1–2.
[31] Chang, *op. cit.*, p. 464.
[32] "Ultra-modern Christianity" (in Chinese), *Hsin ch'ao* (*The Renaissance*), I, No. 5 (May, 1919), 749–60.

the personality and doctrines of Jesus, has many merits. Even Ch'en Tu-hsiu, arch-critic of Christianity, urges his fellow Chinese to cultivate the great spirits of Jesus—the spirit of sacrifice, the spirit of forgiveness, and the spirit of love.[33] He says that in the unfortunate relations between Christianity and China in the previous several centuries, China made greater mistakes. It is amazing that a Communist leader should have such tender words for Christianity. As a leader of the Renaissance, Ch'en's objective appraisal of Christianity did much to sober the Chinese, both Christians and anti-Christians. Similarly admiring the "magnificent personality of Jesus," T'ien Han spoke from the personal point of view. Calling himself a pantheist, he declared that he could "not live without God." [34] And from the practical point of view, Chou Tso-jen says that Christianity is an excellent force for spiritual reform in China. Some people may be reformed through science, art, or social movements, he says, but religion touches all. He warns, however, that China should not accept a God that is merely a modern version of the Taoist Jade Emperor, and China should take great care to avoid the emergence of a clerical autocracy.[35]

These fair remarks show that Chinese intellectuals were approaching religion more objectively and were appreciating its real value. Nevertheless, in the minds of Chinese intellectuals science was still the chief and determining factor in life. If the true position of religion is to be understood, the supremacy of science must be challenged. It was.

The Controversy over Science and Philosophy of Life. The reaction against making science an almighty god did not come on behalf of religion, but its favorable effect on religion is obvious. In 1923 a long controversy was carried on

[33] *La Jeunesse,* VII, No. 3 (February, 1920), 15–22.
[34] *Shao-nien Chung-kuo,* II, No. 8 (February, 1921), 57.
[35] A private letter published in *Nü ch'ing-nien* ("Young Women"), XV, No. 1 (July 15, 1936), 18.

over science and philosophy of life. It was touched off by a lecture on "Philosophy of Life" by Chang Chün-mai (Carsun Chang), in which he contrasted science with life. The former, he says, is objective, logical, analytical, and is bound by the law of cause and effect, and arises from the uniformity of Nature. Life, on the other hand, has the five qualities of subjectivity, intuitiveness, synthesizing power, free will, and personal unity, none of which can be provided by science.[36] While the lecture gave science due recognition, it was a direct blow to its supreme position. Immediately V. K. Ting (Ting Wen-chiang, 1888–1936) the geologist, countered with an essay entitled "Metaphysics and Science," in which he declares that "metaphysics is a bewildered spectre, which has been haunting the European continent for the last twenty centuries and which has recently visited China with the whole entourage of banners, symbols, and slogans." He characterizes Chang as a "reincarnation of some Western and some Chinese metaphysical ghosts." He believes that science has been gradually narrowing the sphere of metaphysical speculation and will ultimately replace it completely.[37]

There is more shouting than science in Ting's idolization of science, but the article started a battle royal, lasting more than a year, in which some thirty leading intellectuals were involved, including Hu Shih, Ch'en Tu-hsiu, Chang Tungsun, Liang Ch'i-ch'ao, and Wu Chih-hui.

In defending science Ting was not opposing religion. To him, religion is "the instinct to sacrifice the temporary advantages of the individual for the permanent good of the group." [38] Other champions of science, however, explicitly attacked religion. Ch'en Tu-hsiu asserts that in agricultural society, people generally believe in polytheism. With the

[36] *K'o-hsueh yü jen-sheng-kuan* ("Science and Philosophy of Life"), I, 1–13. For a good abstract of the lecture, see *China Institute Bulletin,* III, No. 2 (November, 1938), 35–37.
[37] *Ibid.*, p. 14. See also *China Institute Bulletin,* III, No. 2, 37–39.
[38] *Ibid.*, p. 38.

development of commerce, monotheism becomes the basic form of religion. As industry and science develop, atheism becomes the rule.[39]

The most celebrated essay in all the polemics, so far as religion is concerned, is that by Wu Chih-hui (Woochefee), under the title "A New Concept of the Universe and Life, Based on a New Belief," which is 164 pages long. As he sees it, the universe is a "black mass," and it is a process of scientific evolution. It is a great stage on which the two-handed animals are actors here and now. Their chief concerns in life are eating and producing children and entertaining friends. There is neither good nor evil and there are neither gods nor devils. The metaphysical spectre and the religious deity are alien invaders of humanity.[40]

Hu Shih considers Wu's humorous and common-sense essay "the most significant event" in the debate. "With one stroke of the pen," Hu remarks, "he ruled out God, banished the soul, and punctured the metaphysical idea that man is the most spiritual of all things." [41] To Hu Shih, Wu's philosophy was eminently agreeable, for Hu's own philosophy of life is "naturalistic" and "scientific." On the basis of our knowledge of various sciences, he states, we should recognize that the universe extends over infinite space and time; that it follows natural laws and needs no supernatural Ruler or Creator; that the struggle for existence in the biological world renders the hypothesis of the benevolent Ruler untenable; that the causes of the evolution of living organisms and human society can be understood historically; that morality and religion are subject to change and that such changes can be scientifically explained; that those religions seeking a future life in Heaven or in the Pure Land are selfish religions

[39] *K'o-hsueh yü jen-sheng-kuan*, I, Introduction, p. 7.

[40] *Ibid.*, pp. 42, 47, 50–55, 129 ff., 137 ff. For an abstract, see *China Institute Bulletin*, III, No. 2, 43–45. See also Hu Shih, *The Chinese Renaissance*, pp. 91–92.

[41] *K'o-hsueh yü jen-sheng-kuan*, I, Introduction, p. 20.

but that living for the sake of mankind and posterity is religion of the highest order.[42]

We have not surveyed the entire controversy, which dealt chiefly with the validity of science, but we have only reviewed those parts affecting religion.[43] Wu's pronouncements, naïve as they are, practically ended the polemics, and Hu's remarks, made in the Preface to the collection (containing some two hundred and fifty thousand words) of the controversial lectures and articles, were taken to be its final conclusion. The total score was definitely in favor of science and against religion. Hu himself observes that "with the exception of a few conservative scholars trained in German philosophy through the Japanese school, the majority of those who took part in this debate were on the side of science, which they held to be capable of dealing with all problems of human life and conduct." [44]

Actually, however, religion won an important battle. In previous discussions on religion, the all-importance of science was taken for granted. In the present debate, however, it was put on the defensive. Furthermore, while the finality of science is still claimed, the futility of religion is no longer accepted, not even by scientists themselves. We have seen that the chief proponent of science, Wang Hsing-kung, concedes a certain place to religion. Hu Shih also approves a religion of a certain type, although he has no use for a religion of the supernatural and mystical variety. The trend was not only one of serious consideration and better understanding of religion but also one of reestablishing its truth. The time was ripe for an affirmation of religion.

[42] *Ibid.*, pp. 25–27. Cf. Hu Shih, "My Credo and Its Evolution," in Einstein *et al.*, *Living Philosophies*, pp. 260–61.

[43] For abstracts of other essays on the controversy, see *China Institute Bulletin*, III, No. 2, 39–50. For a brief story of the debate, see *China*, ed. by MacNair, p. 318; *China Institute Bulletin*, III, No. 1 (October, 1938), 8–11; Kiang, *op. cit.*, pp. 68–74.

[44] Hu Shih, *The Chinese Renaissance*, p. 91.

THE PERIOD OF AFFIRMATION

From a broad perspective one cannot fail to see that through a series of debates Chinese intellectuals moved from the study of religion to defending it and from defending it to affirming it. From 1927 on, the Chinese intellectuals' approach to religion has been understanding, sympathetic, and constructive. This trend is not sudden or unnatural but inevitable, given the historical background and the existing atmosphere.

We must remember that even in anti-religious days the antagonistic opinion was by no means unanimous. We have already noted that in the debate on religion, Chinese intellectuals were about evenly divided. We must remember, too, that as time went on, the debates took on better and better quality. In the controversy over Confucianism before the days of the Renaissance, arguments were sentimental and unscholarly. By 1922, however, arguments on religion were of a much higher intellectual order. Around 1923, the polemics on science and life were carried on on purely logical and philosophical grounds. This increasing intellectuality had a healthful effect on the Chinese mind, and religion is seen in increasingly true perspective. Finally, we must remember that all these debates took place in the first decade of the Renaissance, from 1917 to 1927. It was a period of doubt, debunking, and revolt. Religion was only one of its targets. After a decade of destructiveness, however, Chinese intellectuals turned to constructive efforts. From 1927, the general political and economic situation in China changed from destruction to construction. In the decade which followed, China began slowly to achieve political unity. Civil wars had subsided. Unequal treaties chaining China in a semi-colonial status were gradually abolished. Both economic and political rehabilitation were well on the way. Spiritually a New Life Movement swept the country in 1934–36. In moral concepts the movement was Confucian, since it was based on the traditional cardinal Confucian virtues. In technique and personnel it was Christian. Even though it was politically inspired and therefore cannot be taken as a spontaneous and genuine spiritual movement, still the spiritual atmosphere in China must have been favorable before the government took advantage of it.

At the same time, Chinese intellectuals themselves were making constructive efforts and achieving positive results. Historians and archaeologists were rediscovering the Shang Dynasty (c. 1523–c. 1028 B.C.) in particular and bringing new lights to Chinese history in general. A new literature came to maturity. In the realm of thought, Chang Tung-sun the Neo-Kantian, Chin Yueh-lin the Neo-Realist, Fung Yu-lan the Neo-Confucian Rationalist, and Hsiung Shih-li the Neo-Confucian Idealist were building and perfecting their own philosophical systems. New Buddhism both as a philosophy and as a religion was being produced. What is more, the most important intellectual debate in the 1930s was one between "native culture" and "complete Westernization." It started with a manifesto by ten college professors on "Cultural Reconstruction on the Chinese, Native Basis." [45] It precipitated a nation-wide debate in which most nationally known intellectuals participated, including Hu Shih, who advocated Westernization.[46] The central issues—what culture is, whether it can be categorized as Chinese and Western, whether it can be imported as an isolated and finished product, and in what direction Chinese culture should develop—need not engage our attention. The important point for us is that regardless of whether the intellectuals favored

[45] *Wen-hua yü chien-she* ("Culture and Reconstruction"), I, No. 4 (January 10, 1935), 1–12.

[46] See *Tu-li p'ing-lun* (*Independent Critic*), No. 153 (June, 1935), pp. 5–10; No. 160 (July 21, 1935), pp. 10–16.

"native culture" or "complete Westernization," they recognized religion as an indispensable factor of culture.

Another trend in Chinese thought important for our discussion is the growing attention to the philosophy of religion. Hsu Pao-ch'ien (1892–1944) published his *Talks on Religious Experience,* Tseng Pao-sun published her *Syllabus of a Course on Empirical Religion,* and Hsieh Fu-ya (N. Z. Zia) published his *Philosophy of Religion.* The latter follows closely William James in psychology and Whitehead and Alexander in metaphysics. During the war, Zia, at the invitation of the China Philosophical Society, translated Royce's *The Religious Aspect of Philosophy.*[47]

On the negative side, anti-religious forces had declined. Leading anti-religionists had either disappeared from the scene or had lost their prominence. Ts'ai Yuan-p'ei, having retired, no longer occupied the commanding position among Chinese intellectuals. Ch'en Tu-hsiu, as the leader of the right wing of the Chinese Communist Party, was hunted by both the Nationalists and the left-wing Communists, went underground and was finally seized and imprisoned. The Communists were confined to the hills. The glamor of Bertrand Russell had been dulled by the brilliance of other Western philosophers, and his pedestal was occupied by philosophers like Whitehead. And Wu Chih-hui, although still a much respected elder statesman, no longer exercised the influence on Chinese intellectuals that he had in the past. All in all, the situation was favorable to the reassertion of religion. Although science still retained a very high position in the new Chinese scale of values, religion was given its proper place, and its position was raised higher and higher.

It is in this atmosphere that religion has been affirmed. To indicate this affirmation, suffice it to refer to only a few lead-

[47] Ho Lin, *Tang-tai Chung-kuo che-hsueh* ("Contemporary Chinese Philosophy"), p. 62.

ing intellectuals without repeating the affirmative statements already quoted or referred to in previous sections. Tai Chi-t'ao (1882–1949), scholar and high government official, voiced the general opinion in the 1930s when he said that among the essential elements of a nation are language, customs, and religion, and that the government should accord religion all protection. He further observed that 99 percent of the Chinese had religion.[48] In a similarly affirmative vein, Chang Tung-sun, foremost philosopher, declared that "from history we know that social reforms must be aided by religion or else a psychological force is lacking." [49] To him as to Tai Chi-t'ao, religion is a "necessary factor in a culture." [50] Wu Mi, an intellectual not known to exhibit any personal interest in religion, attaches equal importance to art and religion, and adds that both government and industry need to be made "solid and substantial by a religious spirit." [51] Fung Yu-lan goes a step further and states that "religion is the guarantee of hope for the future" and that such guarantee is "a universal necessity." [52] To these statements, T'ang Chün-i has added that "the true religious spirit is a strong affirmation of the existence of our sin and our limited ability to remove it. From this spirit comes our sense of repentance and pity. From this sense we derive a strong spiritual power which strengthens the practical spirit of morality and culture . . . therefore religion is indispensable to any culture." [53]

With these statements before us, we must view in its proper light Hu Shih's comment that "practically all prom-

[48] "Chinese Religious Reform and National Salvation" (in Chinese), *Hsin Ya-shih-ya* ("New Asia"), V, No. 5 (May, 1933), 2.
[49] *Chih-shih yü wen-hua* ("Knowledge and Culture"), p. 117.
[50] *Ibid.*, p. 62.
[51] *Chien-kuo tao-pao* ("Reconstruction Journal"), I, No. 1 (January, 1934), 8.
[52] *Hsin li-hsueh* ("New Rational Philosophy"), p. 286.
[53] T'ang chün-i, "The Religious Spirit and the Civilization of Mankind" (in Chinese), *Min-chu p'ing-lun* (*Democratic Review*), I, No. 9 (March, 1950), 451–52, 456.

inent leaders of thought in China today [1933] are openly agnostics and even atheists. . . . The educated people in China are indifferent to religion and . . . the whole intellectual tendency there is not favorable to any religious movement or revival." [54] Undoubtedly he was thinking of religion as a system of superstitions and dogmas or the belief in Creation. But so far as religion on a higher level is concerned, in view of the increasingly better understanding of religion, the growing insistence upon religion as an essential component of culture, and the rise of new intellectual systems, notably New Buddhist Idealism, New Neo-Confucian Rationalism, and New Neo-Confucian Idealism, all of which culminate in the identification of man and Heaven, it is safe to say that the anti-religious forces among Chinese intellectuals have been weakening and that religion is being affirmed.

What is the religion that is being affirmed? It is difficult to know what it is. Chinese literature is not much help because it is distinctly secular. In Indian, Persian, and Western literature, great expressions about God have been full and abundant. In Chinese literature, however, such expressions are isolated and few.[55] Many, if not most, great creations in Western literature, music, and art have religious subjects. On the other hand, those in China have been largely secular, with the exceptions of Buddhist sculpture and painting. Nor do books on Chinese religion offer much assistance. There is not a single essay in any language on the subject of the religion of Chinese intellectuals. To be sure, E. H. Parker devoted a chapter of his *Studies on Chinese Religion* to the Chinese literati and religion. He notes that the Chinese literati believe truth to be relative, that they have been free

[54] Hu Shih, *The Chinese Renaissance*, p. 78.

[55] As noted by James Legge long ago. See his *The Religions of China* (1880), p. 249.

from intellectual prejudices in religious and ethical matters, and that their ancestor worship is not true "worship." Alarmed at their rejection of collective worship, confession, and pardon of sin as necessary for a blessed life, Parker sadly concludes that "it is doubtful whether the religious enthusiasm which once revolutionalized Europe has ever touched, or will ever touch, the trained Chinese intellectual." [56] James Legge, already quoted, realizes that to the educated Chinese, offerings are not connected with any idea of propitiation or expiation but are tributes of duty and gratitude.[57] Joseph Edkins has pointed out that Chinese scholars would accept rational principles of Christianity, even the Trinity, but not miracles and the divinity of Christ.[58] But none of these writers has much to say about the positive content of the Chinese intelligentsia's religion. There is a whole chapter on the literati in Max Weber's *The Religion of China,* but nothing is said about their religious beliefs or practices. Hu Shih has written a masterly chapter on religion in Chinese life, showing how Chinese intellectuals reacted to religion throughout history, but he ends with the polemics over science and life and does not take into account the later period of religious affirmation.[59]

The intellectuals themselves provide little help. Following Confucius, who "did not talk about . . . heavenly spirits," [60] who "seldom discussed . . . Heavenly Mandates," [61] and whose "discourse about man's nature and the Way of Heaven cannot be heard," [62] the Chinese literati rarely discuss their own religion. Religion is considered strictly a private matter and not a subject for public discourse. Exceedingly few intellectuals have formulated their religious code.

[56] *Studies in Chinese Religion,* pp. 27–28, 39.
[57] See above, p. 143.
[58] *Religion in China,* p. 52.
[59] Hu Shih, *The Chinese Renaissance,* pp. 78–93.
[60] *Lun-yü* (*The Analects*), VII, 20.
[61] *Ibid.,* IX, 1.
[62] *Ibid.,* V, 12.

Hu Shih is the only one who has announced his personal credo, and Fung Yu-lan is the only one who has worked out a philosophy of religion.[63] Under these circumstances, we can only make general observations on the religion of the Chinese intelligentsia.

However, in our observations we find definite aid from two directions. One is what religious beliefs and practices the Chinese intellectuals surely reject. From previous references and quotations, it is clear that they frown upon all forms of superstition, idolatry, the belief in original sin, Creation, an anthropomorphic god, heavens and hells, and miracles. Their religion does not consist of the practice of offering, praying, chanting, and confessing. It is not a system of creeds, ceremonies, and dogmas. It is not an organization with membership, baptism, a clergy, a missionary zeal, and a monastic order. It is not one particular religion claiming the only or the highest truth.

From another direction comes positive help in several ways. There is a whole body of ancient religious teaching which has dominated twenty centuries of Chinese religious thought and is no less dominant today. We can trace the religious tendencies in the religion of the masses which faithfully reflect the basic religious convictions of the Chinese race. The expanding concept of the identification of the individual and the universe is common to all new developments in Buddhism and Neo-Confucianism in twentieth-century China. And statements by contemporary intellectuals leave no doubt as to what constitutes their religion. On the basis of all these, we may formulate the religion of the Chinese literati as (1) religion as sanction of ethics, (2) religion as fulfillment of human nature, and (3) religion as realization of the Principle (*Li*).

Religion as Sanction of Ethics. The ethical emphasis in

[63] *Hsin li-hsueh*, pp. 269–89.

Chinese religion is proverbial. We see it in traditional religious teachings, especially Confucianism and Taoism. We see it in the persistent tendencies in the religion of the masses. In a real sense, both the this-worldly and the ethical tendencies in all Chinese religions, including Buddhism, are but a reaffirmation of a long tradition. It has, indeed, been the literati who have steered religion toward social and moral relations and have kept religion firmly rooted on the human world. To them, religion is a sanction of ethics.

By "sanction of ethics" is meant not merely the ancient idea of retribution as expressed in the age-old proverb, "To the good doer all blessings are sent and to the evil doer all miseries," or the saying, "When you plant melons, you reap melons, and when you plant beans, you reap beans." Such concepts are very powerful among the masses, reinforced by the belief in reward and punishment in heavens and hells. While completely disowning such belief, the enlightened Chinese feel that the doer of good enjoys happiness and the doer of evil will ultimately suffer from sorrow, even if only in his own mind.

To the Chinese intellectuals, religion as a sanction of ethics has specific meanings. As previously stated, the best distinction of the religion of the masses and that of the enlightened is that the former is characterized by *pai* (worship), whereas the latter is characterized by *chi* (sacrifice).[64] Traditionally the concept of sacrifice includes three ideas; namely, that it is a fulfillment of human relations, that it helps us to "remember our origins," and that it is a "foundation of moral teaching."

To understand these concepts we have to go back to Confucius. He told his pupils to "respect spirits but keep them at a distance." [65] "When he offered sacrifice to his ancestors," we are told, "he felt as if they were present bodily, and when

[64] See above, p. 143.

[65] *Analects*, VI, 20.

he offered sacrifice to the other spirits, he felt as if the deities were present bodily." [66] These sayings are understood by some Western writers to mean that Confucius was insincere or impious. To the Chinese, however, they mean that Confucius emphasized sacrifice as an end in itself. The idea is that so long as the act expresses a proper feeling toward the object of sacrifice, whether or not the object is really present is immaterial. As the Confucian Classic *Li chi* (*The Book of Propriety*) puts it, "Sacrifice is not something coming from outside, but issues from one's heart." "The heart of sacrifice," the Classic continues, "means that externally all things attain their utmost, and internally the will attains its utmost. This is the true spirit in sacrificing." [67] Hsun Tzu (fl. 298–238 B.C.) explains the meaning of sacrifice quite clearly. "Sacrificial rites," he says, "are the expression of a man's will, emotion, remembrance, and love. They represent the height of loyalty, faithfulness, love, and respect. . . . With sorrow and reverence, one serves the dead as he serves the living, and serves the departed as he serves the present. What is served has neither appearance nor shadow, and yet the social order is completed in this way." [68]

To subordinate the object of worship to the act of worship is not to deny the existence of the object. As Confucius insisted, we should feel that the object is bodily there. According to the *Chung-yung* (*The Doctrine of the Mean*), Confucius said, "How abundantly do spiritual beings display their power! Invisible to the eyes and impalpable to the senses, they enter into all things. It is this fact that causes all people to fast and purify themselves, and with solemnity of dress institute services of sacrifice and religious worship. Like the rush of mighty rivers, they seem to be above us and

[66] *Analects*, III, 12.
[67] *Li chi* (*The Book of Propriety*), Chap. 26.
[68] *Hsun Tzu*, Chap. 19. Cf. *The Works of Hsuntze*, trans. by Homer H. Dubs, pp. 245–46.

around us." [69] We should feel that the spirits are there. But whether they are there or not, the important thing is sacrifice itself.

Sacrifice is important, first of all, because it is a fulfillment of human relations. Confucius said, "To serve those now dead as if they were living, and those departed as if they were still with us: this is the highest achievement of true filial piety." [70] In other words, honoring ancestors is a way to fulfill the relationship which has been interrupted but should not be terminated by death. In the past, the educated performed ceremonies before ancestral altars, not to seek blessings or to supply deceased parents with material needs, but to demonstrate the proper feeling of filial piety and respect. Today few intellectuals perform such ceremonies. They have been replaced with memorial meetings or simply a moment of silence. The form of sacrifice has changed. But the central conviction, that human relations are not cut off by death and need to be continually fulfilled, is none the less alive.

Sacrifice is important also because it helps one to "remember his origin." According to *The Book of Propriety*, "all things originate from Heaven and all men originate from their ancestors. . . . The sacrifice . . . is to express gratitude toward the originators and recall our beginning." [71] Hsun Tzu said, "Rites are rooted in three things. Heaven and Earth are the origin of life; ancestors are the origin of human beings; and rulers and teachers are the origin of ordered government. . . . Hence the rites are to serve Heaven above and Earth below, honor our ancestors, and make eminent our rulers and teachers. These are the three foundations of rites." [72] Even the naturalistic Wang Ch'ung (A.D. 27–c. 100) echoed, "We trace our origin and serve the dead,

[69] *Chung-yung* (*The Doctrine of the Mean*), XVI, 1–3.
[70] *Ibid.*, Chap. 13.
[71] *Li chi*, Chap. 11.
[72] *Hsun Tzu*, Chap. 19. Cf. Dubs' translation, p. 220.

because we dare not forget our origin. . . . There are not necessarily spirits to enjoy the sacrifice." [73] Sacrifice, then, is an expression of gratitude, a reminder of our origin. In modern expression, rulers and teachers have lost their eminence. But the feeling of gratitude and the desire to remember are not any weaker now than in the past. The three minutes of silence, very common in modern memorial meetings, is devoted to an expression of such feelings.

But the most important reason for sacrifice is that it is a "foundation of moral teaching." As has been pointed out already, sacrificing to ancestors has a moral effect on filial piety. According to Confucius' pupil Tseng Tzu, "If people are careful about funeral rites and remember their ancestors in sacrifices, the morals of the people will resume their proper excellence." [74] To put it differently, religion induces people to greater and better moral deeds. Significantly, the Chinese term for religion is *chiao*, which means to teach. This is the meaning of the ancient saying that "the ancient sages established teaching on the ways of the gods." As Hu Shih explains, "Teaching a moral life is the essential thing; and the ways of the gods are merely one of the possible means of sanctioning the teaching. That is in substance the Chinese concept of religion." [75]

To show that the modern Chinese attitude towards religion as a sanction of ethics is substantially the same as that of the ancient sayings, reference to a few contemporary writers will be sufficient. Liang Ch'i-ch'ao, who has exerted perhaps a greater influence on Chinese intellectuals in the twentieth century than any other writer with the possible exception of Hu Shih, conceives of religion principally as a moral force. He says that religion has a fivefold function. It unites

[73] *Lun-heng* ("Critical Essays"), Vol. XXV, Chap. 3. For an English translation, see Alfred Forke, trans., *Lun-Heng.*

[74] *Analects,* I, 9.

[75] Hu Shih, *The Chinese Renaissance,* p. 79.

people together, gives man hope, directs man to freedom and emancipation, restrains man from doing evil, and gives man courage, power, and strength.[76] His view that religion makes a better human being and a better society needs no further comment.

T'ang Chün-i, a young and brilliant intellectual, has noted that in Chinese religion the honoring of ancestors and teachers has assumed greater importance than in most countries. This, he explains, is due to the Chinese deep sense of human relations. Because of this feeling, temples for Confucius and other teachers have been built all over the country, and most homes have the tablet for "Heaven, Earth, Ruler, Parents, Teachers." [77] Although modern intellectuals no longer visit temples, they have retained the religious attitude of reverence towards great men of the past. This is clearly demonstrated in the weekly memorial service to Sun Yat-sen. They participate in the service—and no intellectual is known to have refused on anti-religious grounds to participate—not because they think Sun Yat-sen is a god but because they believe that the service continues the fulfillment of human relations, helps us to remember the sources of our being and strength, and impels us to better behavior.

These ideas have been put on a philosophical plane by Fung Yu-lan. In a chapter in his *Hsin li-hsueh* [78] he has outlined his own philosophy of religion and comes to a conclusion surprisingly similar to traditional concepts. Following the great Neo-Confucianist Chu Hsi (1130–1200), he defines *shen*, heavenly spirits as understood traditionally, as "what is coming and expanding" and *kuei*, earthly spirits, as "what is going away and contracting." However, Chu Hsi

[76] *Yin-ping-shih wen-chi, ho-chi* ("Collections of Works by Liang Ch'i-ch'ao"), *Wen-chi*, X, 81; XVII, 81–84.

[77] *Chung-hsi che-hsueh ssu-hsiang chih pi-chiao yen-chiu chi* ("Essays on the Comparative Studies of Chinese and Western Philosophical Thought"), p. 220.

[78] Pp. 268–89.

says that "in sacrifice, when the heavenly (*shen*) and earthly (*kuei*) spirits are moved, it means that the force that has contracted can again expand." [79] Fung does not accept the theory that what has contracted or gone can expand or come again, but he maintains that what is gone is still related to the present. "Sacrifice is to strengthen this relationship," he says, "so that what is gone seems to appear at present." [80] This is desirable because mankind always has the memory of and feeling for what is gone. "For this reason, no matter how social systems have changed, sacrifice is indispensable." [81] "In ordinary sacrifice," he says, "the object is *kuei*, that is, what is gone or contracted, which is individual. In religion, the object of sacrifice is *shen*, or what is to come and expand. This *shen* may well be *kuei* that appears to us as *shen*. But in the imagination of those who sacrifice, it becomes a kind of perfect model. As such it transcends the individual. The thinking, recollection, and admiration of such a model will enable one to transcend his own individual level of existence . . . and rise from ordinary existence to that of a sage." [82]

In other words, in sacrifice we think of those spirits or forces that have gone and are to come, and in such thoughts they appear to us as ideal examples following which we may live a perfect life. The ultimate goal of religion, then, is man's moral perfection. Religion is therefore essentially ethical and social. This emphasis leaves no room for fanatic and mystical experience. Any abnormal practice like asceticism, celibacy, and self-immolation are ruled out. Organizations, creeds, and ceremonies may be helpful but should be kept to a minimum and should in no case be considered primary, since they are morally neutral. The ideas of prayer, confession, pardon, and grace are deemed as detrimental to the sense of

[79] *Yü lei* ("Conversations Topically Arranged"), Chap. 3.
[80] Fung, *Hsin li-hsueh*, p. 286.
[81] *Ibid.*, p. 287.
[82] *Ibid.*, p. 288.

individual moral responsibility. While faith, piety, and meditation are of great value, the basic way to salvation is a morally good life and good society.

Religion as Fulfillment of Human Nature. From the above it is clear that the goal of Chinese religion, especially as understood and practiced by the intelligentsia, is human perfection. We may go a step further and say that to the Chinese intellectuals the fulfillment of human nature *is* religion.

Like the idea of sacrifice, this idea is nothing new. It goes back to the Confucian Classic, *The Doctrine of the Mean.* Here we read that "what is decreed by Heaven is what we call human nature. To fulfill the law of human nature is what we call the Way (Tao). To cultivate the Way is what we call *chiao* or teaching." [83] "Only those who are their absolute true selves (*ch'eng*) in the world," it goes on to say, "can fulfill their own nature. Those who fulfill their own nature can fulfill the nature of things. Those who fulfill the nature of things can assist Heaven and Earth in transforming and nourishing things. And those who are able to assist Heaven and Earth in transforming and nourishing will form a triad with Heaven and Earth." [84] To these sayings Mencius added, "He who develops his own mind to the utmost knows his nature. Knowing nature, he knows Heaven. To preserve one's mind and nourish one's nature is the way to serve Heaven." [85] And to bring the matter to a climax, he declared, "There is nothing more enjoyable than to return to one's own self and be true (*ch'eng*) to it." [86]

This trend of thought as underscored in ancient Confucianism has remained a central feature in Chinese religious thought. It finds its modern expression in contemporary Neo-Confucianism as revived and reconstructed by Fung Yu-lan.

[83] *Chung-yung* (*The Doctrine of the Mean*), I, 1.
[84] *Ibid.*, XXII.
[85] *Meng Tzu* (*The Works of Mencius*), Vol. VII, Part I, Chap. 1.
[86] *Ibid.*, VII, Part I, Chap. 4.

"People in the moral sphere fulfill human relations and human duties. In doing so, they investigate human Principle to the utmost and fulfill human nature. People in the transcendental sphere serve Heaven and assist in the natural transformation of things. In doing so they investigate the Principle of the universe and fulfill the nature of the universe. . . . To penetrate the mysteries and know the transformation of the universe is to complete the work of the universe. . . . All this is serving Heaven." [87] In his *Hsin li-hsueh* he says,

> From the viewpoint of Heaven, the things a man ought to do are fully in accord with man's Principle. Shao Yung [1011–77] said that the sage is man in the highest degree. By a man in the highest degree is meant a perfect man, that is, a man who can fulfill the nature of man and realize the Principle of man to the limit. . . . These activities must be carried out in social life. In social life the most social activities of man are moral activities. Such moral activities can be viewed from two angles, from the viewpoint towards society and from the viewpoint towards Heaven. From the viewpoint towards society, man's moral activity is to fulfill his duty as a member of society. From the viewpoint towards Heaven, his moral activity is to fulfill his duty as a member of the universe and this is the way to fulfill the way of man. From this viewpoint, man's moral deeds are identical with serving Heaven.[88]

Here we have a reaffirmation of the traditional idea that the way to serve Heaven is to become a morally perfect man, that is, to develop one's moral nature to the fullest extent. From *The Doctrine of the Mean* and Mencius through the Sung Neo-Confucianists, especially Shao Yung, Chang Heng-ch'ü (1020–77) and Ch'eng Ming-tao (1032–85), to contemporary Neo-Confucianists, the idea has been persistent. Hsiung Shih-li, leader of modern Neo-Confucian

[87] *Hsin yuan-jen* ("A New Treatise on the Nature of Man"), p .94.
[88] *Hsin li-hsueh*, pp. 301–2.

Idealism, also expresses similar conviction. He says, "One's self-nature is true and real. There is no need to search for a Heavenly Lord outside oneself. One can develop one's own nature to the fullest extent. One need not desire for Nirvana." [89]

Not only in Confucianism but in Buddhism also the idea of the realization of human nature is basic. One of the most important changes from Indian Buddhism to Chinese Buddhism is that from individual salvation to universal salvation. Universal salvation is possible only if all beings have the Buddha-nature. This is the epoch-making contribution of the Chinese monk Tao-sheng (d. 434), who upon reading the doctrine in the six-chapter version of the *Mahaparinirvanasutra* that Buddha-nature was denied a group of beings called *icchantika,* vigorously attacked it. His conviction that *all* beings had Buddha-nature did not waver even when he was excommunicated. But he was vindicated when the complete *Mahaparinirvanasutra* was introduced into China. Ever since Tao-sheng, the doctrine of universal salvation has become the most important tenet of Chinese Buddhism as well as the strongest basis for Buddhist spiritual democracy and world brotherhood.

If Buddha-nature is all-pervading and common to everybody, it is a logical step to reach the conclusion that Buddha-nature is within oneself. This is a great discovery of the Meditation School of Buddhism. Hence the key teaching of the school is "directly pointing to the human mind and to become a Buddha by seeing one's own Buddha-nature."

In Taoism, too, the idea of realization of human nature is of primary importance. The ultimate goal of both Lao Tzu and Chuang Tzu is to preserve the essence and vitality of man. We have noted that Taoism as a religion aims at the

[89] *Tu-ching shih-yao* ("Important Guides for the Study of Classics"), II, 53B.

realization of the Three Original Principles, Essence, Vital Force, and Spirit. We have seen how the philosophical development of Taoism through Wei Po-yang and Ko Hung and the development of alchemy were directed to the same objective. We have also seen in the Southern School of Taoism the emphasis on the cultivation of man's nature and, in the Northern School, the emphasis on the cultivation and development of man's vital power.[90] Unless we appreciate the central emphasis of Taoism on human nature, we are bound to be puzzled by certain peculiar phenomena in the Taoist school. For example, Taoism, unlike most religions, has respected the body and has developed a system of physical culture as well as a detailed dietary. For centuries it has been the center in China of the art of boxing. It has been suspected that the Taoist practice of alchemy and pseudo-scientific experiment may be partly responsible for the emergence of modern science.[91] Taoist attempts to convert base metals into gold, their recipes and formulas for preparing pills of immortality, and their use of herbs for medical purposes, were all calculated to preserve one's nature. Today the original goal of the cultivation of human nature has long been forgotten. However, to the few educated Taoists and the few Chinese intellectuals inclined toward the Taoist way of life, Taoism is fundamentally a way of realizing one's true and pure nature.

Thus the fulfillment of human nature is the way to attain Tao, achieve Buddhahood, or serve Heaven. The implications of such a doctrine are clear. Religion is fundamentally humanistic and this-worldly. It requires no Heaven or Hell. Salvation is to be found within oneself. One must achieve it through his own effort, making unnecessary any system of clergy, evangelism, conversion, or missionary movement.

[90] See above, pp. 149–51.
[91] L. Carrington Goodrich, *A Short History of the Chinese People*, p. 71).

But why is the fulfillment of human nature the way to serve Heaven? To answer this question we have to proceed to the third aspect of the religion of the intellectual; namely, the realization of Principle.

Religion as the Realization of Principle. Fulfillment of human nature is the way to serve Heaven, for the simple reason that individual nature is identical with universal nature. What is endowed in man is of the same essence as the true nature of the entire universe. Called Tao in Taoism, Thusness in Buddhism, and *Li* in Confucianism, it is Reason, Law, Principle. We have already discussed the recurrent idea in Buddhism that the wave is identical with the ocean and that Thusness in the One and the Many is the same. We have also referred more than once to the Neo-Confucian aphorisms that "the mind is the universe" and that "Heaven and Earth and the ten thousand things form one body." [92] In the words of both Ch'eng Ming-tao and Ch'eng I-ch'uan (1033–1107), "We say that all things are one Reality because all things have the same *Li* in them," and, "The *Li* of a thing is one with the *Li* of all things." [93] Such ideas run through the entire course of Chinese thought. As Chang Tung-sun has pointed out, "the concept of all things forming one body has been a persistent tendency in Chinese thought from the beginning to the end." [94] It underlies practically all contemporary movements of thought in China. Whether in New Buddhist Idealism, Neo-Confucian Idealism, or Neo-Confucian Rationalism, the idea of the unity of man and Heaven occupies a focal position. It is not an exaggeration to say that it represents the common belief of Chinese intellectuals.

To fulfill human nature is to serve Heaven, because human nature follows *Li*, and *Li* is identical with Heaven.

[92] See above, pp. 32, 33, 41, 42, and 48.
[93] *Ch'eng-shih i-shu* ("Literary Remains of the Ch'eng Brothers"), Chap. 18.
[94] *Chih-shih yü wen-hua*, p. 117.

"Heaven is *Li*," says Ch'eng Ming-tao.[95] "The ten thousand things are nothing but the *Li* of Heaven. . . . When we refer to the self-nature of Heaven, we say the Way of Heaven. When we refer to what Heaven endows in the ten thousand things, we say the Mandates of Heaven." [96] They are all aspects of Heaven, the One, the Absolute or what Fung calls the Great Whole.[97] Those who realize this Whole are "citizens of Heaven."

This *Li*, or Heaven, is not to be interpreted as a mere abstract principle. It is moral, because it is the completion of *jen*, or goodness. It produces and reproduces, and that is the greatest of virtues. As such, it "arouses in us certain emotions," as Fung says.[98]

How is *Li* to be realized? It is achieved through the investigation of *Li* to the fullest extent and at the same time through living a life of *jen*. As Fung says, investigation of things will lead to the realization of *Li*, which in turn will lead to full realization of one's nature and "serving Heaven." [99] As Ch'eng Ming-tao says, "The man of *jen* forms one body with all things." [100]

Two questions arise from this All-is-One and One-is-All philosophy. The first is whether such a philosophy is atheistic. It is unmistakably rationalistic. Hu Shih has skillfully traced the development of Chinese religious thought toward rationalism. He has conclusively shown that the original Chinese religion was a very simple religion, consisting in a worship of ancestors, certain spirits, and Heaven. It was simplified by the naturalism of Lao Tzu and the humanism of Confucius and Confucianists of the Han Dynasty (202 B.C.–A.D. 220) tried to simplify it further by making it a religion of filial piety. An elaborate, spectacular, and fanatic

[95] *Ch'eng-shih i-shu*, Chap. 11.
[96] *Ibid.*
[97] See above, pp. 47–48.
[98] *Hsin li-hsueh*, p. 38.
[99] *Ibid.*, p. 294.
[100] *Ch'eng-shih i-shu*, Chap. 2.

kind of Buddhism temporarily overwhelmed the Chinese, but the native rationalistic mentality of the Chinese intelligentsia gradually reasserted itself and revolted against Buddhism. The Meditation School of Buddhism attempted to simplify religion to two essential elements: meditation and insight, and Neo-Confucianism in the eleventh and twelfth centuries turned these Buddhist elements into a philosophy of individual perfection and social advance through intellectual training. This rationalistic temper, Hu Shih points out, is still very strong today.[101]

During the debates on religion, many a Chinese rationalist assumed that a rationalist had to be an atheist. Such, of course, is not necessarily the case. Neo-Confucianism, for example, is extremely rationalistic, but it is not atheistic. It not only encourages worship but also positively affirms the existence of the object of worship. Some one remarked to Chu Hsi that in sacrifice we merely show our attitude of respect; there is not really any spirit. He replied, "By spirit we mean the mystery of the ten thousand things. The entire universe is filled with this spirit." [102] Modern intellectuals are not exactly Neo-Confucianists, although most of them come close to it in their general religious outlook. They participate only in simple services of worship. They do not believe in spirits as they are understood by the ignorant masses. But there is no doubt that they believe in a power above physical existence.

The other problem that arises is the question of personal immortality. If individual nature is identical with universal nature, is there any personal immortality? Do Chinese intellectuals believe in it? Here the Chinese intellectuals differ radically from the masses. The latter still have the Buddhist

[101] Hu Shih, *The Chinese Renaissance*, pp. 80–88.
[102] Chu Hsi, *Chu Tzu ch'üan-shu* ("Complete Works of Chu Hsi"), Vol. XXXIX.

belief in transmigration and the traditional doctrine of *hun* and *p'o*. The ancient belief was that at death a white (*po*) light leaves the human body and joins the moon's light. To this was added later the concept of *hun*, which etymologically includes the element of *yun* (cloud), which is more active than light. Thus, according to the traditional theory, *hun* is the active and positive part of the soul corresponding to *yang*, or the active cosmic principle, and *p'o* is the passive and negative part of the soul corresponding to *yin*, or the passive cosmic principle. *Hun* is the soul of man's vital force (*ch'i*) which is expressed in man's intelligence and power of breathing, whereas *p'o* is the spirit of man's physical nature expressed in his body and his physical movements. When *hun* predominates, the spirit of man becomes *shen*, or heavenly spirit, and when *p'o* predominates, it becomes *kuei*, or earthly spirit. This is the general supposition of the masses. It is reinforced by the Buddhist belief in heavens and hells inhabited by *shen* and *kuei*, respectively.

The Chinese intellectuals, however, totally reject such notions. To them, human immortality has nothing to do with existence in Paradise. Fundamentally they discard the theory of the indestructibility of the soul. The question was settled once and for all in the sixth century, when Fan Chen wrote his famous treatise on "The Destructibility of the Soul" [103] and declared that "there cannot be soul without the body any more than there can be sharpness without the knife." It started a lengthy and bitter controversy.[104] Ultimately, Chinese scholars supported Fan's conclusion.

In the place of the belief in the immortality of the individual soul, Chinese intellectuals entertain two beliefs in immortality. One is social and ethical and the other meta-

[103] "Shen-mieh lun," in *Liang shu* ("History of Liang"), biography of Fan Chen (fl. A.D. 502).

[104] Seng-yu, ed., *Hung-ming chi* ("Essays on Elucidating the Doctrine"), Chap. 9.

physical. The metaphysical doctrine can be traced to *The Book of Changes* but was firmly established by Neo-Confucianists of the Sung period (960–1279) as the philosophical theories of *kuei* and *shen*. Etymologically *shen* means to expand and *kuei* means to return. Thus they are respectively *yang* and *yin*. In ancient and medieval times, the concentration of the vital force (*ch'i*) of *yang* to produce things was considered as an extension of *shen*, whereas the dissipation of the drifting *hun* and the diminishing *p'o*, resulting in change, is the *kuei* that is returning (to the elements). This doctrine was elaborated on at length by Chang Heng-ch'ü. "*Kuei* and *shen* are the natural function of the principles of *yin* and *yang*, in the sense that coldness is an example of *kuei* while hotness is an example of *shen*." [105] "To come into being from non-being," he says, "is the nature of *shen*, and to change from being to non-being is the nature of *kuei*." [106] According to Chu Hsi, "*kuei* and *shen* are the increase and decrease of the two universal forces of *yin* and *yang*." "From the standpoint of the two forces, *shen* is the efficacy of *yang*, and *kuei* is the efficacy of *yin*. From the standpoint of the one universal force, what has become and extended is *shen*, and what has departed and returned [to its origin] is *kuei*." [107] In short, what has become and is unfathomable is *shen*, and what has gone is *kuei*. These interpretations of *kuei shen* and *yin yang* were completely unknown to de Groot and other Western writers who understood them only in animistic terms.[108] This is a serious misunderstanding, because the rationalistic and naturalistic concepts of *kuei* and *shen* generally held by Chinese intellectuals

[105] *Cheng-meng* ("Correct Doctrines for Beginners"), Chap. 1.
[106] *Ibid.*, Chap. 5.
[107] *Chu Tzu ch'üan-shu*, Vol. LI. For a good account of Chu Hsi's theory of immortality, see Derk Bodde, "The Chinese View of Immortality: Its Expression by Chu Hsi and Its Relationship to Buddhist Thought," *Review of Religion*, VI, No. 4 (May, 1942), 369–83.
[108] J. J. M. de Groot, *The Religion of the Chinese*, pp. 3, 18–19.

are entirely different from the concepts of spirits roaming the universe as understood by the ignorant masses.

In our own day, these concepts have been developed by Fung Yu-lan. Following the Neo-Confucianists, he regards what is coming into existence as *shen* and what is going out of existence as *kuei*.[109] However, to Chu Hsi and others, *kuei* and *shen* are correspondingly the declining and growing tendencies in things. For example, "Flowers are *shen* when they are growing, *kuei* when they are withering. Similarly, a man is *shen* when young and *kuei* when old." [110] Fung, however, strictly identifies the future as *shen* and the past as *kuei*. Since the past is permanent and irreducible, all things and human beings are in a sense immortal.[111] Since the past is intimately related to the present and can influence the future, *kuei* is therefore real and alive, able to affect our daily existence.[112] Such a doctrine of immortality is thoroughly rationalistic and naturalistic.

The social and ethical theory goes back to the ancient Classic *Tso chuan*. To the question, "What is immortality?" the answer in the Classic is that "the best is to accomplish virtue, the next best is to accomplish work, and the next best is to accomplish words. This is called immortality." [113] In the last twenty-four centuries, this doctrine has represented the common code among the educated Chinese. Hu Shih calls it the doctrine of the Immortality of Worth, Work, and Words. In his essay, "Immortality, My Religion!" he fully accepts it but enlarges it to be the Immortality of Society, for he thinks the immortality of virtue, work, and wisdom too limited to the individual and therefore too narrow in scope. In its place there should be and is the immortality of the Great Self.[114] As he says in his "Credo," "the indi-

[109] *Hsin li-hsueh*, p. 270.
[110] *Yü lei*, Chap. 3.
[111] *Hsin li-hsueh*, p. 272.
[112] *Ibid.*, pp. 272–73.
[113] *Tso chuan* ("Tso's Commentary"), Duke Hsiang, 24th year.
[114] "Immortality, My Religion!" (in Chinese), *La Jeunesse*, VI, No. 2 (February, 1919), 99–102.

vidual self is subject to death and decay, but the sum total of individual achievements lives on in the immortality of the Larger Self." This, he says, is his religion.[115]

Hu is too much of a humanist to go beyond society and enlarge the Larger Self to include the entire universe. Logically, however, his theory inevitably ends in the typical Chinese concept of the unity of man and Heaven.

The above characterization of the religion of the Chinese intelligentsia as sanction of ethics, fulfillment of human nature, and realization of *Li* may not fit the religious pattern of any particular intellectual, but the three features faithfully reflect Chinese thought in the last eight hundred years and especially in the last thirty years, as is evidenced in the new Buddhist and Confucian intellectual movements. These features cut across Taoism, Buddhism, and Confucianism. To be sure, the characterization is heavily weighted with Neo-Confucian thought, but as Ho Lin has correctly pointed out, "The development of Confucianism in the broad sense is the main current in contemporary Chinese thought." [116] If it is argued that Neo-Confucianism is a system of philosophy, not a religion, let it be remembered that it emphasizes a contemplative life and promotes traditional religion. E. R. Hughes has observed that while all this may appear to be pure naturalistic philosophy and not religion, yet there is religion to be found in it. He points out that the basic emphasis on reason in the world welded to reason in man within can be a very religious concept, as in the philosophy of Thomas Aquinas.[117] He compares it to Stoicism in the days of the Roman Empire, which began as a set of philosophical theories and developed into a religion.[118]

[115] "My Credo and Its Evolution," in Einstein *et al.*, *Living Philosophies*, pp. 260–61.
[116] Chu K'o-cheng *et al.*, *Hsien-tai hsueh-shu wen-hua kai-lun* ("Introduction to Contemporary Thought and Culture"), p. 19.
[117] E. R. and K. Hughes, *Religion in China*, p. 90.
[118] *Ibid.*, p. 83.

It goes without saying that this religion is extremely naturalistic, rationalistic, and humanistic. It is therefore free from myths, supernatural deities, and irrational miracles. Because its ultimate conclusion is the unity of man and Heaven, a concept common to Confucianism, Taoism, and Buddhism, it is truly syncretic.

Such a religion poses certain problems for foreign religions that have not yet entered into the stream of Chinese thought, notably, Islam and Christianity. Neither has had real contact with Chinese intellectuals, Islam chiefly because its followers, mostly poor, have not had the opportunity for education, and Christianity chiefly because it champions the cause of the masses. Few mature Chinese intellectuals have been converted to Christianity, although many Christians are themselves intellectuals. This is partly due to the intellectuals' distaste for belonging to any particular religion, and partly due to the lack of communication between Chinese intellectuals and Christianity. In Christian reports on Chinese reactions to Christianity, the opinions of the Chinese literati have been completely ignored. In the exciting year when Chinese intellectuals were openly debating religion in Peking, reports from that city on Chinese attitudes towards Christianity made no mention of them.[119] The glaring omission is amazing. So long as foreign religions fail to come in touch with the Chinese intelligentsia, they will have failed to reach the nerve center of the Chinese people, for, as was said before, it has been the intellectuals who have determined the development of Chinese religion. How certain Christian doctrines, such as incarnation, atonement, and sin, can be presented to Chinese intellectuals is a real problem. Realizing its great difficulty, Francis Wei, a Chinese Christian leader, urges concentration on the greatness of Jesus instead of on doctrinal presentation.[120] This is wise counsel, for the

[119] *China Mission Year Book*, 1923, p. 17.
[120] Francis Wei, *The Spirit of Chinese Culture*, p. 117.

inspiring power and exemplary character of Jesus, like much of the good work done by the church in education and medicine, is generally and favorably accepted by the Chinese intellectuals. Here an agreeable point of contact can be found. Until foreign religions come to grips with Chinese intellectuals, they will remain foreign religions on Chinese soil, neither influencing nor being influenced by Chinese religious life to any great degree. On the other hand, when a foreign religion enters the midst of Chinese intellectuals, it can enrich Chinese religious life and be enriched by it. Buddhism has been a beautiful example. In the meantime, the religion of the Chinese intellectual faces a future of uncertainty.

THE PERIOD OF UNCERTAINTY

Few can be certain about the nature of this period of uncertainty. There are too many imponderables to make prediction safe. We have already dealt specifically with Confucianism and Buddhism under the Communist regime in China.[121] In dealing with religion in general here, we can only list certain facts, both favorable and unfavorable. On the favorable side, the Common Principles of the People's Republic guarantee freedom of religion. By governmental order, no temples are to be destroyed or images removed. Churches and temples are allowed to own land so long as proceeds from it are used for religious purposes. In the enforcement of government measures religious institutions and secular institutions are treated alike.

On the other hand, the Communist Party has reiterated its familiar tenet that religion is the opium of the people. Its philosophy is basically materialistic. The new government insists on the freedom of anti-religion along with the freedom of religion. There are evidences already of state control of

[121] See above, pp. 52–53, 90–91, and 168.

religious life. A Bureau of Religious Affairs has been set up under the Committee on Culture and Education. The government is openly persecuting the Catholic religion, through the closing of churches, confiscation of property, and expulsion and execution of Catholic missionaries. It has terminated the religious activities of Protestant missionaries. It has nationalized both Protestant and Catholic schools and philanthropic institutions. It has required the Chinese Protestant and Catholic churches to sever their ties with the West. And it is attempting to conform Christian doctrines to Marxism. Paralleling the government's policy of an independent Chinese church, Chinese Christian intellectuals have started a "religious reform" movement. This began in September, 1950, with the declaration by Protestant leaders Chao Tzu-ch'en (T. C. Chao) and Wu Yao-tsung (Y. T. Wu). Two months later, Father Wang Liang-tso of Szechuan and five hundred other Catholics proposed the now well-known three principles of "self-administration," "self-support," and "self-propagation." There can be no doubt about the sincerity of Chinese Christian leaders in striving for financial and administrative independence and for a mature, self-reliant Christianity of their own. However, the Communist government has skillfully directed the movement to mean ultimate control by the state, financial dependence on the state, and propagation in line with the ideology of the state. At present, the Chinese Communists are telling Chinese Christian intellectuals to argue that since both Christianity and Communism work for social justice and since Jesus was a member of the proletariat, therefore good Christians must support Communism.

Whether or not Chinese Christian intellectuals will be finally converted remains to be seen. With reference to the religion of the Chinese non-Christian intellectuals, however, several significant things can be said. Since it is profoundly rationalistic and naturalistic, it should be easy for it to get along with a philosophy that prides itself on its scientific attitude. Humanism in Chinese religion should have no quarrel with an ideology that professes to stand for the welfare of the masses. Since there is no organization in this religion, there will be no conflict between the church and the state. And since it is essentially a private philosophy of life, it will be largely immune from governmental control. Besides, there are many religious intellectuals serving in or cooperating with the new government, such as Chang Tung-sun, T'ien Han, T'ang Yung-t'ung, Fung Yu-lan, C. W. Luh, and Liang Sou-ming, to name only those mentioned in this book. No one knows the future status of Chinese intellectuals in the new order. According to Mao Tse-tung, "Chinese Communists may form an anti-imperialist united front politically with certain idealists and disciples of religions, but can never approve their idealism or religious teachings." [122] That was in 1941. In 1945, he said, "We Communists shall join hands with all intellectuals irrespective of class, religion, or political affiliation." [123] And in 1948 he declared that "dogmas can never fertilize a field or feed a dog. Chinese intellectuals will have to forego dogmas, and construct their own theories on the basis of the reality of Chinese history and revolution from the point of view and with the method of Marxism-Leninism." [124] If the reality of Chinese history is the deciding factor, then the future of the religion of the Chinese intellectual can be reasonably sure. In the past fifty years, among the realities of Chinese history and Chinese revolution, two things stand out. One is that Chinese intellectuals defeated the movement to im-

[122] Mao Tse-tung, *New Democracy*, p. 61. The original edition, in Chinese, was published in 1941.
[123] Mao Tse-tung, *The Fight for a New China*, p. 64.
[124] *Kuan yü chih-shih fan-tzu ti kai-tsao* ("On Reforming the Intellectuals") (Hong Kong, Cheng-pao, 1948), pp. 26–27.

pose a state religion on them. The other is that their own effort to replace religion with aesthetic education and science encountered opposition from their own ranks and was eventually overshadowed by their own affirmation of religion. Will the new rulers of China force Marxism on the Chinese intellectuals as a state "religion"? Will they attempt to replace religion with dialectic materialism? We do not know the answers to these questions. The suspicion is that they will, but we do not know what the results will be. All we can say is that if history repeats itself, the Chinese intellectuals will have neither a state religion nor a scientific or aesthetic substitute for religion. They will keep their own kind of religion going, and they will keep it free.

Bibliography

1. WORKS IN WESTERN LANGUAGES

Ali, Ahmed. Muslim China. Karachi, Pakistan Institute of International Affairs, 1949.

Asaṅga. Mahāyānasamparigraha. Trans. by Étienne Lamotte as Le Somme du grand véhicule. 2 vols. Louvain, Bureaux du Muséon, 1938–39. Bibliothèque du Muséon, Vol. VII.

Aśvaghosha. Aśvaghosha's Discourse on the Awakening of Faith in the Mahāyāna. Trans. by Teitaro Suzuki. Chicago, Open Court, 1900.

—— The Awakening of Faith in the Mahāyāna Doctrine. Trans. by Timothy Richard and Yang Wen Hwui. 2d ed. Shanghai, Christian Literature Society, 1918.

Beal, Samuel. A Catena of Buddhist Scriptures from the Chinese. London, 1871.

Bodde, Derk, "Chinese Muslim Minority," *Far Eastern Survey*, XV, No. 18 (September 11, 1946), 281–84.

—— "Chinese Muslims in Occupied China," *Far Eastern Survey*, XV, No. 21 (October 23, 1946), 330–33.

—— "The Chinese View of Immortality: Its Expression by Chu Hsi and Its Relationship to Buddhist Thought," *Review of Religion*, VI, No. 4 (May, 1942), 369–83.

—— "Japan and the Muslims of China," *Far Eastern Survey*, XV, No. 20 (October 9, 1946), 311–13.

Botham, Mark E., "Modern Movements among Chinese Mohammedans," *Moslem World*, XIII, No. 3 (July, 1923), 291–99.

Braden, Charles Samuel. Modern Tendencies in World Religions. New York, Macmillan, 1933.

Briere, O., "Les Courants philosophiques en Chine depuis 50 ans (1898–1950)," *Bulletin de l'Université l'Aurore,* Série III, Tome X, No. 40 (October, 1949), 561–654.

Broeck, Janet Rinaker Ten, and Yiu Tung, "A Taoist Inscription of the Yuan Dynasty: The Tao-Chiao Pei," *T'oung Pao,* XL, Nos. 1–3 (1950), 60–122.

Broomhall, Marshall. Islam in China, a Neglected Problem. London, Morgan & Scott, 1910.

Bruce, J. Percy. Chu Hsi and His Masters. London, Probsthain, 1923.

"Buddhism," in *China Handbook,* 1937–45, pp. 25–26.

Cady, Lyman Van Law. The Philosophy of Lu Hsiang-shan, a Neo-Confucian Monistic Idealist. New York, Union Theological Seminary, 1939. Manuscript.

Chan, Wing-tsit, articles in *The Dictionary of Philosophy,* ed. by Dagobert D. Runes (New York, Philosophical Library, 1942).

—— "Buddhist Terminology" and "Chinese Terminology," in *An Encyclopedia of Religion,* ed. by Vergilius Ferm (New York, Philosophical Library, 1945), pp. 91–110, 142–58.

—— "The Harmony of Religions," *Bostonian,* April, 1950, pp. 19, 43–44. Reprinted in *World Outlook,* June, 1950, pp. 10–12; *Christian Leader,* CXXXII (July, 1950), 230–32; *Chinese Press,* July 28, August 4, 1950.

—— "Neo-Confucianism," in *China,* ed. by Harley Farnsworth MacNair (Berkeley, University of California Press, 1946), pp. 254–65.

—— "Philosophies of China," in *Twentieth Century Philosophy,* ed. by Dagobert D. Runes (New York, Philosophical Library, 1943), pp. 563–67.

—— "Trends in Contemporary Philosophy," in *China,* ed. by Harley Farnsworth MacNair (Berkeley, University of California Press, 1946), pp. 312–30.

Chao, T. C., "Religious Situation, 1930," in *China Christian Year Book,* 1931, pp. 63–76.

Ch'ien Tuan-shêng. The Government and Politics of China. Cambridge, Harvard University Press, 1950.

"Chinese Moslem Leaders," *China at War,* VII, No. 6 (December, 1941), 80–81.
Christy, Arthur, "Old Religions Made New," *Asia,* XXXV, No. 8 (August, 1935), 526–30.
Chu Hsi. The Philosophy of Human Nature, by Chu Hsi. Trans. by J. Percy Bruce. London, Probsthain, 1922.
Chuang Tzŭ. Chuang Tzŭ. Trans. by Fung Yu-lan as Chuang Tzŭ, a New Selected Translation with an Exposition of the Philosophy of Kuo Hsiang. Shanghai, Commercial Press, 1931.
—— Trans. by Herbert A. Giles as Chuang Tzŭ, Mystic, Moralist, and Social Reformer. 2d ed., rev. Shanghai, Kelly & Walsh, 1926.
Chung-yung. Trans. by James Legge as The Doctrine of the Mean, in *The Chinese Classics,* Vol. I, 2d ed. (Oxford, 1893).
—— Trans. by E. R. Hughes as The Mean-in-Action, in *The Great Learning and The Mean-in-Action* (New York, Dutton, 1943), pp. 105–144.
Clennell, W. J. The Historical Development of Religion in China. London, Unwin, 1917.
Confucius. Lun-yü. Trans. by Arthur Waley as The Analects of Confucius. London, Allen & Unwin, 1938.
—— Trans. by James Legge as Confucian Analects, in *The Chinese Classics,* Vol. I, 2d ed. (Oxford, 1893). Also in *The Four Books* (Shanghai, Commercial Press, 1933).
Cranston, Ruth. World Faith. New York, Harper, 1949.
Creel, H. G. Confucius, the Man and the Myth. New York, John Day, 1949.
Cressy, Earl H., "Recent Developments in the Religions of China," *The Journal of Bible and Religion,* XV, No. 1 (April, 1947), 75–80.
Day, Clarence Burton. Chinese Peasant Cults. Shanghai, Kelly & Walsh, 1940.
de Groot, J. J. M. Religion in China. New York, Putnam, 1912.
—— The Religion of the Chinese. New York, Macmillan, 1910.
—— The Religious System of China. 6 vols. Leyden, Brill, 1892–1910.

De Korne, John C. The Fellowship of Goodness. Grand Rapids, The Author, 1941.

Doré, Henri. Researches into Chinese Superstitions. 18 vols. Shanghai, T'usewei Press, 1914–38.

Dubs, Homer H., "The Dates of Confucius' Birth," *Asia Major*, n. s., I, Part II (April, 1949), 143–46.

Edkins, Joseph. Religion in China, Containing a Brief Account of the Three Religions of the Chinese. 4th ed., rev. London, 1893.

Eliot, Sir Charles. Hinduism and Buddhism, an Historical Sketch. 3 vols. London, Arnold, 1921.

Everett, John R. Religion in Human Experience. New York, Holt, 1950.

Forke, Alfred. Geschichte der neueren chinesischen Philosophie. Hamburg, De Gruyter, 1938.

Four Books, The. Confucian Analects, The Great Learning, The Doctrine of the Mean, and Works of Mencius. With English translation and notes by James Legge. Shanghai, Commercial Press, 1933.

Friess, Horace L., and Herbert W. Schneider. Religion in Various Cultures. New York, Holt, 1932.

Fung Yu-lan. A History of Chinese Philosophy, the Period of the Philosophers (from the Beginning to about 100 B.C.). Trans. by Derk Bodde. Peking, Henry Vetch, 1937.

—— "I Discovered Marxism-Leninism," *People's China*, I, No. 6 (March 16, 1950), 10–11, 21.

—— "The Philosophy of Chu Hsi," trans. by Derk Bodde, *Harvard Journal of Asiatic Studies*, VII, No. 1 (April, 1942), 1–51.

—— A Short History of Chinese Philosophy. Ed. by Derk Bodde. New York, Macmillan, 1948.

—— The Spirit of Chinese Philosophy. Trans. by E. R. Hughes. London, Kegan Paul, 1947.

Gibb, H. A. R. Modern Trends in Islam. Chicago, University of Chicago Press, 1947.

Glick, Carl, and Hong Sheng-hwa. Swords of Silence; Chinese Secret Societies Past and Present. New York, McGraw-Hill, 1947.

Goodrich, Grace, "Nuns of North China," *Asia*, XXXVII, No. 2 (February, 1937), 90–93.

Goodrich, L. Carrington. A Short History of the Chinese People. Rev. ed. New York, Harper, 1951.

Ha Kuo-tung, "Mohammedanism," in *Chinese Year Book*, 1936–37, pp. 1499–1505.

Hamilton, Clarence H., "Buddhism," in *China*, ed. by Harley Farnsworth MacNair (Berkeley, University of California Press, 1946), pp. 290–300.

—— Buddhism in India, Ceylon, China and Japan, a Reading Guide. Chicago, University of Chicago Press, 1931.

Hartmann, M., "Muhammadenism (in China)," in *Encyclopedia of Religion and Ethics*, ed. by James Hastings (New York, Scribner, 1916), VIII, 888–95.

Haydon, A. Eustace, ed. Modern Trends in World-Religions. Chicago, University of Chicago Press, 1934.

Hocking, William Ernest. Living Religions and a World Faith. New York, Macmillan, 1940.

Hodous, Lewis. Buddhism and Buddhists in China. New York, Macmillan, 1924.

—— "Confucianism" and "Taoism," in *The Great Religions of the Modern World*, ed. by Edward J. Jurji (Princeton, Princeton University Press, 1946), pp. 1–23, 24–43.

—— Folkways in China. London, Probsthain, 1929.

Hsü, P. C. Ethical Realism in Neo-Confucian Thought. Peking, The Author, 1933.

Hsüan-tsang, trans. Vijñaptimātratāsiddhi, le siddhi de Hiuan-Tsang. Trans. into French by Louis de La Vallée Poussin. 2 vols. Paris, Geuthner, 1928–29.

Hsün Tzŭ. Hsün Tzŭ. Trans. by Homer H. Dubs as The Works of Hsüntze. London, Probsthain, 1928.

Hu Shih. The Chinese Renaissance. Chicago, University of Chicago Press, 1934.

—— "The Establishment of Confucianism as a State Religion during the Han Dynasty," *Journal of the North China Branch of the Royal Asiatic Society*, LX (1929), 20–41.

—— "My Credo and Its Evolution," in Albert Einstein *et al.*,

Living Philosophies (New York, Simon & Schuster, 1931), pp. 235–64.

Huang, Siu-chi. Lu Hsiang-shan, a Twelfth Century Chinese Idealist Philosopher. New Haven, American Oriental Society, 1944.

Hughes, E. R., and K. Hughes. Religion in China. London, Hutchinson House, 1950.

I ching. Trans. by James Legge as The Yi King, in *The Sacred Books of the East,* Vol. XVI (London, 1882).

—— Trans. by Z. D. Sung as The Text of Yi King. Shanghai, China Modern Education Co., 1935.

Keith, A. Berriedale. Buddhist Philosophy in India and Ceylon. Oxford, Clarendon Press, 1923.

Kiang Wên-han. The Chinese Student Movement. New York, King's Crown Press, 1948.

Ko Hung. Pao-p'u Tzŭ. Trans. by Tenney L. Davis and Ch'ên Kuo-fu as "The Inner Chapters of Pao-p'u-tzŭ," *Proceedings of the American Academy of Arts and Sciences,* LXXIV (1941), 297–325.

—— Trans. by Eugene Feifel as "Pao-p'u Tzŭ," in *Monumenta Serica,* No. 6 (1941), pp. 113–211; No. 9 (1944), pp. 1–33; No. 11 (1946), pp. 1–32.

Latourette, Kenneth Scott. The Chinese, Their History and Culture. 3d ed., rev. New York, Macmillan, 1946.

Lee, Shao Chang. Popular Buddhism in China. Shanghai, Commercial Press, 1939.

Legge, James. The Religions of China; Confucianism and Taoism Described and Compared with Christianity. London, 1880.

Li chi. Trans. by James Legge as The Li Ki, in *The Sacred Books of the East,* Vols. XXVII and XXVIII (London, 1885).

Liao Tai-ch'u, "The Ko Lao Hui in Szechuan," *Pacific Affairs,* XX, No. 2 (June, 1947), 161–73.

Lin, Mousheng Hsitien, "Recent Intellectual Movements in China," *China Institute Bulletin,* III, No. 1 (October, 1938), 3–19.

Lin Yutang. The Wisdom of China and India. New York, Random House, 1942.

McDaniel, C. Yates, "Buddhism Makes Its Place in the New Era," *Asia,* XXXV, No. 6 (August, 1935), 536–41.

Madhyāntavibhanga, Chap. 1. Trans. by Th. Stcherbatsky as Discourse on Discrimination between Middle and Extremes. Moscow, Academy of Sciences of USSR Press, 1936.

—— Trans. into English by D. L. Friedmann as Analysis of the Middle Path and the Extremes. Utrecht, 1937.

Mao Tsê-tung. China's New Democracy. New York, New Century, 1945.

—— The Fight for a New China. New York, New Century, 1945.

Maspero, Henri, "The Mythology of Modern China," in J. Hackin *et al., Asiatic Mythology* (London, Harrap, 1932), pp. 252–384.

—— "Le Songe et l'ambassade de l'empereur Ming," *Bulletin de l'École Française d'Extrème-Orient,* X (1910), 95–130.

Mei, Y. P., "Stronghold of Muslim China," *Moslem World,* XXXI, No. 2 (April, 1941), 181–84.

Mencius. Mêng Tzŭ. Trans. by James Legge as The Works of Mencius, in *The Chinese Classics,* Vol. II, 2d ed. (Oxford, 1893). Also in *The Four Books* (Shanghai Commercial Press, 1933).

Miao, C. S., "Current Religious Thought," in *China Christian Year Book,* 1928, pp. 41–46.

Millican, Frank R., "Modern Religious Movements in Non-Christian Religions," in *China Christian Year Book,* 1934–35, pp. 110–19.

—— "Recent Development in Religious Thought," in *China Christian Year Book,* 1929, pp. 122–41.

—— "T'ai Hsü and Modern Buddhism," *Chinese Recorder,* LIV, No. 6 (June, 1923), 326–33.

"Mohammedanism," in *China Handbook,* 1950, pp. 26–27.

Nāgārjuna. Mādhyamikaśāstra. Trans. by Max Walleser as Die mittlere Lehre. Heidelberg, 1912.

Noss, John B. Man's Religions. New York, Macmillan, 1949.

Pan Wei-tung. The Chinese Constitution. Washington, Catholic University of America, 1945.

Parker, E. H. Studies in Chinese Religion. London, Chapman & Hall, 1910.

Pickens, Claude L. Annotated Bibliography of Literature on Islam in China. Hankow, Society of Friends of the Moslems in China, 1950.

Pickens, Elizabeth Z., "Moslems in China," *Moslem World*, XXXIV, No. 4 (October, 1944), 255–60.

Plopper, Clifford H. Chinese Religion Seen through the Proverb. Shanghai, China Press, 1926.

Prajñāpāramitā. Trans. by F. Max Müller as The Smaller Pragñā-pāramitā-hridaya-sūtra, in *The Sacred Books of the East*, XLIX, Part II (London, 1894), 153–54.

Pratt, James Bissett. The Pilgrimage of Buddhism and a Buddhist Pilgrimage. New York, Macmillan, 1928.

Qur'an. Trans. by J. M. Rodwell as The Koran. London, 1861.

Reichelt, Karl Ludvig, "Present Situation in Buddhism," in *China Christian Year Book*, 1932–33, pp. 100–112.

—— Religion in Chinese Garment. Trans. from the Norwegian by Joseph Tetlie. London, Lutterworth Press, 1951.

—— Truth and Tradition in Chinese Buddhism. Trans. from the Norwegian by Kathrina van Waganen Bugge. 4th ed., rev. and enl. Shanghai, Commercial Press, 1934.

Reid, Gilbert, "Recent Religious Movements in China," in *China Mission Year Book*, 1924, pp. 59–66.

—— "Trends in China's Religious Life," in *China Christian Year Book*, 1926, pp. 71–79.

Rhodes, F. H., "A Survey of Islam in China," *Moslem World*, XI, No. 1 (January, 1921), 53–68.

Ring, George C. Religions of the Far East, Their History to the Present Day. Milwaukee, Bruce, 1950.

Saddharmapuṇḍarīkasūtra. Trans. by W. E. Soothill as The Lotus of the Wonderful Law. Oxford, Clarendon Press, 1930.

Schilpp, Paul Arthur, ed. The Philosophy of Alfred North Whitehead. Evanston and Chicago, Northwestern University, 1941.

Shryock, John K. The Origin and Development of the State Cult of Confucius. New York, Century, 1932.

—— The Temples of Anking and Their Cults. Paris, 1931.

Smith, A. H., "The Present Attitude of the Chinese towards Christianity," in *China Mission Year Book*, 1923, pp. 12–17.

Soothill, W. E. The Three Religions of China. 3d ed. London, Oxford University Press, 1929.

Stcherbatsky, Th. The Conception of Buddhist Nirvāṇa. Leningrad, Publishing Office of the Academy of Sciences of the USSR, 1927.

Sun Yat-sen. San Min Chu I, the Three Principles of the People. Trans. by Frank W. Price. Chungking, Ministry of Information of the Republic of China, 1943.

Suzuki, Daisetz Teitaro. Essays in Zen Buddhism. 1st series. London, Luzac, 1927.

—— Manual of Zen Buddhism. Kyoto, Eastern Buddhist Society, 1935.

"Symposium of Science and the Philosophy of Life," *China Institute Bulletin*, III, No. 2 (November, 1938), 35–50.

Takakusu, Junjiro. The Essentials of Buddhist Philosophy. Ed. by Wing-tsit Chan and Charles A. Moore. Honolulu, University of Hawaii, 1947.

Tao-tê ching. Trans. by Arthur Waley as The Way and Its Power, a Study of the Tao Te Ching. London, Allen & Unwin, 1934.

—— Trans. by Lin Yutang as The Book of Tao, in his The Wisdom of Laotse (New York, Modern Library, 1948), pp. 41–325. Also in his The Wisdom of China and India (New York, Random House, 1932), pp. 583–624.

Thomas, Edward J. The History of Buddhist Thought. London, Kegan Paul, 1933.

Tsu, Y. Y., "Present Tendencies in Chinese Buddhism," *Journal of Religion*, I, No. 4 (July, 1921), 497–512.

—— "Trends of Thought and Religion in China," *New Orient*, II (1933), 321–29.

Tucci, Giuseppe, trans. Pre-Diṅnāga Buddhist Texts on Logic from Chinese Sources. Baroda, Oriental Institute, 1929.

Vasubandhu. Triṃśikā. Trans. by Sylvain Lévi as Matériaux pour l'étude du système Vijñaptimātra. Paris, H. Champion, 1932.

—— Viṃsatikā. Trans. by Clarence H. Hamilton as Wei Shih Er Shih Lun or the Treatise in Twenty Stanzas on Representation-Only. New Haven, American Oriental Society, 1938.

Vissière, A., "Études Sino-Mahométanes," *Revue du monde musulman,* Tome treizième (1911), pp. 30–63.

Wang Ch'ung. Lun-hêng. Trans. by Alfred Forke as Lun-Hêng. 2 vols. London, Luzac, 1907 and 1911.

Wang Tch'ang-tche. La Philosophie morale de Wang Yang-ming. Shanghai, T'ou Sè-Wè Press, 1936.

Wang Yang-ming. The Philosophy of Wang Yang-Ming. Trans. by Frederick Goodrich Henke. Chicago, Open Court, 1916.

Ward, J. S. K., and W. G. Sterling. The Hung Society, or the Society of Heaven and Earth. 3 vols. London, Baserville Press, 1925–26.

Weber, Max. The Religion of China. Trans. from the German by Hans H. Gerth. Glencoe, Illinois, Free Press, 1951.

Wei, Francis C. M., "The Present Status of Confucianism," in *China Mission Year Book,* 1924, pp. 67–72.

—— The Spirit of Chinese Culture. New York, Scribner, 1947.

Wei-huan, "Buddhism in Modern China," *T'ien Hsia Monthly,* IX, No. 2 (September, 1939), 140–55.

Whitehead, Alfred North. Process and Reality. New York, Macmillan, 1929.

Winter, H. J. J., "Science, Buddhism and Taoism," *The Aryan Path* XXI, No. 5 (May, 1950) 206–8.

Yang, Y. C. China's Religious Heritage. New York and Nashville, Abingdon-Cokesbury, 1943.

Zen Sophia H. Chen. Symposium on Chinese Culture. Shanghai, China Institute of Pacific Relations, 1931.

Zia, N. Z., "The Anti-Christian Movement in China," in *China Christian Year Book,* 1925, pp. 51–60.

2. BOOKS IN CHINESE (IN TRANSLITERATION)

Numbers in parentheses refer to the equivalents in Section 1 of the list of Chinese characters, below. Certain well-known works are classified by title.

A-mi-t'o ching. (1)
Chang Hêng-ch'ü. Chêng-mêng. (2)
Chang Jung. Mên lun. (3)
Chang, Neander C. S. Kuo-nei chin shih-nien lai chih tsung-chiao ssŭ-ch'ao. Peking, Chinese Language School, 1927. (4)
Chang T'ai-yen. Chang-shih ts'ung-shu. Hangchow, Chekiang Library, 1919. (5)
—— Ch'i-wu lun shih in *Chang-shih ts'ung-shu* (Hangchow, Chekiang Library, 1919). (6)
—— T'ai-yen wên-lu, pieh-lu, in *Chang-shih ts'ung-shu* (Hangchow, Chekiang Library, 1919). (7)
Chang Tung-sun. Chih-shih yü wên-hua. Shanghai, Commercial Press, 1940. (8)
Chao-kao. (9)
Ch'ên Chiao-yu. Ch'ang-ch'un Tao-chiao yüan-liu. 1879. (10)
Ch'ên Yüan. Nan-Sung ch'u Ho-pei hsin Tao-chiao k'ao. Peking, Fu-jên University, 1941. (11)
Ch'êng I-ch'uan and Ch'êng Ming-tao. Ch'êng-shih i-shu. (12)
Chi Chüeh-mi, trans. Han-i Ku-lan ching. Shanghai, Ai-li Garden, 1931. (13)
Ch'ien Mu. Hsien-Ch'in chu-tzŭ hsi-nien. Shanghai, Commercial Press, 1935. (14)
Chin Chi-t'ang. Chung-kuo Hui-chiao shih yen-chiu. Peking, Ch'êng-ta Normal School, 1935. (16)
Chin-kang ching. (17)
Chou Ku-ch'êng. Chung-kuo shih-hsüeh chih chin-hua. Hong Kong, Shêng-huo, 1947. (18)
Chou Yü. Sun-tsung lun. (19)
Chu Hsi. Chu Tzŭ ch'üan-shu. (20)
—— Yü lei. (21)
Chu K'o-chêng *et al.* Hsien-tai hsüeh-shu wên-hua kai-lun. Shanghai, Commercial Press, 1948. (22)

Chuang Tzŭ. (23)
Chung-kuo nien-chien. Shanghai, Commercial Press, 1924. (24)
Chung-yung. (25)
Fa-fang. Wei-shih shih-kuan chi ch'i chê-hsüeh. Wuchang, World Buddhist Institute, 1950. (27)
Fan Chên. Shên-mieh lun. (28)
Fu Ssŭ-nien. Hsing-ming ku-hsün pien-chêng. 2 vols. Shanghai, Commercial Press, 1940. Institute of History and Philology Monographs, Academia Sinica, Series B, No. 5. (29)
Fu T'ung-hsien. Chung-kuo Hui-chiao shih. Shanghai, Commercial Press, 1940. (30)
Fung Yu-lan. Chung-kuo chê-hsüeh shih. Shanghai, Commercial Press, 1934. (31)
—— Chung-kuo chê-hsüeh shih pu. Shanghai, Commercial Press, 1936. (32)
—— Hsin chih-yen. Shanghai, Commercial Press, 1946. (33)
—— Hsin li-hsüeh. Changsha, Commercial Press, 1938. (34)
—— Hsin shih-hsün. Kunming, K'ai-ming, 1940. (35)
—— Hsin shih-lun. Kunming, Commercial Press, 1939. (36)
—— Hsin yüan-jên. Chungking, Commercial Press, 1942. (37)
—— Hsin yüan-tao. Chungking, Commercial Press, 1944. (38)
Ho Lin. Tang-tai Chung-kuo chê-hsüeh. Shanghai, Shêng-li, 1947. (39)
Hsi-lai tsung-p'u. (40)
Hsieh Yu-wei. Hsien-tai chê-hsüeh ming-chu shu-p'ing. Chungking, Shêng-li, 1941. (41)
Hsin ching. (42)
Hsiung Shih-li. Chên-hsin shu. (43)
—— Fo-chia ming-hsiang t'ung-shih. Peking, Peking University, 1937. Also in *Shih-li ts'ung-shu* (n.p., 1947). (44)
—— Hsin wei-shih lun. Chungking, Commercial Press, 1944. Also in *Shih-li ts'ung-shu* (n.p., 1947). (45)
—— P'o p'o hsin wei-shih lun. Peking, Peking University, 1933. Also in *Shih-li ts'ung-shu* (n.p., 1947). (46)
—— Shih-li ts'ung-shu. N.p., 1947. (47)
—— Shih-li yü-yao. N.p., 1947. Also in *Shih-li ts'ung-shu* (n.p., 1947). (48)

—— Tu-ching shih-yao. Shanghai, Chêng-chung, 1948. Also in *Shih-li ts'ung-shu* (n.p., 1947). (49)

—— Yin-ming ta-su shan-chu, in *Shih-li ts'ung-shu* (n.p., 1947). (50)

Hsü tsang-ching. (51)

Hsüan-tsang, trans. Ch'êng wei-shih lun. (52)

Hsün Tzŭ. (53)

Hu Shih. Hu Shih lun-hsüeh chin-chu, 1st series. Shanghai, Commercial Press, 1935. (54)

—— Shuo ju, in *Hu Shih lun-hsüeh chin-chu,* 1st series (Shanghai, Commercial Press, 1935). (55)

Hua-yen ching. (56)

Huang Yen, ed. K'ung-chiao shih-nien ta-shih. Taiyuan, 1924. (57)

Hui-hui lai-yüan. (58)

I ching. (59)

Kao-sêng chuan. (60)

Ko Hung. Pao-p'u Tzŭ. (61)

K'o-hsüeh yü jên-shêng-kuan. Shanghai, Ya-tung, 1923. (62)

Komai Kazuchika. Chung-kuo li-tai shê-hui yen-chiu, trans. by Yang Lien. Shanghai, Commercial Press, 1935. (26)

Ku Huan. I-hsia lun. (63)

Kuan yü chih-shih fên-tzŭ ti kai-tsao. Hong Kong, Chêng-pao, 1948. (64)

K'uei-chi. Ch'êng wei-shih lun shu-chi. (65)

Kuo Chan-po. Chin wu-shih-nien Chung-kuo ssŭ-hsiang shih. Peking, Jên-wên, 1936. (66)

Kuo Mo-jo. Ch'ing-t'ung shih-tai. Chungking, Ch'ün-i, 1946. (67)

—— Shih p'i-p'an shu. Chungking, Ch'ün-i, 1945. (68)

Lao Tzŭ (Tao-tê ching). (69)

Lêng-yen ching. (70)

Li Shih-yü. Hsien-tsai Hua-pei pi-mi tsung-chiao (Religions secrètes contemporaines dans le nord de la Chine). Chengtu, *Studia Serica* Monographs, Series B, No. 4, 1948. (71)

Li T'ieh-chêng, trans. K'o-lan ching. Shanghai, Chung-hua, 1927. (72)

Liang Ch'i-ch'ao. Ta-ch'êng ch'i-hsin lun k'ao-chêng. Shanghai, Commercial Press, 1924. (73)
—— Yin-ping-shih wên-chi, ho chi. Shanghai, Chung-hua, 1936. (74)
Liang shu. (75)
Liang Sou-ming. Tung-hsi wên-hua chi ch'i chê-hsüeh. Shanghai, Commercial Press, 1922). (76)
Liu Chih (Chieh-lien). T'ien-fang Chih-shêng shih-lu. (77)
—— T'ien-fang hsing-li. (78)
—— T'ien-fang tien-li tsê-yao chieh. (79)
Liu Lien-k'o. Pang-hui san-pai-nien ko-ming shih. Macao, Liu-yüan, 1940. (80)
Lo Erh-kang. T'ien-ti Hui wên-hsien lu. Chungking, Chêng-chung, 1943. (81)
Lo Yüan-kun. Chung-kuo chin pai-nien shih. Shanghai, Commercial Press, 1936. (82)
Lu Hsiang-shan. Lu Hsiang-shan hsien-shêng ch'üan-chi. (83)
Lun-yü. (84)
Lü Ch'êng. Fo-tien fan-lun. Shanghai, Commercial Press, 1925. (85)
Ma Fu-ch'u, trans. Han-i pao-ming chên-ching. (86)
Ma I-yü. Chung-kuo Hui-chiao shih-chien. Shanghai, Commercial Press, 1931. (87)
Ma Lin-i. I-ssŭ-lan-chiao kai-lun. Shanghai, Commercial Press, 1934. (88)
Ma Wên-ping (Chu, Chung-hsiu). Ch'ing-chên chih-nan. (89)
Mao Tsê-tung. Hsin min-chu chu-i lun. N.p., 1940. (90)
—— Lun hsin chieh-tuan. N.p., 1939. (91)
Mencius. Mêng Tzŭ. (92)
Min-kuo ta tsang-ching. (93)
Mo Tzŭ. (94)
Ou-yang Ching-wu. Shih-chiao. Chungking, Institute of Inner Learning, 1940. (95)
—— Wei-shih chüeh-tsê t'an. Nanking, Institute of Inner Learning, 1921. (96)
Pai Shou-i. Chung-kuo Hui-chiao hsiao-shih. Chungking, Commercial Press, 1944. (97)

—— Chung-kuo I-ssŭ-lan shih kang-yao. Chengtu, Wên-t'ung, 1946. (98)
Sêng-yu, ed. Hung-ming chi. (99)
Shih chi. (100)
Shih-lieh-ko. T'ien-ti Hui yen-chiu. Shanghai, Commercial Press, 1940. (101)
Shina himitsu kessha no shin jōsei. Shanghai, 1937. (15)
Sun Ch'o. Yü-tao p'ien. (102)
Sun Pên-wên. Chung-kuo chan-shih hsüeh-shu. Chungking, Chêng-chung, 1946. (103)
Sun Yat-sen. Sun Wên hsüeh-shuo. Shanghai, Min-chih, 1928. (104)
Sung shih. (105)
Sung-tsang i-chên. (106)
Ta-Ch'ing t'ung-li. (107)
T'ai-hsü. Fa-hsiang wei-shih hsüeh. Shanghai, Commercial Press, 1938. (108)
—— T'ai-hsü Ta-shih wên-ch'ao, 1st series. Shanghai, Chung-hua, 1927. (109)
T'ang Chün-i. Chung-hsi chê-hsüeh ssŭ-hsiang chih pi-chiao yen-chiu chi. Chungking, Chêng-chung, 1943. (110)
T'ang Yung-t'ung. Han Wei Liang-Chin Nan-Pei-ch'ao Fo-chiao shih. Shanghai, Commercial Press, 1938. (111)
Tao-tê ching (Lao Tzŭ). (112)
Tao-tsang chi-yao. (113)
Tsa a-han ching. (114)
Tsai-li tsung-lun. (115)
Tsang-yao. (116)
Tso chuan. (117)
Wang Chih-hsin. Chung-kuo tsung-chiao ssŭ-hsiang shih ta-kang. Shanghai, Chung-hua, 1933. (118)
Wang Ching-chai (Wên-ch'ing). Ku-lan ching i-chieh. Peking, The Chinese Mohammedan Mutual Progress Association, 1932. (119)
Wang Ch'ung. Lun-hêng. (120)
Wang Yang-ming. Wang Yang-ming ch'üan-chi. (121)
Wei Po-yang. Ts'an-t'ung-ch'i. (122)

Wu Chih-hui (Woochefee). Wu Chih-hui hsüeh-shu lun-chu. Peking, Ch'u-pan Ho-tso Shê, 1925. (123)

Wu Yü. Wu Yü wên-lu. Shanghai, Tung-ya, 1921. (124)

Yin-shun. P'ing Hsiung Shih-li ti Hsin wei-shih lun. Hong Kong, Chêng-wên, 1950. (125)

3. CHINESE PERIODICALS (IN TRANSLITERATION)

Numbers in parentheses refer to the equivalents in Section 2 of the list of Chinese characters, below. Detailed references to the periodicals are found in the footnotes.

Chê-hsüeh (126)
Chên-li yü shêng-ming (127)
Ch'ên-hsi (128)
Chêng-fêng (129)
Chêng-fu kung-pao (130)
Chia-yin (The Tiger) (131)
Chien-kuo tao-pao (132)
Ching-shih pao (133)
Ch'ing-chên yüeh-pao (134)
Chung-kuo Fo-chiao chi-k'an (135)
Chung-yang jih-pao (136)
Chüeh yu-ch'ing (137)
Eastern Miscellany (Tung-fang) (174)
Hai-ch'ao yin (138)
Hsin ch'ao (139)
Hsin ch'ing-nien (La Jeunesse) (140)
Hsin hsi-pei (141)
Hsin-hua yüeh-pao (142)
Hsin-min ts'ung-pao (143)
Hsin t'an (144)
Hsin Ya-hsi-ya (145)
Hua-ch'iao jih-pao (146)
Huai-shêng (147)
Hui-chiao wên-hua (148)
I-chên (149)
I-kuang (150)
I-shih pao (151)
Jên-chien-shih (152)
Jeunesse, La (Hsin ch'ing-nien) (140)
Kuang-hua pan-yüeh-k'an (153)
Kuang-ming jih-pao (154)
K'ung-chiao Hui tsa-chih (155)
Lun-t'an (156)
Min-chu p'ing-lun (157)
Min-kuo jih-pao (158)
Min-Toh (Min-to) (159)
Nei-hsüeh (160)
Nü ch'ing-nien (161)
Pu-jên (162)
Quarterly Bulletin of Chinese Bibliography (T'u-shu chi-k'an) (173)
Shao-nien Chung-kuo (163)
Shê-hui ching-chi yen-chiu (164)
Shêng-ming (165)

Shih-chêng p'ing-lun (166)
Shih-ta yüeh-k'an (167)
Shih-tzŭ hou (168)
Ta-lu (169)
T'ien-shan (170)
Tiger, The (Chia-yin) (131)
Tsai-shêng (171)
Tu-li p'ing-lun (172)
T'u-shu chi-k'an (Quarterly Bulletin of Chinese Bibliography) (173)
Tung-fang (Eastern Miscellany) (174)
Tzŭ-yu chên-hsien (175)
Wah Kiu Yat Po (146)
Wên-hua p'i-p'an (176)
Wên-hua yü chiao-yü (177)
Wên-hua yü chien-shê (178)
Wên Shê (179)
Yen-ching hsüeh-pao (180)
Yung-yen (181)
Yü-kung (182)
Yüeh-hua (183)

Glossary of Chinese Terms and Names (in Transliteration)

Numbers in parentheses refer to the equivalents in Section 3 of the list of Chinese characters, below. For additional names of Chinese writers, see Bibliography, Section 2.

Ahung (*Ahong*) (184)
An Shih-kao (185)
Chan Ssŭ-ting (186)
Chan Wing-tsit (200)
Ch'an (187)
Chang Chün-mai (Carsun Chang) (188)
Chang Hua-shêng (189)
Chang Ling (190)
Chang T'ien-jan (191)
Chang T'u-fu (192)
Chao, T. C. (Tzŭ-ch'ên) (193)
Chê-ho-yeh Chiao (194)
Chên-ju (195)
Chên-yen (196)
Chên-yüan chih ch'i (197)
Ch'ên Ch'i-t'ien (198)
Ch'ên Huan-chang (199)
Ch'ên Tu-hsiu (201)
Chêng Ho (202)
Chêng-i (203)
Ch'êng (204)
Ch'êng Chai-an (205)
Ch'êng-shih (206)
Ch'êng-ta (207)
Chi-tsang (208)
Ch'i (209)
Chiang Ch'ao-tsung (210)
Chiang Shan-t'ung (211)
Chiang Shao-yüan (212)
Chiang T'ien (213)
Chiang Wei-ch'iao (214)
Chiao (215)
Ch'ien Hsüan-t'ung (216)
Ch'ien Tuan-shêng (217)
Chih-i (218)
Chih Kung Tong (219)
Chih-tsang (220)
Ch'ih-sung (221)
Chin-shan (222)
Chin Yüeh-lin (223)

Ching (224)
Ching-an (225)
Ching-ch'üan (226)
Ching Tien-ying (227)
Ching-t'u (228)
Ching-yen (229)
Ch'ing-ching (230)
Ch'ing-liang (231)
Ch'ing Pang (232)
Ch'ing-yu Chiao (233)
Chiu Chiao (234)
Ch'iu Ch'ang-ch'un (235)
Chou Fu-hai (236)
Chou Tso-jên (237)
Chou T'ung-tan (238)
Chu Chih-hsin (239)
Chu Yu-yü (Y. Y. Tsu) (240)
Chung (241)
Chung-kuo Hui-chiao Chiu-kuo Hsieh-hui (242)
Chung-kuo Hui-chiao Chü-chin Hui (243)
Chung-kuo Hui-min Chiu-kuo Hsieh-hui (244)
Chung shu (245)
Chü-shê (246)
Chü-tsan (247)
Ch'üan-chên (248)
Ch'üan-ch'iu Shêng-chiao Ta-t'ung Hui (249)
Fa-chuan (250)
Fa-hsiang (251)
Fa-tsang (252)
Fa-yen (253)
Fa-yüan (254)
Fang (255)
Fang-shih (256)
Fei-ming lun (257)
Fêng-shui (258)
Hai-jên (260)
Hai Wei-liang (261)
Han-shan (262)
Han Shan-t'ung (263)
Han Yü (264)
Hardoon, S. A. (259)
Hêng-chuan (265)
Hsi-hsin (266)
Hsi-hsin Shê (267)
Hsi p'i (268)
Hsia-shih (269)
Hsia Tsêng-yu (270)
Hsiao Pao-chên (271)
Hsieh Fu-ya (272)
Hsien-shou (273)
Hsien-t'ien Tao (274)
Hsien-tz'ŭ (275)
Hsin Chiao (276)
Hsin Chiu-shih Chiao (277)
Hsin-hsin Chiao (278)
Hsing-chih (279)
Hsing-tz'ŭ (280)
Hsü Pao-ch'ien (P. C. Hsu) (281)
Hsü-yün (282)
Hu Têng-chou (283)
Hua-shêng (284)
Hua-yen (285)
Huang Siu-chi (286)
Huang-t'ien Chiao (287)
Huang Tsung-hsi (288)
Hui-nêng (289)
Hui-yüan (290)
Hun-p'o (291)
Hung-i (292)

Hung Mên (Pang) (293)
I-hsin T'ien-tao (294)
I-kuan Tao (295)
Jên (296)
Jên-hsin (297)
Jên-shan (298)
Jüan Yüan (299)
K'an Tsê (300)
K'ang Yu-wei (301)
Kao-min (302)
Ko-lao Hui (303)
Ku Chieh-kang (304)
Kuan-tsung (305)
Kuei (306)
Kuei-i Tao (307)
Kuei Nien-tsu (Po-hua) (308)
K'uei-chi (309)
K'ung-yeh (310)
Lai-kuo (311)
Lee Shao Chang (319)
li (312, 313)
Li Chiao (314)
Li-chih (315)
Li Huang (316)
Li i lien ch'ih (317)
Li Mên (318)
Li T'ing-yü (320)
Li Yü-ying (Shih-tsêng) (321)
Lien-ch'ih (322)
Lin-chi (323)
Lin Chün (324)
Lin Sên (325)
Ling-yin (326)
Liu Hai-ch'an (327)
Liu San-chieh (328)
Liu-shêng Tsung-chiao Ta-t'ung Hui (329)
Liu Tê-jên (330)
Liu Yü-tzŭ (331)
Lu Chêng-hsiang (332)
Lu-hsün (Lusin) (334)
Luh, C. W. (333)
Lü (335)
Lü Tsu (336)
Lü Tung-pin (337)
Ma Ch'i-jung (339)
Ma Hung-tao (340)
Ma I-fu (341)
Ma Kin (Chien) (338)
Ma Ming-hsin (Hsin) (342)
Man-shu (343)
Mao Tzŭ-yüan (344)
Mei, Y. P. (345)
Mi (346)
Mi Fei (347)
Mi-mi (348)
Ming-chêng lun (349)
Ming-yün lun (350)
Na Chung (351)
Nei-hsüeh Yüan (352)
Nieh Shuang-chiang (353)
Ou-i (354)
Pai Ch'ung-hsi (355)
Pao-kuo (356)
Pao-t'ung (357)
Pên-t'i (358)
Po (359)
San-ho (360)
San-lun (361)
San-shih Hsüeh-hui (362)
San-tien (363)
Sêng-chao (364)
Shang-ti (366)
Shao Chang Lee (319)

Shao-lin (367)
Shatien (365)
Shê (368)
Shê-lun (369)
Shên (370)
Shih-chieh Tsung-chiao Ta-t'ung Hui (371)
Shun-yang (372)
Siu-chi Huang (287)
Ssŭ-ming lun (373)
Su Yüan-ying (374)
Sung, Z. D. (375)
Ta-ch'üan (376)
Ta-lin (377)
Ta-tao (378)
Ta-yüan (379)
Ta-yung (380)
Tai Chi-t'ao (381)
T'ai-chi (382)
T'ai-ho (383)
T'ai-i (384)
T'ai-p'ing (385)
T'ai-shêng Hsüan-yüan Huang-ti (386)
T'an Ssŭ-t'ung (387)
T'an Yün-shan (388)
T'ang Chu-hsin (389)
T'ang Huan-chang (390)
Tao-chieh (391)
Tao-hsüan (392)
Tao-shêng (393)
Tao-tê Hsüeh Shê (394)
Tao-tê Shê (395)
Tao-t'i (396)
Tao Yüan (397)
Thien Ti Hwai (410)
Ti (398)
Ti-hsien (399)
Ti-k'u (400)
Ti-lun (401)
T'i-jên (402)
T'i-yung (403)
T'ien (404)
T'ien-chên (405)
T'ien Han (406)
T'ien-li (407)
T'ien-shih (408)
T'ien-t'ai (409)
T'ien-ti Hui (410)
T'ien-t'ung (411)
Ting Fu-pao (412)
Ting-ming lun (413)
Ting Wên-chiang (V. K. Ting) (414)
Tsai-li (415)
Ts'ai P'iao (416)
Ts'ai Yüan-p'ei (417)
Tsan-hsin Chiao (418)
Ts'ao-tung (419)
Tsêng Ch'i (420)
Tsêng Kuo-fan (421)
Tso Tsung-t'ang (422)
Tsu, Y. Y. (240)
Tsung Pai-hua (423)
Tu-shun (424)
T'u Hsiao-shih (425)
Tuan Yung (426)
T'ung-shan Shê (427)
T'ung Tsung (428)
Wan-kuo Tao-tê Hui (429)
Wang Ch'ang-shê (430)
Wang Chê (431)
Wang Chia-shu (432)
Wang-ch'ing (433)

Wang Ch'uan-shan (434)
Wang Ch'ung-yang (435)
Wang Ên-yang (436)
Wang Fu (437)
Wang Hao-jan (438)
Wang Hsing-kung (439)
Wang Hung-yüan (440)
Wang I-ch'ang (441)
Wang I-t'ing (442)
Wang Kuang-ch'i (443)
Wang Liang-tso (444)
Wang Tai-yü (445)
Wang Tch'ang-tche (430)
Wang Tsêng-shan (446)
Wei, Francis C. M. (447)
Wei-shih (448)
Wei-t'o (449)
Wên-ch'ang (450)
Wu Hsin-hêng (451)
Wu Lei-ch'uan (452)
Wu Mi (453)
Wu-nien (454)
Wu-wei (455)
Wu Yao-tsung (John Wu) (456)
Yang (457)
Yang Chung-ming (458)
Yang Kuang-hsien (459)
Yang Shao-yu (460)
Yang Ts'un-jên (461)
Yang Tzŭ-hou (462)
Yang Wên-hui (463)
Yang, Y. C. (464)
Yeh Kung-ch'o (465)
Yen Fu (466)
Yen Wang (467)
Yin (468)
Yin-kuang (469)
Yin Shu-jên (470)
Yin Yen-shêng (471)
Ying (472)
Yü Chia-chü (473)
Yü-fo (474)
Yüan T'ung-li (T. L. Yuan) (475)
Yüeh-hsia (476)
Yün (477)
Zia, N. Z. (272)

Chinese Characters

1. BOOKS

1 阿彌陀經
2 張橫渠 正蒙
3 張融 門論
4 張欽士 國內近十年來之宗教思潮
5 章太炎 章氏叢書
6 (齊物論釋)
7 (太炎文錄別錄)
8 張東蓀 知識與文化
9 召誥
10 陳教友 長春道教源流
11 陳垣 南宋初河北新道教考
12 程伊川程明道 程氏遺書
13 姬覺彌譯 漢譯古蘭經
14 錢穆 先秦諸子繫年
15 支那秘密結社の新情勢

16	金吉堂	中國回教史研究
17	金剛經	
18	周谷城	中國史學之進化
19	周顒	三宗論
20	朱熹	朱子全書
21		語類
22	竺可楨等	現代學術文化概論
23	莊子	
24	中國年鑑	
25	中庸	
26	駒井和愛	中國歷代社會研究
27	法舫	唯識史觀及其哲學
28	范縝	神滅論
29	傅斯年	性命古訓辨正
30	傅統先	中國回教史
31	馮友蘭	中國哲學史
32		中國哲學史補
33		新知言
34		新理學
35		新世訓
36		新事論
37		新原人
38		新原道

39	賀 麟	當代中國哲學
40	西來宗譜	
41	謝幼偉	現代哲學名著述評
42	心 經	
43	熊十力	真心書
44		佛家名相通論
45		新唯識論
46		破破新唯識論
47		(十力叢書)
48		十力語要
49		讀經示要
50		因明大疏刪注
51	續藏經	
52	玄奘譯	成唯識論
53	荀 子	
54	胡 適	胡適論學近著
55		(說儒)
56	華嚴經	
57	黃 巖	孔教十年大事
58	回回來源	
59	易 經	
60	高僧傳	
61	葛 洪	抱朴子

62 科學與人生觀
63 顧歡 夷夏論
64 關於知識份子的改造
65 窺基 成唯識論述記
66 郭湛波 近五十年中國思想史
67 郭沫若 青銅時代
68 十批判書
69 老子 (道德經)
70 楞嚴經
71 李世瑜 現在華北秘密宗教
72 李鐵錚譯 可蘭經
73 梁啟超 大乘起信論考証
74 飲冰室文集合集
75 梁書
76 梁漱溟 東西文化及其哲學
77 劉智, 介廉 天方至聖實錄
78 天方性理
79 天方典禮擇要解
80 劉聯珂 幫會三百年革命史
81 羅爾綱 天地會文獻錄
82 羅元鯤 中國近百年史
83 陸象山 陸象山先生全集
84 論語

85 呂澂 佛典汎論
86 馬復初譯 漢譯寶命真經
87 馬以愚 中國回教史鑑
88 馬鄰翼 伊斯蘭教概論
89 馬文炳,注.仲修 清真指南
90 毛澤東 新民主主義論
91 論新階段
92 孟子
93 民國大藏經
94 墨子
95 歐陽竟无釋教
96 唯識抉擇談
97 白壽彝 中國回教小史
98 中國伊斯蘭史綱要
99 僧佑 弘明集
100 史記
101 施列格 天地會研究
102 孫綽 喻道篇
103 孫本文 中國戰時學術
104 孫文學說
105 宋史
106 宋藏遺珍
107 大清通例

108 太虛 法相唯識學

109 太虛大師文鈔

110 唐君毅 中西哲學思想之比較研究集

111 湯用彤 漢魏兩晉南北朝佛教史

112 道德經

113 道藏輯要

114 雜阿含經

115 在理總論

116 藏要

117 左傳

118 王治心 中國宗教思想史大綱

119 王靜齋, 文清 古蘭經譯解

120 王充 論衡

121 王陽明 王陽明全集

122 魏伯陽 參同契

123 吳稚暉 吳稚暉學術論著

124 吳虞 吳虞文錄

125 印順 評熊十力的新唯識論

2. PERIODICALS

126 哲學
127 真理與生命
128 晨熹
129 正風
130 政府公報
131 甲寅
132 建國導報
133 經世報
134 清真月報
135 中國佛教季刊
136 中央日報
137 覺有情
138 海潮音
139 新潮
140 新青年
141 新西北
142 新華日報
143 新民叢報
144 新壇
145 新亞細亞
146 華僑日報
147 懷聖
148 回教文化
149 伊聯
150 伊光
151 益世報
152 人間世
153 光華半月刊
154 光明日報
155 孔教會雜誌
156 論壇
157 民主評論
158 民國日報
159 民鐸
160 內學
161 女青年
162 不忍
163 少年中國
164 社會經濟研究
165 生命
166 市政評論
167 師大月刊
168 獅子吼
169 大路
170 天山
171 再生
172 獨立評論
173 圖書季刊
174 東方
175 自由陣線
176 文化批判
177 文化與教育
178 文化與建設
179 文社
180 燕京學報
181 庸言

182 禹貢　183 月華

3. CHINESE TERMS AND NAMES

184 阿衡
185 安世高
186 瞻思丁
187 禪
188 張君勱
189 張化聲
190 張陵
191 張天然
192 張屬夫
193 趙紫宸
194 遮持業教
195 真如
196 真言
197 真元之氣
198 陳啟天
199 陳煥章
200 陳榮捷
201 陳獨秀
202 鄭和
203 正一
204 誠
205 程宅安
206 成實
207 成達
208 吉藏
209 氣
210 江朝宗
211 江山童
212 江紹原
213 江天
214 蔣維喬
215 教
216 錢玄同
217 錢端升
218 智顗
219 致公堂
220 智藏
221 持松
222 金山
223 金岳霖
224 敬
225 靜安
226 靜權
227 敬貞瀛
228 淨土
229 靜嚴
230 清淨
231 清涼
232 青幫
233 清油教
234 舊教
235 邱長春
236 周佛海
237 周作人
238 周通旦
239 朱執信
240 朱友漁
241 中
242 中國回教救國協會

243 中國回教俱進會
244 中國回民救國協會
245 忠恕
246 俱舍
247 巨贊
248 全真
249 全球聖教大同會
250 法尊
251 法相
252 法藏
253 法演
254 法源
255 坊
256 方士
257 非命論
258 風水
259 哈同
260 海仁
261 海維諒
262 憨山
263 韓山童
264 韓愈
265 恒轉
266 習心
267 洗心社
268 翕闢
269 俠士
270 夏曾佑
271 蕭抱珍
272 謝扶雅
273 賢首
274 先天道
275 顯慈
276 新教
277 新救世教
278 新新教
279 性智
280 興慈
281 徐寶謙
282 虛雲
283 胡登州
284 化聲
285 華嚴
286 黃秀璣
287 黃天教
288 黃宗羲
289 慧能
290 慧遠
291 魂魄
292 弘一
293 洪門紅幫
294 一心天道
295 一貫道
296 仁
297 任心
298 仁山
299 阮元
300 闞澤
301 康有為
302 高旻
303 哥老會
304 顧頡剛
305 觀宗
306 鬼
307 皈一道
308 桂念祖

(桂伯華)
309 窺基
310 空也
311 來果
312 里
313 理
314 理教
315 理智
316 李贄
317 禮義廉恥
318 理門
319 李紹昌
320 李廷玉
321 李煜瀛
(石曾)
322 蓮池
323 臨濟
324 林鈞
325 林森
326 靈隱
327 劉海蟾
328 劉三傑
329 大聖宗
教大同會
330 劉德仁
331 劉玉子
332 陸徵祥
333 陸志韋
334 魯迅
335 律
336 呂祖
337 呂洞賓
338 馬堅
339 馬啟榮
340 馬宏道
341 馬一浮
342 馬明心,新
343 曼殊
344 茅子元
345 梅貽寶
346 密
347 米芾
348 密密
349 命正論
350 命運論
351 納忠
352 內學院
353 聶雙江
354 耦益
355 白崇禧
356 報國
357 寶通
358 本體
359 白
360 三合
361 三論
362 三時學會
363 三點
364 僧肇
365 沙甸
366 上帝
367 少林
368 攝
369 攝論
370 神
371 世界宗教
大同會
372 純陽
373 俟命論

374 蘇元瑛
375 沈仲濤
376 大全
377 大林
378 大道
379 大圓
380 大勇
381 戴季陶
382 太極
383 太和
384 太一
385 太平
386 太上玄元皇帝
387 譚嗣同
388 譚云山
389 湯住心
390 唐煥章
391 道階
392 道宣
393 道生
394 道德學社
395 道德社
396 道體
397 道院
398 帝
399 諦閑
400 帝誊
401 地論
402 體認
403 體用
404 天
405 天真
406 田漢
407 天理
408 天師
409 天台
410 天地會
411 天童
412 丁福保
413 定命論
414 丁文江
415 在理
416 蔡鏢
417 蔡元培
418 蘄新教
419 曹洞
420 曾琦
421 曾國藩
422 左宗棠
423 宗白華
424 杜順
425 屠孝實
426 段永
427 同善社
428 童琼
429 萬國道德會
430 王昌社
431 王嚞
432 王嘉樹
433 忘情
434 王船山
435 王重陽
436 王恩洋
437 王浮
438 王浩然
439 王星拱
440 王弘願

441 王宜昌
442 王一亭
443 王光祈
444 王良佐
445 王岱輿
446 王曾善
447 韋卓民
448 唯識
449 韋馱
450 文昌
451 吳心恒
452 吳雷川
453 吳宓
454 無念
455 無為
456 吳耀宗
457 陽
458 楊仲明
459 楊光先
460 楊方猷
461 楊存仁
462 楊子厚
463 楊文會
464 楊永清
465 葉恭綽
466 嚴復
467 閻王
468 陰
469 印光
470 尹恕仁
471 尹岩生
472 營
473 余家菊
474 玉佛
475 袁同禮
476 月霞
477 云 雲

Index